Synastry

About the Author

Rod Suskin (South Africa) has been a professional astrologer since 1989. He hosts a radio program, appears every month on national television to talk about astrology, and regularly writes articles on astrology for many major South African newspapers. In 1994 he was commissioned by the official publication of the South African Parliament to create and interpret an astrological chart for the newly democratic country.

Synastry

UNDERSTANDING THE ASTROLOGY OF RELATIONSHIPS

Rod Suskin

Llewellyn Publications
Woodbury, Minnesota

First Edition
First Printing, 2008

Cover design by Gavin Dayton Duffy
Llewellyn is a registered trademark of Llewellyn Worldwide, Ltd.

Chart wheels were produced by the Kepler program with the permission of Cosmic Patterns Software Inc. (www.AstroSoftware.com)

Library of Congress Cataloging-in-Publication Data
Suskin, Rod.
     Synastry : understanding the astrology of relationships / by Rod Suskin.—1st ed.
       p. cm.
     Includes bibliographical references and index.
     ISBN 978-0-7387-1255-0
     1. Synastry. I. Title.
     BF1711.S94 2008

   133.5—dc22
                                                             2007041106

Llewellyn Worldwide does not participate in, endorse, or have any authority or responsibility concerning private business transactions between our authors and the public.

All mail addressed to the author is forwarded but the publisher cannot, unless specifically instructed by the author, give out an address or phone number.

Any Internet references contained in this work are current at publication time, but the publisher cannot guarantee that a specific location will continue to be maintained. Please refer to the publisher's website for links to authors' websites and other sources.

Llewellyn Publications
A Division of Llewellyn Worldwide, Ltd.
2143 Wooddale Drive, Dept. 978-0-7387-1255-0
Woodbury, Minnesota 55125-2989, U.S.A.
www.llewellyn.com

Printed in the United States of America

Other Books by Rod Suskin

Soul Life
(Double Storey Books, 2006)

Cycles of Life
(Llewellyn Publications, 2005)

Soul Talks
(Double Storey Books, 2004)

For P., of whom I am sure.

Contents

Tables and Examples

Charts

Foreword

Synastry is one of the biggest, most important considerations for astrology—the astrology of relationships—yet it is still on the frontier of our learning! Because so many techniques have been conceived and applied trying to grasp synastry, the center of understanding has been lost. We feel bewildered by methods, we feel bewilderment with meaning.

What do we with all the charts? Two individuals with perhaps four horoscope portraits each and then one or two between them! What measurements really *sing*? With so many complications still abounding, what technical reliability can we find?

This is the state of synastry today—*until this wonderful book by Rod Suskin!* Rest easy, now; synastry has been tamed and anchored for all our benefit.

Rod Suskin is perhaps astrology's premier practitioner and spokesperson in South Africa. His many years of teaching have put hundreds of astrologers into professional public service; his writings have focused a practical yet spiritual light into understandings; his pervasive radio broadcasts and lectures have created a Suskin outreach that is formidable. His international relationships with the United States are also well established and, with this new book, will certainly be further illuminated.

Entering this book is really easy. Suskin has a terrific traditional grounding in astrology, which is very important with this frontier issue: it provides the reader with a vocabulary that is tried and tested and holds up to the overlay of special-focus creativity. Suskin presents everything so gradually. Even the page organization of the small units of explanation is compelling; you simply can't open this book and not become immediately intrigued, engrossed, informed.

Above all, Suskin softly engineers the learning with *gradual* presentations of heretofore often complex data. You get a *feel* about the information just as you learn to be comfortable with another person; you get a feel for the relationship and respond accordingly.

It is a delight to see in Suskin's style that memorization of formulae is *not* the rule—as it is in so many old "cookbooks"—but instead, the *understanding of principles and how they interrelate with one another* leads the way! You will see this everywhere. For example, the section on how money is handled—certainly a key dimension of any close relationship—is managed ever so gracefully through simple understanding of astrological principles. The whole spectrum from extravagance to selfishness is covered with just a few planetary and sign archetypes. And you say: "Of course! How simple!"

And how intelligent and real is Suskind's discussion of management of age differences within relationship! He does this through outer planet assessment, and it's a charm.

Yes, Suskin breaks procedures into gradual steppingstones up the mountain, and that can call for many horoscope charts. But what happens within this learning process is that, eventually and quite quickly, with the principles so naturally internalized, *knowledge directs vision*, and we see more with less.

Thank you, Rod. Quite a book!

Noel Tyl

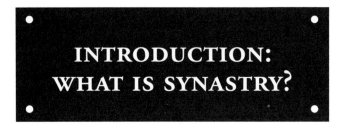

INTRODUCTION: WHAT IS SYNASTRY?

Imagine a magical mirror that brings your values, beliefs, and ideas right out into the open, that makes others examine who you are and shows you what other people think of you. Imagine this mirror has the power to satisfy your desires or bitterly disappoint you.

That Mirror Is a Relationship

Now imagine you have the blueprint for this special mirror, a plan that allows you to understand why all these things are reflected in that way. You can see how it is that others think of you the way they do, and what are the problems that cause your magical reflection to look as it does, and even why looking into it sometimes makes you feel so good.

That Blueprint Is Synastry

Synastry is the astrology of relationships. This book will show you how to create and analyze this blueprint for any relationship. In the process you will take your work as an astrologer to a new level and be able to offer your clients one of the most important and practical services astrologers have at their disposal. You will learn how to understand an individual's relationship patterns, what his or her relationship experiences are likely to be, and most importantly how to use the powerful special techniques that offer astrologers unique insights into specific relationships.

Why Use Synastry?

The synastry blueprint shows what people bring out in each other and where they clash. In fact, it may be the most practical of all astrological techniques because it offers the astrologer and the client a laboratory to test the relationship before it even happens or tools to enhance an existing relationship. With the understanding of what occurs when two charts are put together, we can show the clients how this reflects their experience and bring them the insight they seek.

Outline of the Method in This Book

We will take a thorough approach to relationship analysis. We will cover all the traditional and modern techniques of synastry, with a strong emphasis on using your skills to counsel both parties involved in a relationship. The emphasis in interpretation will be on understanding the relationship dynamics so that individual and joint needs can be met, patterns can be understood, a sense of the future progress of the relationship can be gained, and most importantly the couple can be shown the best possible way to play out the dynamics of all these factors so their needs can be met.

Rather than pursuing a cookbook approach, which many books of this type adopt and which new astrologers become dependent upon, this book aims to teach you a thorough, logical approach to synastry based on solid, tested techniques. You will learn to make your own interpretations that are reliable, accurate, and useful to your clients.

The basic strategy for relationship analysis that this book teaches is:

1. First, analyze the natal chart thoroughly, with a special emphasis on relationship-oriented needs, but also understanding which other natal factors always play a role in relationships.

2. Then, analyze how the *individuals* interact, based on their natal charts. Assess how they might perceive and respond to each other, and which traits will contribute to later patterns in the relationship.

3. Next, make a thorough analysis of how the two *charts* interact.

4. Follow with an analysis of charts that describe the relationship itself.

5. Finally, employ techniques to assess the likely longevity of the relationship.

A synastry consultation is unlike any other—you have two people in front of you who already have a relationship and who have all the patterns firmly in place. A chapter devoted to the special considerations for consulting with a couple will teach you the critical skills that are required to make sense of all this analysis in a way that is useful and meaningful to your clients.

Not only will you need all-new methods of conveying important information, but the fact that a relationship is about practical, everyday, hands-on aspects of the clients' lives means that you will need to provide useful strategies that can be employed immediately to help your clients improve their relationship.

That is the ultimate goal of this book.

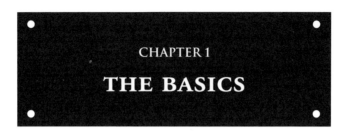

CHAPTER 1

THE BASICS

Love is one of the great mysteries of life; it can be a great frustration or a great joy. Astrology offers a way to penetrate the mystery that is meaningful and can offer the individual the possibility to gain some understanding of an important but often confusing aspect of life.

In This Chapter

- Why people come to astrologers to analyze their relationship and what astrology can offer them.
- What compatibility really means.
- First impressions and why they often are wrong.
- How to analyze the Ascendant and planets in the first house.
- The important role of Mercury in creating first impressions.

Why the Client Seeks Help

Every practicing astrologer knows that a good percentage of clients want to discuss two areas: love and money, or more precisely, relationships and profession. Some astrologers even make it a point to make some mention of these early in the chart reading so that the client is not distractedly listening and waiting.

Our relationships get to the very core of what it means to be human; they are related to our identity, self-worth, security, even the elusive state called happiness and the enigma of destiny. To be able to provide insight into the essence of being human is a valuable gift the astrologer has to offer, and is a significant responsibility that he or she carries.

Relationships are about more than the pleasures of love and sex or the mutual responsibilities and shared difficulties. They make us examine who we are and require us to expose all sorts of things about ourselves to somebody else; they bring our beliefs, ideas, and values right out into the open; and they show us what other people think about us.

We carry deep cultural beliefs about relationships and particularly about marriage. Marriage is a legal act that fundamentally affects our rights and our status, one of the reasons that governments control who is allowed to marry. Even when a relationship is not "sanctioned" by marriage, relationships lead us to commit our resources and ourselves. They have a permanent effect on our lives and our futures.

Some of our beliefs about relationships are based on past experience. Most people are able to identify patterns in this area of life more clearly than any other—an area of relationships that astrology is particularly good at exposing. Some of these patterns clearly are based on early-life emotional experiences, another area in which astrology can be especially insightful.

Relationships bring into sharp relief how we value ourselves and what we'd like others to think about us. The powerful need for social approval is evident in how proudly we display our partners when we believe they have special status in the eyes of others (perhaps by being attractive or successful), as if that will somehow reflect back on us. Similarly, when we are with someone our friends may consider of a lesser social status than ourselves, we may become secretive and defensive.

Relationships have one other feature that drives clients to seek help. As much as clients may secretly wish to control their partner (hopefully not!), they will settle for being able to anticipate the partner's actions. They want to know how this person will behave and what is likely to be the outcome of having a relationship with him or her.

What Astrology Can Offer

When it comes to relationships, while clients have an idea of how they themselves feel and what they hope and fear about this relationship, they cannot be sure of how their partner feels. This uncertainty is probably the greatest of all motives that drive them to an astrologer, the motive wrapped up in the question "Are we compatible?"

We consider the client's complex network of beliefs, hopes, fears, feelings, experiences, and past experiences. We are able to offer a meaningful form of objectivity that will allow the client to make decisions that are less skewed by passions and emotions. Even though emotions are the very stuff relationships are made of, our feelings in partnership situations are closely related to our insecurities and the "buttons" that our partner presses in the exchange of love.

Which Relationships Can We Analyze?

One significant relationship for many people is their marriage or their romantic relationship. Relationships with siblings can be powerful and often represent a significant bond or ongoing issue in a person's life, just as a relationship with a parent can be one of those extremes, or some complex mix of both. Some people have a lifelong friendship that transcends many of the changes that cause other friendships to wane. All of our relationships deal with our self-worth, insecurity, beliefs, and needs for control and affection: these, and the many others our relationships bring to the surface, are the core issues of being human.

We can use synastry to explore any kind of relationship. Although this book will concentrate on romantic relationships, most of the techniques you will learn here easily can be applied to other types of relationships.

What Is Compatibility?

Most people assume that a successful relationship requires compatibility. They assume that the role of an astrologer in analyzing relationships is to tell them whether their partner is compatible with them, and they often expect the astrologer to give them information like, "You are compatible with Pisceans but not Geminis, and yet your perfect partner is a Scorpio."

If relationships were that simple, we wouldn't need astrologers in the first place. Not only is it meaningless to sum up a person as his or her Sun sign, but the notion of "compatible" is variable according to who defines it.

Is compatibility merely the ability to get along? Are we more compatible with people we are similar to? What is the meaning behind "opposites attract"? Does compatibility mean that there is never any conflict? Has this anything to do with "soul mates" and the idea that there is a specific person just for me somewhere out there in the world? Even if unspoken, many of these questions are in the mind of the client seeking to analyze relationships for compatibility.

In reality, each of us is looking for something a little different. We all have different needs, drives, and experiences. What works for one person might not work for someone else. We often are astonished by our friends' choice of partners, or how their relationship with such an unlikely individual may seem to work.

Whether two people get along harmoniously or not may relate to their preference in relationship style. For example, some people tend to stagnate or become lazy in harmonious relationships and seem to need something more challenging to make them confront their own issues. The astrologer who sees many challenges in a synastry analysis cannot safely assume that this means the individuals are incompatible.

When it comes to compatibility, there clearly is no "one size fits all." There are, however, certain basic principles, which we will specifically look for, that all relationships depend on. For our purposes, these then become our criteria for compatibility—everything else is defined by the unique situation and needs of the individuals concerned. Here are the criteria for compatibility:

- Communication—expressing one's own needs and hearing the partner's needs

- Rapport and nonverbal communication

- Empathy—the ability to understand and relate to the partner's feelings

- Compromise—the ability to adjust one's own needs to allow for the other's needs to be equally met

- The ability to respond to specific needs of the partner

- The likelihood of gaining or improving something (especially oneself) through the relationship

There are a few special criteria that will emerge as we examine different types of relationship, but there is one more assumption we will make in order to seal our definition of compatibility: *a relationship rarely succeeds when the value systems of the individuals concerned are different.* This will be explored in considerable depth during the course of our analysis.

The Difference Between Synastry and Natal Readings

All astrological techniques are derived from the basic astrological concepts: planets, signs, houses, and aspects. Even if you have only a rudimentary knowledge of astrology, you already are equipped to start developing it into a tool that will allow you to understand relationships in a new and powerful way. As you apply this knowledge to working with relationships, you will develop techniques to extend your use of those basic tools:

- Using a natal chart to find specific things that are relevant to the matter you are inquiring about (in this case, relationships) rather than trying to synthesize the whole chart
- Learning to use astrological methods to see how people interact and how one person's chart can have an effect on another person's chart
- Taking your natal methods one step further to develop new charts that work similarly to natal charts but that allow you to analyze a relationship rather than an individual

When it comes to actually dealing with the clients, what makes a synastry reading so different is that you are dealing with two people. There may be other situations in which you will handle more than one chart at a time—in fact, any reading for predictions as well as many other techniques practically require this—but there are very few in which you will have more than one person in your office. This situation may not sound like anything special, but you will discover that it creates a whole new dynamic.

The last chapter of this book is devoted to handling the special dynamics of a synastry reading. Before you even begin to plan a session with your clients, you need to consider your whole approach to relationship work and know in advance your strategy for dealing with the sensitive ethical issues that arise.

First Impressions

Before people have any effect on each other, they see each other through a whole collection of expectations, hopes, desires, and beliefs about other people. Whether we mean to or not, we make a lot of assumptions about other people at the very moment we first meet them. Sometimes we even will go so far as to make decisions or judgments based on this first impression, but usually we will be careful not to jump to any conclusions and most of us will keep an open mind as we learn a little more about who the other person is. Still, that first impression often becomes a foundation for a relationship, or at least for some of what we believe about another person.

Despite the benefits of intuition and experience, first impressions are wrong more often than they are right. There are good reasons for this that can be well understood using astrology, and that makes the analysis of first impressions a useful starting point to examine the earliest beliefs and expectations that may be set up in a relationship. Luckily, analyzing first impressions makes use of the most basic of all astrological methods, so even if you know only a little astrology at this stage, it is a good place to start learning about synastry.

Understanding why we form first impressions, and what is usually wrong with them, will allow you to help your clients understand why their expectations are not always accurate.

Why We Form First Impressions

We all have a genetic program that determines our instinctual behavior. The purpose of such behavior is to provide us with the most basic needs, one of which is self-preservation. We need to determine rapidly whether another being threatens our person or our resources, an instinct we share with all other living creatures. Following this rapid, unconscious assessment, we go on to decide whether this individual may have something we need, or whether this is likely to be an opportunity for gain in the future.

Since one of our needs is to be in a relationship (which includes some of the more basic needs like sex, reproduction, and comfort), it is necessary for this process to kick in. But as we are a lot more sophisticated than other species that are going through the same process, the standards we apply to what determines a threat or what determines an opportunity are quite far removed from those of the animal world. All of our beliefs and expectations, all the baggage we carry, and how we see ourselves help form the filter through which we assess another person and against which we measure the person's suitability.

Actually, it may be considered reasonable to apply this strategy; after all, all that baggage is relevant to describing our basic needs. But it is more complex than that. It's one thing to have a set of standards or a measuring system—but just what is it we are measuring? What is it we know about a total stranger? And how accurate is that knowledge?

Why We Create Impressions in Others

Our inability to accurately assess people through our personal filter is only half the problem. The rest of the problem lies in the fact that each of us deliberately projects an image of ourselves into the world that is far from the whole picture of who we are. Sometimes that image is altogether different from our real self.

We project this image for reasons similar to the ones that make us judge others so early on. Most of the time, our instincts drive us to try to create a good impression. We want them to believe that we meet their criteria, and we also want them to believe specific things about us. We want to be liked and we want to ensure that there is no way that a stranger will realize our flaws and insecurities.

Why First Impressions Often Are Wrong

Between all the biases we have when we "read" another person and all the impressions the person is deliberately trying to make, it is very unlikely that our first impression will be accurate. After all, we are gaining that impression through a lens we already have colored with our own projections.

What chance do we have for success when our beginnings are so fraught with confusion and misjudgment? In fact, it is likely that it is this very illusion-filled process that ensures we actually do have relationships. If we formed an accurate impression of somebody else, baggage and all, we would certainly shy away (if not *run* away) from any involvement. So first impressions are wrong by nature's very design.

The projection is not sustained for long, and as we become more comfortable and familiar with our partners the mask slips and we show more of our real selves. Many of the problems that seem inevitable later in a relationship very often are based on the fact that our partners turn out to be different from who we thought they were at first meeting (and vice versa).

Helping your clients understand what they each tend to project (and why), and how they will perceive the other person, can go a long way to help them deal with the changes that develop later on and to become more compassionate when their partner misreads them.

Appearance Counts: The Ascendant

Even though we generally are aware that judgment of appearance rarely is related to underlying qualities, we often make much of our initial judgment based on the physical attributes of the other person. These include actual "looks" or genetic makeup and more significantly clothes, jewelry, hygiene, etc. Remember, people control how they wish to be seen by others through their choice of how they are going to appear.

Astrologically, appearance is described by the Ascendant. The Ascendant also describes how individuals place themselves in the world, how they tend to react and respond to it.

Analyzing the Ascendant for First Impressions

In this book, we always will assume that you have both parties to the relationship sitting in front of you. Now, for each chart:

- Bearing in mind what you know about the Ascendant and its role in attraction, describe to the client as how he or she wishes to be seen. (In the next chapter you will learn more about how the Ascendant compares with the "real self," but for now your job is just to describe appearances and impressions.)

This table will help you get started by showing you what to look out for, but remember that people are individuals and these are only examples. Use your knowledge of astrology to relate appearance to the rising sign.

Table 1: How the Ascendant Affects First Impressions	
Ascending Sign	**Apparent Characteristics**
Aries	Enthusiastic, brash, easily riled, naive
Taurus	Conservative, lazy, sensual, down-to-earth, likable
Gemini	Talkative, flighty, intellectual, distracted
Cancer	Sensitive, easily hurt, nurturing, emotional
Leo	Warm, knows what's best, takes care of all, self-involved
Virgo	Fussy, helpful, critical, earthy, intellectual
Libra	Friendly, gentle, romantic, considerate, flighty, talkative
Scorpio	Intense, quiet, secretive, mysterious, powerful, confident
Sagittarius	Happy-go-lucky, uncommitted, friendly, warm, experienced
Capricorn	Serious, knowledgeable, practical, reserved, older
Aquarius	Remote, different, idealistic, individualistic, stubborn
Pisces	Quiet, sensitive, willing to cooperate, unfocused, spiritual, emotional

- Planets in the first house modify the Ascendant strongly. In describing the appearance, be sure to consider the influence of these planets. If there is more than one planet here, the planet that is closest to the actual Ascendant will be the strongest influence, but all must be considered. If there are planets in the twelfth house within ten degrees of the Ascendant and in the same sign, they also will have an influence.

Table 2: How Planets in the First House Affect First Impressions	
Planet	**Effect on Characteristics**
Sun	Warm, easy to like, draws attention, bossy, confident, self-involved
Moon	Sensitive, private, emotional, caring, intense
Mercury	Talkative, busy, intellectual, critical
Venus	Easygoing, lazy, romantic, artistic, seductive, feminine
Mars	Confident, aggressive, forceful, determined, masculine
Jupiter	Optimistic, gregarious, wise, generous, fun-loving
Saturn	Serious, seems older, conservative, disapproving, wise, fatherly
Uranus	Eccentric, individualistic, unpredictable, exciting, erratic
Neptune	Dreamy, romantic, glamorous, deceptive, vague, spiritual
Pluto	Intense, powerful, secretive (these people often "hide" Pluto behind likability and good manners, so don't expect this placement to be obvious)

Once you have described the Ascendant of each person in this way, you have set the scene for your clients. You can even discuss with them how they each saw the other and how this concurs with what they have just heard.

This initial description also serves as a great introduction to the whole concept of relationship analysis. Tell your clients that, having seen the outer appearance, you now will help them see a more accurate picture. Be light and gentle—it helps to break the ice and prepare the clients for what can become quite an intense experience of exposure.

Controlling Other People's Impressions of Us

Even though we consciously control our appearance as much as possible, the most immediate way we have to deliberately create an impression is through the use of language. Our choice of what we talk about, the way we talk, and even our tone of voice can be very powerful tools to help create a desired impression. This is particularly true since we tend to believe that what a person says is very revealing about how he or she really thinks. Clearly, at the early stages of an encounter this is anything but true.

The element of the sign that Mercury occupies shows *how* the individual uses language. This can go a long way to explain some of the incorrect perceptions we have of each other, because our style of speaking may not reflect our real values. The following list will give you a sense of how the element affects Mercury and will be especially useful when considering the basic misunderstanding conveyed when Mercury is in a different element from that of the Sun. (In practice, these examples must be made more specific to the actual sign that Mercury occupies.)

Table 3: Effect of the Element of the Mercury Sign	
Element of Mercury Sign	**Style of Speech and Thought Process**
Fire	The style of speech is more dramatic, frank, spontaneous, honest, blunt; the speaker may get excitable and step on toes unintentionally
Earth	Speech is slower and more deliberate; things are thought through; conservative ideas and language are expressed; there is greater emphasis on practicality
Air	Ideas and abstract concepts are readily expressed; the individual is very talkative; there is a lot of conversation about others, ranging from gossip to social concerns
Water	The emphasis is on emotional language, personal experience, and listening rather than speaking

Consider, for example, how an Aries with Mercury in Pisces could convey a more sensitive, emotional impression or how a Gemini with Mercury in Taurus could seem so much quieter and more conservative than he or she really is. It's easier to get a misleading first impression when Mercury is in a different sign than that of the Sun.

- The house that Mercury is in shows what the person tends to be concerned about. He or she is likely to talk about these concerns. This can help create an accurate impression.

- The aspects to Mercury will reveal more about the thought process and communication style. For example, a challenging aspect from Neptune will make it difficult for the individual to express him- or herself clearly. Such a person could be seen as confused or vague; a person with Mercury in aspect with Saturn may be seen as plodding or conservative; and so on.

Remember to keep the context in mind: if you are looking at the "first impression" aspect of Mercury, you are not going to analyze it too deeply. We don't reveal our whole mind at the start any more than we reveal our whole personality. Just consider the overall impression Mercury would make, especially in the context of the Ascendant, which sets the tone for the first impression. The following example will show you how this works. All natal charts are given in appendix C.

EXAMPLE: FIRST IMPRESSIONS CREATE A FALSE IDEA

Helen (chart 6) and Peter (chart 7) met and married in a few short weeks. They sorely misjudged each other and didn't get along from the start, divorcing after only a few years.

Helen has Cancer rising with Uranus in the first house. She wants to be seen as sensitive and nurturing, able to provide and take care of others, and as very home- and family-oriented. She's certainly very individualistic and probably will try to capitalize on her uniqueness to be seen as unusual, perhaps fascinating. Of course, some of these perceptions are out of her control—no doubt some people will think of her as eccentric or strange!

Mercury is strong in her chart because it is in its own sign. It helps her communicate in a rational and analytical fashion and, along with its conjunction to Saturn, makes her style of speech seem deliberate, well thought out, and a little conservative. She even seems practical. That tones down the eccentricity of Uranus and helps convey the traditional family values of her rising sign.

Peter has Sagittarius rising, which contributes to his image of being fun-loving and happy-go-lucky. He seems eager to learn and fascinated by philosophical ideas, foreign places, and adventure. He has no planets in the first house, but you might have noticed how strongly Uranus aspects his Ascendant with an opposition, adding a bit of that eccentric flavor we already have seen in Helen's chart.

Peter's Mercury is in Aquarius. He seems full of fascinating ideas and strongly formed opinions. He's likely to be very talkative and engaging, enthusiastically discussing his ideals for the collective, be it his neighborhood or the whole world. Helen, with her strong intellectual orientation, is likely drawn to this—although it is not that intellectual orientation of hers that is visible to Peter. He's really a more sensitive, emotional person, and no doubt is attracted to her Cancerian appearance.

Finding the "Real" Person

In chapter 4 we will see that once we start expressing our needs and expectations in a relationship, the "real" self emerges and provides a potentially serious challenge to the couple.

For now, let's see if we can identify more of that real self and how we can make a more accurate astrological comparison of the two charts.

CHAPTER 2

RELATIONSHIPS AND THE INDIVIDUAL

By taking a disciplined "first principles" approach, we will discover that the natal chart alone provides plenty of valuable information about the individual's relationships. If the *promise* of the natal chart is well understood, it can allow the student to confidently move on to the techniques of synastry and the analysis of several additional charts.

In This Chapter

- How the chart as a whole shows the individual's relationship orientation.
- Knowing when planets are strong or weak.
- Reading the Sun, Moon, and Ascendant for basic needs.
- How needs determine our relationship behavior.

The Promise of the Natal Chart

A basic assumption in astrology is that *the natal chart shows the promise of the individual's entire life*. While we may use special techniques like synastry or the vast array of predictive methods so daunting to the novice, the natal chart represents the life pattern from which everything must unfold. No matter what all the other charts and methods reveal, they can only develop further the potentials of the nativity. A thorough grasp of each partner's natal chart is the most essential ingredient in relationship analysis.

In analyzing the natal chart to discover the individual's relationship potential, there are two basic principles to consider: first, the chart as a whole must be examined, and second, characteristics of the chart that relate specifically to relationships must be analyzed.

The Chart as a Whole

Human beings are not easily compartmentalized. Our emotions and feelings are not somehow separate from the rest of us; our relationships are not a separate part of our lives. On the contrary, they affect every single aspect of our lives and touch the deepest, most personal parts of our psyche. When we enter into a relationship with another person, we bring a whole host of needs, expectations, beliefs, and baggage. Our day jobs and life goals shape these and shape our everyday activities. In short, there is no part of us that is irrelevant to the way we will behave in our relationships, and the way we will experience them.

Let's review the key features of the overall analysis that are especially important in the consideration of relationship matters.[1]

Hemisphere Emphasis

Although hemisphere emphasis is the most general of patterns in a chart, it has particular relevance to how the individual relates to others.

- An emphasis of planets in the eastern hemisphere (houses ten through three) shows a strong focus on oneself, on personal goals and individual needs. This is especially true when most of the planets are in houses eleven through two.

- An emphasis of planets in the western hemisphere (houses four through nine) shows an emphasis on other people and relationships. This is even more emphatic when most of the planets are in houses five through eight.

- An emphasis of planets in the northern or southern hemisphere is less relevant to relationships, but does help you understand if the individual is more extroverted (houses seven through eleven emphasized) or introverted (houses one through five emphasized). This will be useful when comparing charts of different people.

---

1. For a comprehensive guide to chart analysis, an excellent text is Kevin Burk's *Astrology: Understanding the Birth Chart* (St. Paul, MN: Llewellyn Publications, 2001).

Strong or Weak Planets

Planets are the most important features in the chart, and a good understanding of how they are operating in a chart will give you the most accurate results and help you sort out the endless possible meanings planets seem to be capable of having.

The traditional principles of rulership are the best way to understand how the planets are exerting their influence, and although those rules can become complex and detailed, they can be simplified into a highly effective two-step check that will let you discover whether a planet is acting mostly positively or mostly negatively, and whether it has a strong role or a weak role in the chart.

- Step One—Positive or negative: A planet manifests its best characteristics when it is in a sign that it rules or in which it is exalted. This is called *essential dignity*. A planet tends to have a more negative influence when it is in a sign opposite the one it rules (detriment) or opposite the one in which it is exalted (fall.) When interpreting a planet, consider how the sign affects how the planet expresses itself, and if any of these rulership rules apply, then remember how they create the tendency toward positive or negative manifestation. Remember, people are not two-dimensional: never interpret a planet as *all* good or *all* bad; just think of a tendency toward the positive keywords or the negative ones.

- Step Two—Strong or weak: It's one thing to be positive or negative, but you still need to consider how much opportunity the planet has to express these qualities. Planets have the strongest role when they are in the angular houses and when they are direct in motion (that is, not retrograde). This is called *accidental dignity*.[2] Being retrograde or in a cadent house weakens the planet's role. So in your interpretation of a planet, you also should consider how the house meaning tells you where in life the planet's characteristics are expressed, and whether they are a strong influence (affecting many things in life and so very important) or not. Again, be realistic—planets in cadent houses won't just disappear; they are just less important than the angular ones.

- You should look at all the planets right at the beginning and assess them with this two-step approach.

---

2. Both essential and accidental dignity have many more factors than those discussed here. Some of those will come up later in this book. Studying and applying the dignities thoroughly from one of the beginner books referenced in appendix A can be a great way to get a very clear guideline to accurate planetary interpretations.

Other Emphasized Chart Features

Whenever there is emphasis in a chart, whether it be many planets in a single house, a planet that is especially strong, or a planet that has aspects to most other planets, this emphasized feature will play a part in all areas of the individual's life. That means that it also will play a part in relationships, whether or not the planet or house is specifically associated with relationships. So, for example, if someone has an emphasized tenth house, the focus of the person's attention and experience will be on work, which will have an effect on his or her personal life (perhaps because the person will not pay enough attention to his or her partner, or will have relationships with co-workers, or something similar).

EXAMPLE: A PRELIMINARY ASSESSMENT OF THE CHART AS A WHOLE

The chart of Louise (chart 1) will be looked at in some depth throughout the course of this book. Before we can do that, we need to gain an overall sense of the chart.

Most of the planets in Louise's chart are below the horizon in houses two through five. This shows that she inclines toward privacy and introversion. There also is a greater emphasis on the western hemisphere, houses four through nine, telling us that Louise is quite oriented toward her interactions with others and that relationships are important to her.

A quick check on the planets shows us that quite a few of them are in signs that could bring out their negative qualities:

• The Sun is in its fall position (Libra). For the Sun, this is "negative" only because Librans are more concerned with relationships than themselves (and the Sun prefers to be focused on the self—think of its strong positions in Leo and Aries and you'll know why!). So there's no need to worry too much about the Sun's fall. It is in an angular house, making its Libran social nature very strong.

• The Moon also is in its fall. Scorpio makes it very perceptive and sensitive. What are the negative, fallen characteristics? There could be too great a need for control, which is really just insecurity, and which could lead to intensity and even manipulation. The Moon is in a succedent house, meaning it has regular strength, neither too much nor too little.

• Mercury is in Libra, converting those Libran social needs into great conversational tools. It also is angular, making it a strong influence, although it's retrograde, which dampens some of that strength slightly. If you were comparing its strength with that of another angular planet, that retrograde fact would help you decide which one has the upper hand.

- Venus is in detriment (Scorpio), which may bring out more of that troublesome effort to control things. She may have more difficulties with some of her relationships and less pleasure than the Libran would like.

- Mars is another planet in fall. In Cancer, its characteristics of drive, aggression, and ambition are unfocused, and it is hard to get a sense of direction. This can lead to feelings of frustration or resentfulness, especially since her goals are often turned toward nurturing her partner rather than pursuing her own ambitions.

- Jupiter and Saturn are both in signs that they rule, bringing out their better sides. Jupiter in Pisces creates a love of learning and gives faith and compassion; Saturn in Aquarius brings out concerns for the collective and the community, and helps the Libran sense of fairness be expressed. They both are retrograde, which weakens their influence just a bit, and although Jupiter is cadent, the ninth house is not really so weak—it's right up there at the top of the chart where all influences are strong.

- The outer planets Uranus and Pluto are cadent, helping to weaken their often-troublesome influence, but Neptune is in a regular-strength house and closely involved with two important planets, the Moon and Venus. It has the potential to cause confusion and poor boundaries or even deception in romance (it's in the fifth house of romance).

- When considering other emphasized chart features, we would consider that Moon-Neptune-Venus conjunction to be a standout feature—your eye is immediately drawn to it.

The Primary Needs: Sun and Moon

Now that we have a sense of the chart as a whole and the person as a whole, we are almost ready to start comparing the charts through the process of synastry. To bring our sense of the individual into much sharper focus, it is useful to take a look first at the two most important planets, the Sun and the Moon. These describe key needs and behaviors and one's sense of self.

Many of our drives are geared toward fulfilling basic needs that are established largely in the earliest stages of life. Although new needs will continue to develop in life, many of those that must be met through our interpersonal relationships are part of the very first experiences in life.

Astrologically, the Moon symbolizes the earliest part of life, and although the Sun's potentials will not mature fully until adulthood, the Sun, too, is a powerful driving force that already is noticeable in the later childhood years. Together, the luminaries are the most fundamental indicators of the essence of the self.

Forming relationships is among the most personal of our drives. It is here where the self is exposed, where the true identity is required to express itself. We can "put on" a professional façade at work and a social one in public, but in relationships we eventually have little option but to be ourselves. Thus the luminaries are the most crucial aspects to examine in the individual chart.

The Sun and the Moon do not simply represent the abstract notion of "self"; they embody the most essential needs of the individual. These needs must be met no matter what area of life is being considered. In fact, when it comes to relationships, the Moon is an especially important consideration, since it represents primary emotional needs. These are the same needs that are pursued from our earliest years.

Part of the search for a satisfactory partnership is seeking for basic emotional needs to be met. Most of those basic needs can be understood by looking at the Moon in the chart. In practice, a relationship that does not support the most basic needs of the Moon is going to prove dissatisfying and may not last very long. The individual will feel that the partner does not understand him or her or is not sensitive.

The Sun's needs are also primary. While the Moon can represent the inner needs that we seek to satisfy, the Sun's needs are projected into the world and are considerably more obvious and demanding. The Sun says, "This is who I am!", while the Moon says, "If you really knew me, you'd do this for me."

Noel Tyl suggests that the Sun and Moon must be capable of blending their energies in a harmonious way. The Moon's needs must be capable of being met by the Sun, through the Sun's drives and means of expression. An individual with the Sun and Moon in very different elements may have difficulty establishing this inner sense of harmony, while similar or compatible elements will blend much more successfully.[3] Although the individual

---

3. Noel Tyl, *Synthesis & Counseling in Astrology* (St. Paul, MN: Llewellyn Publications, 1994).

alone is responsible for finding a way to blend these two energies harmoniously, a way to blend the energies also will be sought through the partner.

Steps to Analyze the Sun and Moon

When analyzing any planet, start with the steps described earlier in the section "Strong or Weak Planets." In this case, we also want to consider the issue of whether the Sun and Moon meet each other's needs:

- First, look at each luminary and consider what needs each one has in the sign that it is in. Table 4 provides some keywords relevant to relationships to help you get started.

- Also keep in mind the dignity of the planet: if the luminary is in its own sign or its exalted sign, the person may be more able to actively pursue and satisfy his or her needs, while if it is in detriment or fall, this is not as easy.

- Needs are closely related to actual experiences in life—so the house of the luminary is also very important to understand the needs. Table 5 will help you identify some of those needs.

- Now compare the Sun and Moon by considering whether their basic needs are compatible. Ask yourself, is this individual's Sun, in terms of its sign and house, capable of meeting the needs demanded by this Moon, in terms of sign and house? It can be helpful to consider the elements when making this comparison. Very basic needs are related to the elemental principles, and it helps if the two luminaries agree at this level. Table 4 can help you find basic similarities or dissimilarities.

- Finally, consider whether the luminaries actually have an aspect between them. The conjunction, sextile, and trine can work together and usually occur when the elements are compatible. Squares and oppositions are challenging because the needs of each luminary are in conflict. Even though oppositions generally involve compatible elements, the opposite houses show that the needs will be looked for in very different places, and the opposite signs show they will be sought in very different ways.

Table 4: Needs of the Luminaries in Each Sign	
Sign	**Keywords for Basic Needs**
Aries	Success, immediate results, express self, feel free to do anything
Taurus	Security, comfort, stability, material well-being, certainty
Gemini	Express opinions, make changes, socialize, intellectual stimulation
Cancer	Emotional security, domestic harmony, nurture and provide
Leo	Attention, acknowledgment, control, affection
Virgo	Sense of order, be helpful or useful, be needed
Libra	Social success, friendship, relationship, romanticism, create harmony
Scorpio	Control, access to resources, catalyze changes
Sagittarius	Freedom, new experiences, new ideas, fun, spiritual growth
Capricorn	Security, certainty, structure, responsibility, sense of importance
Aquarius	New ways of being and doing, group activities, participate, express ideals
Pisces	Romanticism, spiritual growth, peacefulness, seclusion, be of service

Table 5: Needs of the Luminaries in Each House	
House	**Keywords for Basic Needs**
1	Recognition, independence, dominance, appreciation
2	Material security, sense of purpose and self-worth, strong values, indulgence
3	Identify with others, communicate, new environments, change
4	Domestic security, family connections, sense of roots, privacy
5	Pleasure, fun, romance, children, sexual expression
6	Serve others, good health, feel useful
7	Relationships and partnerships, interdependence, social connections
8	Find resources, feel powerful, depend on others

9	Travel, study, experience new things, feel free, grow spiritually
10	Recognition, achievement, status, power, popularity, influence
11	Social success, friendship, pursue and fulfill ideals, be part of something
12	Seclusion, privacy, make sacrifices, grow spiritually

Interpreting Compatible or Incompatible Needs

In the majority of people, the similarities between the Sun and Moon are a mixture of needs that support each other and needs that don't. It is likely that some of the incompatible needs will produce some inner conflict. Since it is hard for us to know clearly what we need at all times, these conflicting needs can make us try to find satisfaction of our needs in ways that cause more problems than they solve.

For example, we may simply engage in behavior that seeks to satisfy the needs of one luminary, but in so doing, unsettles the needs of the other luminary. Perhaps we'll even find a partner who seems to satisfy them for us. The problem is that this approach addresses only one luminary's needs, and the other luminary's needs may become even more frustrated as other incompatible needs are overlooked, later to cause fresh problems. It may even be that the way the partner satisfies our needs causes problems.

Of course, if all our needs were harmonious and easily satisfied, we probably would end up complacent and lazy. Clearly, the tension between different kinds of needs and varying abilities to meet them creates the energy and motivation for many of our basic drives.

That means you should be careful not to interpret these conflicts as if they were life-threatening or challenging the possibility for successful relationships. Rather, they simply help us identify very basic motivations, which can be one of the most powerful ways to help clients understand themselves and their relationships.

It is hard to gain perspective in our own lives, so the conflicts arising out of these basic issues often seem fundamental and unchangeable. That's not the case. Understanding basic needs will help you get to the bottom of inner conflicts and the frustration people can feel toward their partners in straightforward, everyday terms. It also can help clients find more practical ways to satisfy their own needs.

Once you can identify the frustration as a basic need looking for fulfillment, you also can encourage clients to find practical ways to try to meet the needs in the context of their relationship. (A simple example is shown at the beginning of the next chapter.)

EXAMPLE: SUN AND MOON WITH CONFLICTING NEEDS

Louise (chart 1) is an attractive, graceful artist with a Libra Sun and Scorpio Moon. These luminaries function very differently. They are not aspected, except by semisextile, which does not indicate compatible needs, and they both are in the sign of their fall, implying that it is difficult for Louise to satisfy those needs.

Louise has a strongly passionate, creative, and sexual nature that, with a badly dignified Moon, is very difficult to fulfill. The Neptune and detrimented Venus conjunct the Moon leads to fruitless sexual and romantic fantasy and illusion and a tendency to make sacrifices. She probably has great ideals about romance and children.

The Libra Sun is largely after different things than the Moon, seeking traditional security in the fourth house. This need is strong because the Sun is strong, being in an angular house. It emphasizes her Libran qualities like equanimity, while the dark and mysterious fallen Moon stirs desires.

The weaker (not angular) position of the Moon makes those desires less pressing and helps prevent the Sun-Moon differences from becoming too much of an issue. Still, she finds it hard to fulfill her inner needs, which may seem polarized to her.

How Needs Are Made Visible to Others

It's one thing to be able to identify all these needs, but it's not as if individuals consciously go around searching for them to be met, or have a neat little list that they can check off against the person they have met. If life were that simple, there would be very little need for relationship counseling at all.

Besides, the needs that seem so obvious to the astrologer are actually a network of partly conscious and mostly unconscious factors that are intimately bound into the remainder of the personality. Neither the individual who has the needs nor the rest of the world can clearly identify what they are. On top of that, as we saw in the last chapter, we often go about presenting an altogether different self to the world, especially when we are in pursuit of partnership.

Our desire to create a good first impression means that we tend to do the exact opposite of what our needs and drives demand. We present to the world a very different image from who we really are: remember, we also use the Ascendant and Mercury to try to control how others perceive us. Not only that, but rather than trying to find ways to indicate what we are looking for in a partner, *we tend to imagine what others are looking for and then make the effort to look as if we represent that very holy grail.*

Is it any wonder relationships are such a minefield? Not only is our idea of what people are looking for likely to be inaccurate, but in effect we are our own worst enemies because we are trying to create what we think someone else wants rather than pursuing what we ourselves want.

Another Look at the Ascendant

We need to look at the Ascendant again in light of these essential needs that we have identified.

- Consider whether the Ascendant can project what the Sun and Moon show is needed. How accurate is the picture of the person that the Ascendant shows?

- It is especially important to compare the Sun with the Ascendant. The Sun is a more authentic projection of our drives and efforts to pursue our needs, but the Ascendant can conceal this real self in order to create an impression calculated to attract the "right" person.

- Take note if the Ascendant seems more similar to or compatible with one of the luminaries than the other. The needs of that luminary then will become more obvious or the individual will more directly try to satisfy them, while the needs of the other luminary may become neglected or may seem even more invisible to other people and perhaps even to the chart owner.

EXAMPLE: WHAT DOES LOUISE PROJECT?

Louise's Gemini Ascendant will give her the appearance of being gregarious, highly communicative, and eager to be liked by others. This is not so different from the Libra Sun's needs for social interaction, harmonious relationships, and a sense of security.

Of course, since the Sun and Ascendant are both in air signs, this ability of the Ascendant to reflect and project real needs that Louise has is not surprising, and will help her pursue and satisfy some of her needs. On the other hand, the Scorpio Moon finds little expression through that Ascendant, and its needs and desires become even harder to find in the friendly but not very deep world that she creates around herself.

Drawing Some Conclusions

We have looked at the luminaries and the Ascendant is some detail, and made an initial analysis of Mercury. Even though we have barely touched the surface of the chart, we have developed quite a thorough understanding of how the most essential personality characteristics contribute to the basic drives that underlie much of what we are looking for in our pursuit of relationship success.

You already can provide each individual in a relationship with a pertinent picture of some basic relationship dynamics, but to make it relevant to a specific relationship, you need to start making some comparisons.

CHAPTER 3

FIRST STEPS IN COMPARISONS

Now it's time to actually begin the work of synastry. Soon you will learn the specific technical methods to compare different charts, but the first comparisons you must make will be based on natal astrology and common sense.

In This Chapter

- Comparing elements to determine personality style.
- Comparing the Sun, Moon, and Ascendant.
- Which personality characteristics cause the biggest compatibility issues, and how to find them astrologically.
- Expressing information to clients.
- Deciding how much to say.

Initial Comparisons

The first thing to do when examining how people get on and how likely they are to have a successful relationship is simply to compare those personality characteristics that are most likely to affect everyday interactions. At first, comparing only the elements will give you a sense of the style of behavior, and then you can go further to consider the same trait in each person in the relationship and the extent to which they are similar or contrasting in that way.

Start with Elements Alone

Comparing the elements is easy and direct, and in many cases will give your clients an easy way to enter into the process of synastry. It allows your clients to understand the basics of comparison and helps to relax them and draw them in as participants rather than mere listeners. Most people relate to the general descriptions of the dominant element in their chart, especially when it is contextualized to their own particular Sun, Moon, or Ascendant causing that emphasis.[1] The natal chart is the final arbiter of just how much you will stress the emphasis of elements, and the accent should be on comparing and contrasting the interaction of the elements.

The simplest approach to this is best, especially at first. Once you get more experience in synastry, you may not even want to take this individual step but rather build it in to the steps that follow.

Comparing Elements

The elements are so basic that, even without astrological knowledge, understanding how they interact is a matter of common sense. Although strictly speaking the use of the elements to generalize about the personality "type" is an oversimplification, in practice it proves useful and accurate.

To get a sense of elemental interaction, think of the elements as literal substances that are being mixed. These guidelines will help you translate that into human terms. There are three types of interaction: elements that mix easily are highly compatible; elements that can be mixed but don't naturally mix are compatible when effort is applied; and elements that won't mix at all are not compatible or are disinterested. Remember, you are generalizing at this stage: don't assume you are talking about compatible or incompatible *people*. The elements are better understood as *styles* of interacting with the world that help create values and experiences.

---

1. Advanced or scholarly readers may use the more comprehensive traditional methods of assessing temperament. See Appendix A: Further Reading for recommended books on temperament.

Highly Compatible Elements

Highly compatible elements are separated by a conjunction, sextile, trine, or opposition.

- **The same element dominates**. When a couple have the same elemental strength, they are similar in the way they do things and their overall personality styles. This makes it easy for them to get along, and at first they will perceive each other as very similar. It is possible to have too many similarities. The basic elemental quality can become overemphasized and lead to stalemates in dealing with problems, or the similarities can make it seem that your own issues are in fact your partner's (since he or she has similar issues). Too much fire can lead to high levels of interpersonal conflict; too much earth makes for intransigence and resistance to growth; too much air and it's all talk and no action, with lots of argument about ideas or principles; too much water and the relationship sinks in an emotional quagmire, with both people taking everything personally and never really relating as a couple, or alternately losing their sense of individuality completely.

- **Naturally compatible elements**. These are the elements that have some interdependence, making for the best type of compatibility in relationships. The individuals have different energy styles, but they easily interpolate with each other. Different but compatible values and goals make for a relationship that has fewer problems and more opportunities to work together toward shared goals. Fire and air cause each other to grow (air feeds fire and fire makes air expand). Both individuals value knowledge and experience but pursue them in different ways. Both deal with things intellectually, also with different styles, but with a high potential for mutual understanding. Earth and water also depend on each other for growth (think of plants in the soil). Together they make clay, the basis for life symbolically. They both relate to the world emotionally and personally, making interpersonal dynamics and relationship success high up in the value system.

Elements That Are Compatible with Effort

These are elements that don't naturally mix, but when made to mix they can lead to a constructive outcome. They are separated by a semisextile or a square. When they mix, they create a combination of problems and benefits. Effort must always be maintained for the benefits to be apparent.

- **Air and water** usually remain apart, but air can be dissolved into water by natural forces (it dissolves into rainwater this way) or by effort (soda is made like this). Water-dominated people may lack the skills to talk about or understand their feelings, but can learn to do so with the help of an air partner, while the air partner can learn to relate a little more emotionally.

- **Earth and fire** can actually hurt each other—earth puts out fire while fire dries out earth. But together they can create a powerful force. Astrologers often talk about the "steamroller" effect produced by the successful combination of these elements or of the useful, long-lasting ceramics that depend on their interaction. The fire individual benefits by being grounded and made to see practical concerns, while the earth person learns to be more spontaneous and energetic.

Not Compatible or Disinterested Elements

Some elements will not mix at all. This does not mean there is no hope for the partnership—remember that we are still at the stage of introductory generalities—but it does mean that there always will be conscious effort required to overcome the perception that the other person is irredeemably different in every way.

- **Earth and air** have no meeting point at all. They have no way of mixing (unless you consider a sandstorm to be a mix). In people, this combination is a little like polite strangers meeting at a cocktail party. Their approach to life is different, but they are capable of understanding each other. Still, any relationship between them will lack emotional investment or passion. This combination is good only for acquaintances, colleagues, or casual friends.

- **Fire and water** have an inimical relationship—they will each destroy each other. Actually, this potentially is an exciting relationship: think of the sizzling and the steam when the two elements join. But in the long run they have very different styles of emotionality and can create complex codependent relationships that have much more interaction than earth and air but may not be good for each partner's personal growth.

Comparing Sun, Moon, and Ascendant

The elemental emphasis in a chart often is reflected in the fact that the dominant element usually is represented in the Sun, Moon, or Ascendant. These are chart fundamentals that can go some way to describe essential qualities of the individual all on their own. You have already analyzed them quite thoroughly for each chart—you can now combine this with your knowledge gained from elemental analysis and apply that knowledge to the process of comparison.

1. Compare Ascendants, talking about how each one tends to approach the world. Use their elemental interaction to describe how these two approaches may or may not be compatible.

2. Compare Sun signs. Clients readily relate to this information. The elemental interaction provides the basic message of whether they are compatible, and you can elaborate if you have found either of them to be typical of their Sun sign.

3. Compare Moon signs. You can now talk specifically about emotional needs and behaviors, information that is directly related to relationships. It also is useful to consider to what extent the two Moons support and respond to each other, as you did with each Sun-Moon pair in the individual charts. You may find that an individual's Sun-Moon relationship does not lend itself to needs being met, but the needs may well be satisfied by the partner's luminary positions. Later we will look more closely at this comparison.

4. Take note when one partner has one of these three chart points in the same sign as that point or one of the other points in the partner's chart. These are powerful points of similarity that you can highlight and use later to help the partners build understanding of each other. These similarities often will override the apparent differences you have discovered in the more generalized comparison of elements. Similarity at such a fundamental level creates an ability to relate to each other very early on and may circumvent some of the issues of first impressions.

EXAMPLE: COMPARING SUN, MOON, AND ASCENDANT

Maggie (chart 8) has an earthy chart, with her Sun in Capricorn, Moon in Scorpio, and Ascendant in Virgo. Ken (chart 9) has his Sun in Aquarius, Moon in Leo, and Ascendant in Capricorn. He is predominantly air. Although their elemental mix has little that's good and twelve years separate them, her Ascendant compared with his Sun and Ascendant continues to create enough similarity for them to stay in a long-term relationship.

Their Moons are in highly incompatible elements and will produce a lot of conflict—although their basic emotional values are probably similar (they are both fixed signs and need security). They handle the world in a similar fashion (both Ascendants are earth), but of course they perceive more similarities than are really there (between their Suns and Moons alone there is little elemental compatibility).

Conveying Information to Clients

We eventually will get deeper into the many dynamics of talking about relationships with clients, but at this early stage in the reading I have found it useful to simply describe this comparison to the couple and allow them to share their experiences of basic interaction based on the description of the interaction of these traits. Here's a recent example from my client Anne:

EXAMPLE: DIFFERENT BASIC NEEDS

Anne has the Moon in Taurus; her son Raymond has it in Leo (charts not shown). I told them, "Ray needs warmth and attention and Anne needs security and comfort." Anne immediately responded, "When he is emotional and needs pampering and attention, I give him food, which doesn't do anything for him, so he always says I never understand him."

Before any of the work has even been started, they already have gained insight into their relationship, like the fact that their Moons are square to each other (Taurus squares Leo).

Comparing Individual Characteristics

There are some personal characteristics that have a strong influence on the way we manage our relationships. In the next chapter we will look at aspects of the individual chart representing fundamental qualities that have an influence on relationships, but there also are personality features that are less fundamental to the values, beliefs, and expectations but that equally affect the outcome of the relationship. We'll start with these, because their effects are clear and apparent right from the start without going as deeply into the personality as we will do in the next chapter.

Some of these may represent issues you want to discuss in private with your client, and it always is better to have seen each member of the partnership privately before the synastry consultation. But since these characteristics are so closely related to what happens in a relationship (and often to what goes wrong in a relationship), they are also characteristics that can be compared in the way we have been doing in this chapter. Unlike the fundamental characteristics discussed in the next chapter, these do not underlie all aspects of our lives. They may surface only when we are in a relationship or in our interactions with other people.

In all cases, you will weigh these qualities in the individual charts. Look for supporting factors—remember, accuracy improves when more than one chart factor says the same thing. Always remember to check the accidental dignity (see chapter 2) of a planet you are holding responsible for some quality; a planet gets the opportunity to express its influence only if accidental dignity is reasonably high. Also remember to look at the *ruler of a house* (the planet that rules the sign on the cusp of the house) for more information about the areas related to that house.

- **The need for independence** often undermines the search for a successful relationship. A strong Uranus (especially in the first or seventh house or closely aspecting the Sun or Moon) represents this need, as do dominant fire signs (especially Aries and Sagittarius, and especially when the Sun or Moon is in one of these signs). An emphasized Sun, or a few personal planets in the first house, can create a strong focus on pursuing personal needs and desires. The Sun or Moon in Aquarius also makes for a pretty independent streak.

- **A tendency to be dependent or needy** is the opposite extreme. This can be symbolized by many personal planets in the water element or by a weak Moon. Possessiveness also can be signaled by such a Moon, or an emphasis on the signs Cancer and Taurus (they are the signs that need security).

- **Willingness and ability to commit.** Another kind of opposite to independence is commitment. Commitment is critical to long-term relationship success. Emphasized Capricorn or Saturn, especially when well aspected with the Sun, Moon, or Venus, as well as strong earth qualities on the whole, all contribute to this characteristic even when the commitment may feel like a burden to the person. Indicators similar to those for independence can show an inability or unwillingness to commit.

- **Ways of expressing emotion.** Different styles of emotional expression go a long way to create communication difficulties, but they often get mistaken for more fundamental differences (such as different value systems or needs). It can be extremely useful for a couple to understand their different ways of expressing emotion.

  Very emotionally expressive people are usually strong in fire and have quite a bit of water in the chart. There also may be harmonious aspects between Moon and Mercury, which allows Mercury, the communicator, to express what the emotional Moon is feeling, especially if Mars also aspects them, adding passion and intensity to the feelings. Air and earth may be prominent for less expressive people, but those who tend not to display emotion often have Saturn strongly placed—it may be aspecting or ruling the personal planets, or its signs, Capricorn and Aquarius, may dominate the chart.

- **Sexual needs.** We will discuss the interplay of sexual drives in greater detail in the next chapter. At this stage, it is useful to see if one of the partners has an especially powerful sex drive, as a difference in this drive can become a major obstacle for some even if many other indicators of compatibility exist. The strong sex drive can be indicated by a powerful Venus or Mars, but this is especially so if both are strong and aspecting each other. Scorpio also is associated with sex, as it is the sign that rules the sexual organs, so when emphasized by personal planets (especially Venus and Mars) it can add fuel to the sex drive. This is also the case when the fifth house is heavily occupied or its ruler is very strong.

  A weaker sex drive is signified by the same qualities that show lack of emotional expression (see previous point), especially when Saturn aspects Venus or sits in Scorpio or the fifth house.

- **Jealousy.** The need to guard what is our own is a primal need that almost everybody has to learn to manage. Jealousy is famously responsible for destroying relationships because it so often leads to possessiveness, control, and a host of irrational behaviors. Astrologically, a strong Mars, Scorpio, or Pluto signifies jealousy, especially if a strong, negative Saturn is in the picture. A challenged but powerful second house or its ruler could create the need to cling to one's possessions—including the partner—and even the eighth house in a similar condition could do the same (it is the house of what the partner has, which one may also feel the need to own and control).

- **How money is handled.** A different approach to the saving and spending of money can be a very destructive force in a relationship. Extravagance is a fiery quality, especially when Sagittarius is emphasized, although Leo also can indicate excessive generosity. Jupiter and Venus when weakly placed or in a square or opposition to each other also incline toward spending or poor control of financial resources. A conservative approach to money—even selfishness—can be indicated when Saturn or Capricorn are powerful; Jupiter or Venus in Virgo, a sign in which both of them are weak (it is Jupiter's detriment and Venus's fall), also can be responsible.

Although these are important personality issues when considering potential relationship problems, remember that they are also basic human traits that most people have in varying degrees, and that many people increasingly master with time. This particular list is an adaptation from one by Derek and Julia Parker.[2] There are many more you might be able to think of, and a few that will be mentioned only in later chapters where they are more relevant to specific areas of analysis.

Don't make a big deal out of these issues; they may not be as problematic as they look in the chart (things rarely are).

EXAMPLES: DIFFERENT INDIVIDUAL CHARACTERISTICS

Dan (chart 10) and Janice (chart 11) have been married for over fifteen years. Despite the strong attraction between them (we'll look at their charts a few times in the coming chapters), there are some fundamental differences: she is very generous with those she loves, while he tends to hold tightly to all he has.

Janice's generous and sharing nature is evident in her conjunction of Jupiter in the first and a strong Venus in air, and an extremely strong and expressive Mercury makes it easy for her to express her nature and give of herself.

Dan is predominantly Scorpio (three planets are there, including the Sun) with reticent Taurus rising. He has Venus in selfish Capricorn and the dark eighth house, both adding to the hidden Scorpionic nature. Mercury is in detriment, making it hard for him to find the right words to express himself.

---

2. This list appears in *Parkers' Astrology* (see appendix A).

Dan has a number of factors suggesting possessiveness and jealousy: Scorpio is on the seventh cusp of marriage, with its ruler in its own sign but in the difficult sixth house, and Pluto has high accidental dignity. He also has a lot of earth and water.

Joanne Woodward (chart 12) and Paul Newman (chart 13) show how a careful look at these matters reveals inherent compatibility. Though they have been married for over forty-five years and are famously happy, Woodward has declared that they have nothing in common.

So they like different things. Does it matter?

- Their need for independence is similar, with strong first houses in Capricorn ruled by a strong Saturn and the luminaries in Aquarius—but this is the kind of independence that does not oppose relationship, but rather gives them the need for their own pursuits.

- These same indicators give strong qualities of commitment and responsibility.

- They have similar emotional styles, with strong water elements highlighting Pisces, Cancer on the seventh with Pluto emphasized by accidental dignity on the seventh, and strong earth with low fire. They're probably equally possessive, which perhaps prevents their independence from threatening the relationship.

- Their sexual natures are similarly strong and positive, suggesting how they can satisfy each other. Her Venus is the ruler of the fifth and is exalted in Pisces, with Jupiter actually *in* the fifth. Jupiter's detriment in Gemini shows there is one snag, possibly related to secrecy (Jupiter rules her twelfth). His ruler of the fifth is Mercury, which is prominently placed with the two beneficial planets Venus and Jupiter. His Jupiter is similarly troubled—this time by being in fall in Capricorn—and probably also because of secrecy since it again rules the twelfth! They even share similar problems.

- Their financial patterns are similar, although less relevant since they earn their own fortunes. Both have a strong Saturn ruling the second and the Moon in the second, giving wealth. Woodward's very strong second house is weakened only by the square with poorly dignified Jupiter; she probably spends her money on pleasures. His second-house strength is undermined by the spending potential of its ruler, Uranus, but is balanced by the Venus-Jupiter conjunction in conservative Capricorn. Independently wealthy, they are unlikely to be troubled by money, but if this were a more ordinary couple we would be a little concerned about Neptune in her eighth house of partner's money, considering that his Uranus is in the second.

An analysis of the fundamentals reveals the "mystery" of why such apparently dissimilar people are not that different after all.

How Much Should You Say?

Each situation is a little different. Although I make many recommendations in this book, you must consider the actual situation to be your main guide. For example, when dealing with people who have met only recently and are in the stages of seeing much more appearance than reality, is it your job to burst the bubble? More specifically, should you reveal qualities like jealousy or difficulty expressing emotion? It is unlikely that it is desirable to know all at this stage in a relationship, whether or not the couple think they have come to hear the whole truth. There is probably a good reason why these qualities are discovered in each other only in small stages.

With a couple who have been together for years, it usually is very useful to discuss all these qualities in an honest but diplomatic way. Just discuss and compare as you have been doing with all the personal traits, and allow each partner to contribute personal experiences of that aspect if he or she wants. Chapter 9 will take you step by step through planning a constructive session.

The Foundation in Place

You have uncovered a lot of meaningful information that you easily can shape into a powerful and useful session for your clients, yet you barely have started the work of synastry. When you learn how to put the charts together, you will find the issues that are unique to each particular relationship and the unique methods that will help resolve them.

Before you can do that effectively, you need to go further than these compatibility characteristics and start exploring much deeper, core issues that relate to our beliefs and expectations about a relationship.

CHAPTER 4

THE FOUNDATIONS
OF RELATING

While it's true that we can get a good understanding of basic compatibility be comparing the essentials of people's personalities, relationships are in reality much more complex than that. Compatibility is not based on the simple principles of similarity or difference alone, but rather on the complex network of emotions and experience that we build throughout our lives and that makes us who we are.

Many of our actions and expectations are based on fundamental aspects of ourselves that are the same in whichever relationship we have and that may critically determine the success or failure of our relationships. These are the factors we will now explore.

In This Chapter

- The importance of communication.
- How the value system is at the root of all relationship matters.
- Reading the fifth house and the other succedent houses for critical life issues affecting relationships: values, self-worth, love, pleasure, children, and sex.
- Determining whether conditions exist for a lasting marriage.

Communicating Feelings

As human beings, we all experience emotions. What varies among us, and what has a very strong bearing on relationships, is the extent to which we understand our emotions and the ability and willingness we have to communicate them. Having strong feelings and even knowing and understanding them, while this can be a growth milestone for some people, is only the beginning when it comes to relating these feelings to others.

Communicating what we feel can be the most challenging part of a relationship, and for many relationships this eventually becomes the make-or-break issue. Sometimes poor communication or misunderstanding is enough to seriously damage a relationship.

Mercury is the planet that describes both understanding and communication. By examining its relationship with the Moon, we are able to see how easy and likely understanding and expression of emotions will be.

Analyzing Communication Using Mercury and the Moon

The relationship between Mercury and the Moon shows whether this understanding of emotions or lack of it is applied to one's own life. More importantly, it also shows whether or not feelings tend to be expressed.

You already have looked at both of these planets and can now build on your analysis by examining how they relate to each other:

- Look again at your notes about the Moon, and now consider that Moon in that sign and house with regard to the basic idea of the emotional self that you are already familiar with. Don't forget to keep in mind what you have established as the basic needs of that Moon—communicating those needs successfully can be an important reason for success or failure in relationships, and the Moon-Mercury relationship can show whether those needs are properly communicated.

- Analyze Mercury the way you did the Moon in chapter 2. Look at the sign it is in, and expand your description of the element into a more detailed description of Mercury in that particular sign.

- Look at the essential dignity and accidental dignity of Mercury, as we have been doing, and ask yourself whether this person clearly says what he or she means (Mercury has good essential dignity) and whether the person actually gets around to saying it (Mercury has good accidental dignity). If Mercury is in fall or detriment, it means the person's style of speech may not effectively communicate the feelings; for example, Mercury in Pisces may be vague or in Sagittarius may be too blunt.

- Now look at the aspect between Moon and Mercury, if there is one. The harmonious aspects (the sextile and trine) allow emotions to be successfully communicated, especially since the individual identifies with his or her own feelings. These people are able to be persuasive and convincing and can even use their understanding of themselves and others to their advantage.

- Conjunctions sometimes can show a perfect harmony between head and heart, although they are more likely to give strong instincts while making a person rather obsessive. These people can hold on to their ideas and beliefs about themselves passionately. They can express their feelings very directly, but find it difficult to see themselves objectively and distinguish thoughts from feelings.

- Squares show either a disinclination to talk about feelings at all or a difficulty in finding the right words to communicate those feelings, often creating further misunderstanding and a vicious cycle of problems. Oppositions can be similar, although more often they reveal an individual at odds with his or her feelings. These people don't know how to fit their feelings into the bigger picture and may not relate to them at all, although they sometimes go to the other extreme and are "all emotion," with no rational ability to make use of the feelings and move forward.

- If the Moon and Mercury are each in a sign ruled by the other (this is called *mutual reception*), or even if only one of them is in the other's sign (*reception*), this can act like a very harmonious aspect and will improve the relationship between them.

The Value System

Although there may be specific relationship expectations that arise from early life experience, the most fundamental of our foundations is the value system. The things we hold dear, our moral and ethical values, what we will consider acceptable in another human being, and perhaps most importantly what we do with our resources—all these are key in determining the success of our relationships. (It is important to remember, however, that they do not necessarily determine who we will become attracted to; in fact, it is not unusual to be attracted to people who embody the very opposite of our value system.)

Of course, the reason for this is that Venus rules all the things that we love and hold dear, and that therefore lie at the very heart of our value system. Venus also rules passion, romance, and sex.

Venus's position by sign, its essential dignity, and its house position are crucial in establishing these values. As you did with Mercury, start your analysis by looking at the element and then extend that into the sign.

Table 6: Element of Venus and the Value System	
Element of Venus Sign	**Basic Values**
Earth	The values tend to be more traditional. The individual feels very secure in these values, which may be seen by others as highly principled, and often becomes impassioned about them. This is strongest when Venus is in its own sign of Taurus.
Water	The values also are rather traditional, but are more personal and emotional. This is strongest when Venus is in Pisces, its sign of exaltation. Relationships themselves are a value.
Air	Air brings out the social side of Venus, especially when Venus is in its own sign of Libra. This sociability means that the individual will have few problems meeting people and may even enter into relationships quite easily, but the high need for social stimulation may be a threat to the security of the relationship.
Fire	Fire suits the need for pleasure that is characteristic of Venus, but may not be good for the security and exclusivity that generally are required for meaningful relationships to work. For example, with Venus in Aries, impulsively entering into relationships may be an issue.

Self-Worth

One of the key value systems is based on the saving and spending of money. Differences in spending habits can be enough to bring a relationship to its knees and is a common source of stress. To the astrologer, though, money usually is part of a much deeper issue: self-worth.

Money is the perfect symbol for how we value things, and the way we manage our money (and handle our other possessions) usually reflects our unconscious assessment of our own value. For example, people who undercharge for their services may not feel they are good enough at what they do, while people who charge more than average clearly feel that they are above average at their jobs.

People who have poor self-worth tend to be less discriminating about their choice of partners for the same reason—they do not consider themselves worthy of the person they are attracted to or might consider their ideal match. They often see the partner as better than themselves, especially if the partner is someone who tends to have high self-worth. *In fact, these individuals are likely to overlook all the other flaws, even serious problems, when the partner's self-worth is much greater than their own.*

This makes the assessment of self-worth one of the key issues in your analysis of the natal chart. It is assessed using these criteria:

- Planets in the second house have the strongest influence. Consider the inherent nature of the planet (for example, the difficult planet Saturn has a debilitating effect here, while Jupiter has a good effect) as well as the essential dignity it has in the sign it is in.

- Consider the aspects this planet receives, especially if it receives oppositions from planets in the eighth (the partner's self-worth) or squares from the fifth- or eleventh-house planets. The fifth deals with the ability to express love, while the eleventh shows the capacity to receive love. Poor self-worth often relates to an inability to receive the love of others.

- Finally, consider the *ruler* of the second house in the same way.

- The Sun, as the planet of "self," also can be a significator for self-worth. In particular, the aspects of the Sun can have a significant effect. Challenging aspects from Saturn or the outer planets could impair the self-worth.

EXAMPLE: DIFFICULTY MEETING NEEDS

Louise (chart 1) has her challenging Moon as the ruler of her second house (remember that it is in fall and conjunct Neptune). She has a fallen Mars inside the second house, contributing to a poor sense of worth connected to her inner emotional and strong sexual needs (the Moon in the fifth in Scorpio). Mercury as no connection to that Moon, so the deep Scorpionic feelings remain unexpressed. Yet as the chart ruler in an angular house, Mercury is strongly expressive of her Mercurial and Libran mental qualities. This helps her Gemini Ascendant create an impression based on her better qualities, but doesn't help the real needs become known, and can become an issue in her relationships.

Love, Sex, and Pleasure

Our personal needs and beliefs go a long way to explain the relationship we make, but perhaps the most significant need is the need for a relationship itself. A variety of chart factors pertain directly to this need, but one of the most basic human needs is to love and be loved. The fifth and eleventh houses reveal this experience.

Analyzing these houses will give you a useful understanding of how these issues most directly affect expectations about relationships and the actual experience of loving someone. In fact, the fifth house in particular has a very important place in relationship analysis because it describes things that are important experiences and potential "issues" in any relationship.

In analysis, consider how the planets in the fifth and the ruler of the fifth might affect:

- Experiencing and expressing fun and pleasure.
- The importance of sex and the nature of its expression.
- Beliefs and attitudes about romance.
- Expectations regarding children.

Matters of romanticism and children are the more fundamental issues of this house. The "fun" aspect of the fifth means that planets cause a stark contrast in the experience of pleasure depending on whether they are benefic or malefic. Venus is the planet that is the significator for the same pleasurable things as those of the fifth house, so first examine it again in the light of these fifth-house matters:

- The relationship between Venus and the other planets is highly descriptive of sexuality and sexual expression. This is particularly true of aspects between Venus and Mars. Conjunctions and sextiles produce a passion that helps make a relationship work, and the trine speaks of the ability to harmonize the sexual drive with that of the partner. Even "difficult" aspects may sometimes be good for passion, although they often cause confusion between platonic and romantic love. The square and opposition can indicate that sex is overemphasized in the quest for a mate, or that promiscuity will be the source of problems.

- Venus's aspects with Saturn, particularly the challenging aspects, can produce coldness in sexual expression, while Venus's aspects with the outer planets can indicate unusual needs or experiences (see "Beyond Pleasure" later in this chapter).

Now look at the actual ruler of the fifth and the planets in that house. These are the important things to keep in mind for each planet:

- The luminaries strongly emphasize the need for pleasure and the satisfaction taken in it. They both provide the ability to take delight in simple things and in the physical and fun side of a relationship. In their negative (debilitated) state, they may lead to overidentification with these things, making it difficult to deal with the adult side of the relationship and potentially creating issues of irresponsibility or selfishness. There also can be too much emphasis on sexual needs, unbalancing the relationship.

- Venus in the house also will emphasize the need for pleasure. If it receives positive aspects or is positively dignified, there will be easy and natural opportunities to express these needs. Sexual experience is likely to be positive, and there is a likelihood of attracting partners with a similar taste for pleasure and a compatible style of sexual expression. If, however, Venus is poorly aspected or debilitated, the appetite for pleasure and sex may be difficult to satisfy or may lead the individual into fruitless pursuits or a disproportionate focus on sex in his or her relationships. For example, with Venus in Aries, the search for pleasure may be selfish. This may lead to a lack of consideration for the partner, or incline the individual toward short-term sexual relationships. In Scorpio, sexual passions may dominate or tastes may be perverted.

- Although Mars generally is challenging, it sometimes can be beneficial in the fifth house. Since this house deals with activities such as sports and creative endeavors, Mars's strong energy is helpful. When Mars has good dignity and aspects, this energy will produce positive and beneficial results and help the individual pursue specific (although still often selfish) pleasure-seeking goals. In a debilitated condition, selfishness becomes a problem, and there also may be destructive behavior and sexual perversion: in Taurus, the individual may have confidence problems with sex or feel frustrated in the effort to succeed in this area, while in Libra, Mars makes the individual's needs incompatible with the way he or she handles social situations. Flirtatiousness may be too aggressive or sexually suggestive, or the person may fail to assert his or her needs altogether.

- Jupiter also emphasizes the needs of this house and provides much joy and pleasure, while its debilities are less likely to highlight troublesome sexual problems. Rather, Jupiter in Gemini or Virgo will accentuate the rational and analytical qualities, making it difficult for the individual to enjoy him- or herself. A well-placed Jupiter will not only provide for a much more positive experience of sex and pleasure, but also will allow these pleasures to contribute positively to the individual's growth.

- Saturn can make it very difficult for the person to experience pleasure at all. Even when positively placed, these people have difficulty in expressing themselves or even just "playing." In its debilitated state, Saturn can deny sexual relationships completely or can make sex the source of issues and problems in relationships. Relationships usually will lack the fun aspect and seem like a chore or worse. With good dignity or aspects, Saturn helps the individual take relationships more seriously; sex is not frivolous but rather is associated with meaningful and lasting relationships. This still means that sexual experience is limited, which may not be the individual's choosing. In such cases, an understanding of the Saturn placement will be particularly helpful.

- The outer planets Uranus, Neptune, and Pluto create challenges in whatever house they are placed. In the fifth, any one of them will make these pleasure and sexual matters a serious, even major issue for the couple. These planets are discussed in detail in chapter 6.

Connecting Self-Worth and Love

Love is not a one-way street. The ability to receive love is just as important to relationship success, and just as in a professional relationship, both parties must contribute and should benefit.

The most critical commodity in the personal relationship is love. Although we could spend a few volumes trying to define love, for practical purposes we can consider the expression of affection and regard as the essential ingredient we are looking for.

The feelings we experience when another person loves us can be one of the strongest motivators for having a relationship at all. Many people show a great difference in their ability to show love for others compared with their ability to receive it. Although receiving love may not sound like an ability, to be able to accept the love of another person requires that an individual considers him- or herself *worthy* of it.

Unworthiness is similar to the guilt we may feel if somebody gives us something very expensive. We may feel that it imposes obligations on us, that we are unable to afford to give something of equal value; many people describe the feeling as embarrassment. When love is the commodity, though, the problem may be even greater: how do we measure the value of what we give in return? How do we know when the gift we are giving is considered equal in value? The simplest way to resolve such dilemmas is to avoid situations in which we have to receive, or perhaps to give as much as we possibly can.

Such "solutions" clearly create more problems than they solve. As with a business partner, if there is an unequal distribution of outlay and of reward, then one person will inevitably feel exploited or plain sorry for him- or herself, or may end up in a destructive pattern of losing out to others. The person may even tend to attract people who deliberately take advantage of this imbalance, or who have very different value systems. Even when such relationships begin on the most equal of terms, though, they inevitably end in disaster.

Of course, this is a self-worth issue. If we value ourselves very highly, we will readily accept valuable gifts of love. Also, we will have a higher standard of the *quality* of that love, which we assess by seeing whom the love comes from or in what way that love is given.

You already have explored the self-worth issues by looking at the second house. Now look at them specifically in the context of how they relate to being loved. The eleventh house is the focus of our analysis of this issue:

- Planets in the eleventh house should be analyzed in the same way you have analyzed planets in the fifth. Consider their essential dignity and their aspects to assess whether it is easy for the individual to accept love, and what the quality of it is likely to be. For example, a dignified Venus here will show good-quality love easily received, while a dignified Saturn may show love coming from an older person or late in life, or love of a more traditional nature. An ill-dignified or badly aspected Saturn, though, could indicate failure to receive love or issues about receiving love (probably connected to early life or the parents).

- Aspects between eleventh-house planets and second-house planets are the most important. Such aspects are usually squares, and allow you to make a more precise assessment of exactly how the difficulties in receiving love are related to self-worth matters.

Occasionally, these aspects are sextiles or trines, which indicate a sense of worthiness and show love received to be a healthy reflection of that sense of worth.

- Oppositions between eleventh- and fifth-house planets show a clear picture of the balance between love given and love received. The nature of each planet (and its dignity, of course) will help you decide what types of problems create an imbalance. Take note if either is the ruler of the other—the issues described by this planet will be more dominant and could be a key to unlocking problems.

- When analyzing aspects, remember that you also can look at what other houses are ruled by the planets in the fifth or eleventh. This will help you see in which other areas of life the problems may actually manifest.

- Aspects between eleventh-house planets and eighth-house ones allow you to identify when issues in receiving love are related to the partner's resources or to the partner's efforts to acquire some power over the individual.

- It is not uncommon for T-squares to cause planets in three of the succedent houses to aspect each other. When this is the case, or in the case of the rarer but more powerful grand cross covering all four of these houses, this aspect pattern will become the focus of relationship issues. It will prove invaluable to the client to spend plenty of time delineating in detail the issues that arise out of the relationships between planets in these houses.

Children

For many people, having children is an important goal in their relationships. For some, this goal may even be irrespective of whether they are in a permanent relationship or not. There are also those who specifically wish not to have children, which can produce issues since they may well become involved in relationships with people who do want them.

While it will be necessary to consider all goals and how they may be modified by a relationship, children are of course different. They are a product of a relationship, and they become an integral part of it; they may even constitute one of the main reasons why many people choose to get married.

Bear in mind that nowadays the social pressure to marry in order to have children is considerably less, and it is important not to make assumptions about your clients or to impose your beliefs and ideas onto them. It is a common and acceptable goal to have children in a "common law" marriage or even when single. Gay couples are able to adopt children in many places, or they may choose to have their own—they are even able to marry in more and more places around the world.

Another issue that must be kept in mind is that children are a sensitive issue for many people, especially people who are unable to have children or who have had great difficulty having them. In discussing the likelihood of having children, make it clear to the client that astrologers link emotional and physical issues as part of one whole individual. There is plenty of evidence to show that emotional changes apparently can release physical problems in childbearing (for example, cases of people who have had difficulty conceiving who finally adopt, only to become pregnant soon thereafter).

The rulership of children in the fifth house is a reflection of the connection between relationships and children. Children are people we give love to and hold dear in our hearts. The analysis of the fifth house must take into account the individual's goals with respect to children and the likelihood that the person actually will have children, as these can be matters that seriously influence the choice of partners, the willingness to enter into a relationship, as well as the ever-critical self-worth issues (since planets in the fifth tend to square those in the second, as we have seen).

When analyzing the fifth house, goals and the willingness for and likelihood of having children should be considered:

- The benefics Sun, Moon, Mercury, Jupiter, and Venus contribute to the desire for children, and make it highly likely that these people will actually have them.

- The influence of the other planets may not necessarily prevent or deny children; however, they may limit the number of children, or make children become a difficult issue in the individual's life. In some cases, they may indicate difficulties in the lives of the children themselves. Remember, good essential dignity and aspects from benefics make these planets a lot friendlier.

EXAMPLES: SUCCEDENT HOUSE ISSUES

Louise (chart 1) has strongly emphasized succedent houses. We have already looked at some of the issues involving the rulers of three of her succedent houses—Moon, Mars, and Venus. Saturn, the ruler of the remaining succedent cusp, the eighth, is placed in dignity (its own sign) in its own house and in a square with the Moon-Neptune conjunction. We would expect her self-worth issues and unexpressed desires to contribute to finding partners who have many more resources than she (that dignified Saturn in its own house describes her partner's resources).

She has a strong desire for children, certainly indicated by those fifth-house planets and the ruler of the first (Mercury) being in the sign of Venus, the fifth-house ruler. But Louise is likely to find it very hard to have them—there is just too much debility around the fifth-house planets and the fifth-house ruler. That urge has been powerful since early adulthood, but by her early forties it still had not been fulfilled.

Steven Spielberg (chart 2) has a similar fifth house and is noted for his love of children. The difference is that he has Jupiter there instead of Neptune, and it strongly improves the fortunes of Venus. Jupiter trines the Midheaven, which it rules, giving him success related to the fifth. Similarly, his first-house ruler (the first house gives us a sense of identity) is in the fifth—it's the Moon, trine the Ascendant, which it rules. The fact that these planets aspect their own cusps strengthens them, especially since they are benefics. Even still, the Moon and Venus are in fall and detriment, respectively. Of Spielberg's seven children, only the first is his biological child. The benefics allowed him to adopt many, which remains an option for Louise.

Beyond Pleasure

There can be little doubt that the succedent houses hold the core issues of what constitute the deeper relationship-oriented drives. Clearly, since self-worth is the fundamental issue that is reflected one way or another in our analysis of the second, fifth, and eleventh houses, the eighth house also must play a critical role.

The aspect of the eighth that pertains to issues that can arise in a sexual relationship is power. In any relationship there is a certain amount of jostling for power or control, and in some relationships this can become a pathological dynamic where the couple engage in power plays, often giving one of the partners an inordinate amount of influence over the other's life.

Controlling the purse strings is a simple way to exert control in a relationship, and this is the house of the partner's resources (such as money.) Imbalance of financial resources is potentially a serious issue. Since the eighth house is opposite the second, this issue is a direct assault on self-worth. Obviously, being supported by another or having that person dole out what money can be spent can easily undermine self-worth.

But there are also times when sex is a power issue, and this is when the analysis of it moves to this house. The withholding and granting of sex can be used as a means of control, especially by the partner who feels financially controlled by the other. Sex also raises issues of body image for some people, another matter of self-worth that can stand in the way of a healthy sexual relationship.

- Difficult planets in the eighth warn of these power issues, especially Mars, Saturn, and Pluto, all of which identify a partner who will attempt to gain power. However, these planets may be modified by good aspects and by high dignity, which would relocate much of the power to the chart's owner and make power issues less threatening.

- Neptune also warns of power problems, but these are more insidious. There can be sacrifices made, or the partner may unconsciously be given the power over resources. Neptune in this house often signifies a partner who has poor control over his or her finances and who draws the individual into troubling financial situations.

- Uranus also may produce similar financial issues, and can sometimes show a partner who uses unpredictability, change, and selfish acts as a way of maintaining dominance.

- The luminaries or the benefics here are adversely affected by this placement, especially with regard to the houses they rule, but they generally promise a much healthier power relationship and benefits from the partner's resources. They rarely relate to sexual matters at all.

It is important to see how astrology links the issues of the succedent houses. The planets in these houses usually oppose or square each other—which is most telling, as the houses of self-worth and unbalanced control (second and eighth) square the houses of love, sex, pleasure, and friendship (the fifth and eleventh). Sex as a power issue challenges sex as a pleasure principle. In any individual, therefore, the desire to give and receive love and the need to control in order to feel self-worth are in conflict, and planets in these houses (or aspects between the rulers of these houses) will bring these issues to the surface in every relationship the individual becomes involved in.

Venus's aspects with the outer planets also can show issues in which sex becomes a force in the relationship beyond pleasure and procreation. Venus is the natural significator for sex, although occasionally we also can use Mars to analyze the sex *drive* itself.

- Venus's aspects with the outer planets may produce results similar to those of planets being located in the eighth, although this is more clearly connected to sexual matters.

In positive aspect with Uranus, Venus shows partners (or the desire for them) who are unusual and individualistic; with Neptune, the partners seem to be romantic ideals; and with Pluto, they are powerful and sexy.

- The negative aspects with Venus (and occasionally the positive ones too) have more challenging implications. With Uranus, the need for individuality competes with the need for relationship, with the result that the individual often pursues people who are unavailable or far away. This unconsciously satisfies the need for independence, although effectively it is a bit like the individual shooting him- or herself in the foot. There is a need for "unconventional" sexual expression.

- Challenging Venus-Neptune contacts lead to romantic idealism and a consequent unrealistic approach to both the partner and relationships in general. This often leads to high expectations followed by great disappointments, as well as a tendency to make sacrifices in relationships.

- Venus-Pluto contacts can indicate serious power issues most likely involving control through sexual expression. This is another indicator of negative patterns in sexual relationships, or a partner whose sexual behavior pattern is detrimental to the relationship. Power issues are very real and have an eventual transformative effect, although usually at a high price. Many early relationships may end in a power struggle until the individual learns to share power equally.

Marriage and One-to-One Relationships

By far the most important astrological significator for relationships is the seventh house. As the traditional house of marriage, it can be used to analyze all important one-to-one relationships and is the best indicator of what to expect in those relationships that go beyond the first flush of romance seen in the fifth house. Of course, love and pleasure are important ingredients in a successful relationship, but since relationships are a reflection of very deep and primal needs, they should be reflected in the more important areas of the chart.

Since this relationship house is angular, the experiences it brings must have a strong impact on our lives. In every chart, the angular houses are the most significant ones. Not only do these houses relate to the areas most immediate and critical in our everyday lives, but they also describe the development of the identity and how that identity is placed in the world.

The first house (including the planets in it and the Ascendant itself) is the most important identity house of all. As our projected persona, it reflects how we see ourselves and how we want others to see us. That means it has a strong impact on who we attract into our lives as well as how those people experience us, an experience that ultimately will have a strong impact on both the relationship and even our sense of identity. This clearly shows how the first house draws on the seventh, and indicates that, at least to some extent, our sense of self actually depends on our relationship experience.

Planets in and Ruling the Seventh House

As the house opposite our identity house, the seventh house describes our relationships, which reflect us back to ourselves. In relationships we see ourselves doing and saying things we never imagine we would. Through our partner's feedback and responses, we discover that how others see us is very different from how we see ourselves. This also explains why we tend to attract certain types of people into our lives, and hopefully the opportunity to see ourselves mirrored (this is the ultimate "warts and all" reflection) will give us opportunities for self-knowledge and growth.

Interpretation of this house is of immediate, practical value to the client and can be very revealing. You usually will find that the client experiences this part of the reading as highly accurate and pertinent, partly because what is going on in our personal lives always seems to occupy the forefront of our attention.

Planets in the seventh house are very descriptive of the relationship experience and even the types of people we attract. Table 7 gives some examples of how the planets manifest as other people. Here are some additional considerations:

- The Sun or the Moon in the seventh house indicates that the individual overidentifies with relationships and usually enters into them prematurely (especially when it's the Moon in this position). The identity is somewhat dependent on the partner. While this can make for very strong connections with the spouse, it can lead to problems of being unable to function as an individual.

- Traditional benefics Jupiter and Venus promise very positive relationship experiences, especially since Venus is also the natural significator for marriage. However, the *idea* of marriage may be more attractive than the difficult practicalities marriage involves.

- Traditional malefics Mars and Saturn can be very destructive, as this is an angular house and problems here have the capacity to affect all of life, not just partnership. A badly dignified Mars may be the most challenging, producing conflict and, at its worst, violence from the partner. A challenged Saturn often represents partners who have a profoundly dampening effect and eventually are experienced as an obstacle or a burden. In some cases, a difficult Saturn in this house indicates that marriage is unlikely—although when there finally is a partnership, it can last for a very long time. Sometimes it may merely show that long-term relationships will come only much later in life. A positively placed Saturn in the seventh gives a relationship staying power through life's changes, improving over time.

- The outer planets may make for difficult relationships. Not only can they represent partners that are challenging, but being in the seventh house gives them accidental dignity and the capacity to be an unduly strong influence on the whole of the individual's life (for the most part, these planets are otherwise quite impersonal, which is appropriate for such challenging and unruly influences).

- Uranus in the seventh shows a need for independence that can work against efforts to find relationship, or can indicate relationships that are not readily acceptable to others because of their unconventionality. It also can show unusual partnerships and relationships that are exciting and provoke growth and change.

- Neptune in the seventh sows confusion and can lead the individual to pursue the "wrong type" of partner. There can be deception or overidealized romanticism that leads the individual into unnecessary sacrifice. Neptune rarely is positive here.

- Pluto in the seventh produces a fascination for powerful people, although it also may cause these individuals to attract weaker, needy people who proceed to gradually drain them of their own power (especially in early adulthood). Relationships may have a pattern of trauma and dramatic, drawn-out endings, and occasionally Pluto may even indicate an abusive partner (challenging aspects with other malefics can hint at this, especially when the personal planets are also involved in these aspects). Occasionally, Pluto in the seventh may mean the native is the power figure or the abuser, although this is much less common. Like the other challenging planets, Pluto can indicate that there will not be a marriage or that it will come very late. If Pluto is well aspected or not particularly challenged, it is not unusual for it to represent extremely long-lasting relationships in which difficulties are overcome.

- By now you should be getting into the habit of checking the ruler of the house in the same way you have examined the planets in the house. In this case, it also is important to see whether an aspect exists between the rulers of the seventh and the first. If it does, this aspect shows you how the individual tends to relate to partners, and whether these relationships are easy or hard. Positive aspects indicate a strong likelihood of marriage, which is practically a certainty if the two planets also are in mutual reception.

Table 7: Keywords for Planets Symbolizing People	
Sun	Strong sense of self, masculine, warm, self-centered
Moon	Sensitive, emotional, feminine, changeable
Mercury	Young, talkative, intellectual
Venus	Passive, beautiful, easy to get along with
Mars	Aggressive, exciting, dangerous, domineering
Jupiter	Philosophical, wealthy, a teacher, benevolent
Saturn	Older, restrictive, authoritative, reserved, stable
Uranus	Unconventional, disruptive, independent, exciting, unpredictable
Neptune	Mystical, vague, deceptive, romantic
Pluto	Powerful, transformative, challenging, dangerous, controlling

EXAMPLES: USING DIGNITY TO UNDERSTAND
THE SEVENTH-HOUSE PLANETS

Actor-director Ron Howard (chart 3) has had a long and loving marriage with his childhood sweetheart. He has Saturn and Neptune in the seventh house, which at first glance may seem a little dangerous to a good marriage.

A closer examination reveals that Saturn is probably the reason they have such a strong bond after more than thirty years. Representing the person he marries, it may refer to someone known for a long time. It has no special dignity, but it is in a tight trine with the ever-important Sun, ruler of his fifth house of romance and sex. The ruler of the fifth in the eleventh house of love received suggests strong mutual feelings with a partner, and of course the eleventh is ruled by Saturn, which is in the house of marriage.

Even more importantly, Venus, ruler of his seventh house, is highly dignified by being in its exaltation sign of Pisces. Its placement in the twelfth house may be a little alarming, but traditional texts tell us that Venus has some dignity there, probably because matters of love and sex are private and behind closed doors.[3]

Of course, no marriage is free of problems. Neptune in the seventh with its square to the detrimented Moon will probably be the source of some of those problems, but the strong Saturn provides all the glue they need for a lasting marriage.

O.J. Simpson (chart 4) has had notoriously unsuccessful and violent relationships with women. His chart has a distinctly eastern hemisphere emphasis (emphasizing self more than others), with no planets in the seventh house. The ruler of the seventh is Saturn, detrimented (in Leo) in the twelfth house (loss and imprisonment) and conjunct Pluto. The bad dignity of Saturn contributes to the actual manifestation of these problems.[4]

Likelihood and Lastingness of Marriage

The question of whether a relationship will lead to marriage or even last is best analyzed when looking at the specific relationship, as we will see in the following chapters. But we tend to have similar experiences many times in our lives. Some people are inclined to long-lasting partnerships; others tend to have many shorter ones, while still others have both.

The Moon and Venus already have shown themselves to be among the most important things to look at in relationship analysis. Not only can they describe the partner and the marriage experience, but they can even help indicate whether a relationship is likely to last.

---

3. Traditionally, each planet is a significator for one or two houses, just as the planets signify "things" like marriage. Venus is the traditional significator for the fifth and twelfth houses.

4. How does Simpson manage to get acquitted so often? Saturn has two saving graces: it is in its own minor dignity of *face*, allowing it to "save face," and it has the accidental dignity of *joy* in the twelfth house—allowing it to benefit in this house when no other planet can. These kinds of details are often overlooked but are very revealing, and show how valuable it is to study and use dignity further as you become more experienced with astrology.

- When working with Venus and the Moon, the simplest analysis is to compare them with Saturn, the planet of solitude and bachelorhood. If Saturn is strong by accidental dignity while Venus and the Moon are weak in both accidental and essential dignity, and one of them has a challenging aspect from Saturn (especially a conjunction, which in Saturn's case is challenging to any planet), then marriage or long-term partnership is unlikely.

- A strong Saturn may also indicate that relationships last for a very long time. When Saturn is well placed and is connected to Venus or other relationship factors, the relationship is characterized by loyalty and long-lastingness. When there is a difficult Saturn, the person may feel stuck or trapped in a relationship, or may simply stagnate and stay in a relationship long past the expiration date.

- Other traditional indicators for marriage being unlikely or short-lived (and more than one of these should be present) include Saturn in the seventh, Saturn and Mars in difficult aspect and inhabiting or ruling the first and seventh houses, and the luminaries or Venus poorly dignified and in difficult aspect with Saturn or Mars or with an outer planet.

- Any case in which Saturn or Uranus is strong and is connected to a weaker Venus is unlikely to produce a lasting marriage. In fact, if Uranus is strong and personal enough (say, conjunct the Sun or the Ascendant, or in the seventh), it will make individuality paramount and commitment difficult. This could mean no marriage or multiple marriages (because of divorce).

- A strong Neptune magnifies romanticism: when configured with the Sun, Moon, or Venus, marriage is very likely although the individual probably has unrealistic beliefs and expectations about it.

EXAMPLES: MARRIAGE THAT LASTS

Ron Howard (chart 3) probably can thank Saturn for his long-lasting marriage. Even though Saturn has no special dignity, it is well aspected and is the ruler of the eleventh ("love received"). The ruler of his seventh, Venus, is in exaltation in Pisces.

Marian (chart 5) celebrated her fiftieth wedding anniversary in 2006. Her seventh house is uninhabited, but its ruler, Venus, is well placed in the ninth, a very positive house. Venus here has the minor dignity of face, and its ruler, the other benefic (Jupiter), is very highly dignified both essentially (in its exaltation) and accidentally (in the angular fourth house). Venus's aspects are a grand trine with Mars and Uranus and a sextile with the all-important Moon. Neptune also engages in a weak square, probably the source of whatever problems that do exist in her marriage. Not surprisingly, she traveled overseas, where she married (the ninth-house Venus and the aspect of Uranus representing a person of a different culture).

All this would be enough to imply longevity of marriage, but let's not forget Saturn: it is very highly dignified, ruling the Sun and Moon and the almuten (most dignified planet) of the seventh-house cusp.

Learning about Ourselves

Relationships are one of the most immediate and powerful ways that we have to confront otherwise-unseen aspects of ourselves, as well as to learn about basic issues that probably affect other areas of our lives too (like self-worth does). There can be no doubt that the natal factors you have analyzed will be the predominant influences on the experience of every relationship. Whether we like it or not, we experience patterns in our lives, and even though individual relationships may vary, they often can be seen to have something in common, or at the very least to reflect personal issues that are described in the natal chart.

But we do learn, and we do have the capacity to consciously influence our patterns. We grow wiser and more self-knowing, and we make different choices. Despite our patterns, every new relationship is an opportunity for redemption, for change.

Each relationship is a chance to try again, to know and answer to our true selves. Now that you have helped your clients understand some of the important aspects of the true self that are so relevant to relationships, it is time to finally start comparing the charts more thoroughly, using the techniques of synastry.

CHAPTER 5

BASIC CHART COMPARISON

By far the most important (and the most useful) work in synastry is the study of the way the planets in one person's chart interact with those in the partner's chart. Now that we have a clear picture of each person in the relationship, especially those aspects of their personalities relevant to relating, we can thoroughly compare the charts using the astrological technique of synastry.

In This Chapter

Synastry is about the effects of one chart on another chart:

- How to draw up synastry wheels.
- How planets affect the houses of the partner's chart.
- Selecting and measuring aspects between charts.
- The effects of aspects and planets.
- How different areas of life together are shown.
- Comparing characteristics with synastry and synthesizing the information by analyzing key areas.

What Does Synastry Involve?

Synastry is often thought of as a complex art, probably because it involves the use of two charts at the same time. That certainly makes it more challenging than a straightforward natal reading, but it is not nearly as complex as it seems.

In fact, most of astrology is based on the same set of simple components: planets in sign, house, and aspect. Even the complicated mathematical methods or non-planet chart points astrologers create like parts or midpoints are based on these same core principles.

So in learning synastry you already know most of the techniques involved. Unlike the often complex ideas that lie behind the various methods of prediction, there are no special concepts or units of measurement involved in this type of chart comparison. Synastry uses the tools of natal astrology with no modification. The only adaptation you will make is the way you make your interpretations.

The Method of Comparison

The basic method of comparing charts usually is learned for the first time when you study prediction. Most methods of prediction require you to compare a newly calculated chart (progressions or transits, say) to the original natal chart. The method of comparison involves two basic principles:

1. See where (by sign and house) the planets of the new chart fall in the houses of the original chart.

2. Measure the aspects made from the planets in the newly calculated chart to the planets in the original chart.

This is the identical process you will use in synastry analysis, except rather than using new charts based on the original natal chart, you will use two natal charts—the charts of the couple whose synastry you are analyzing.

Making the Necessary Calculations

In order to make your calculations, follow these steps using your computer:

1. Calculate the two natal charts.

2. Calculate the aspects made between the two charts. This will produce an aspect grid similar to the one produced when you calculate progressions to a natal chart. The is-

sues around which aspect and what orb will be discussed when we look more closely at these aspects later in this chapter.

3. Draw up a double-ringed wheel with the planets of one chart in the inner wheel and the planets of the second chart in the outer wheel.

4. Now repeat step 3 with a second double wheel, but this time place the planets from the second chart in the inner wheel and the planets of the first chart in the outer wheel.

The principles of analysis will follow the same principles usually used in natal analysis. We will interpret the house positions of the planets before we get into the finer work of the interchart aspects.

The Effect on Each Other

A lot of very useful information can be gleaned from looking at the wheels alone, where you can see how the planets of one individual fall in the houses of the other. Just as with transits, it is as if the planets of one individual activate the natal houses of the other individual.

When analyzing natal houses, our chief concern lies in which planets occupy the houses, always the strongest influence over the affairs of that house. Beginner astrologers often are concerned with empty houses, as if somehow that aspect of life could be missing, until they learn about house rulers. Even then, the basic principle that a planet occupying a house has a stronger effect than the planet ruling the house makes the interpretation of occupied houses easier than that of unoccupied ones. This will make the first stages of the synastry analysis relatively easy.

The overall meaning of this type of comparison is that *the positions of another person's planets in our own chart show the lasting effect that person will have on us*. It is the basis of why we seem to be a somewhat different person in each of our relationships. We are different—we have different house emphases in each relationship. We sometimes find that we are much more powerful and effective in our lives in one relationship, whereas another seems to drain the life out of us. Perhaps the first person's planets land in all our angular houses, where they are strong and can make things happen, while the second person's planets occupy all our cadent houses, where they can't easily be expressed. You already can see how quickly and easily the power of synastry can be accessed.

When examining the wheel this way:

- Look where one person's planets fall in the angular houses of the partner. These planets will be felt as a strong impact on the area of life signified by the house involved, although they also will have the general effect of making it seem like the partner has had a strong impact on the person's life as a whole.

- Planets that fall in houses that already contain natal planets will modify the existing planets according to their own nature. So, for example, if your partner's Uranus falls in a house containing Mars, the effect of Mars will be magnified, whereas if Venus had fallen there it would have eased the harsh nature of Mars, although of course it still would have some Martian effect.

- Pay special attention when the partner's planet falls very close to the natal planet. These conjunctions will have a stronger effect, which will be explored when we look at the interchart aspects.

- Planets falling in houses that are empty in the natal chart will activate that house in a manner similar to how you would interpret that planet natally in that house.

While making these interpretations, bear in mind that you should not describe the effect as if it is a permanent one. Our partners do not make us into "new people." When you start working with more advanced methods involving directions, you will need to consider how long-lasting the effect of another person will be, and how long it may take before the effect manifests.

We do learn lessons from our partners, some of which stick and some that seem to keep returning in barely changed forms. We do and say things we never would with other people. We learn ways of doing things that stay with us forever. We may have our best or our worst brought out. But all these effects are not really changes: *they are potentials that already are implicit in our own natal charts.*

When your partner's Mercury sits in your third house, you may be more communicative with that person than you are with others, and you may even learn to be more communicative all round, but the way you communicate will still be described by your own third house: the sign on the cusp, its ruler, and the natal planets that are there.

EXAMPLE: A RELATIONSHIP CAN HAVE
A STRONG EFFECT ON SOMEONE

Brett (chart 14) was more interested in fun and pleasure than in having a relationship, as his emphasis of Sagittarius, Pisces, Scorpio, and the ninth house would suggest. Alan (chart 15) had had his fill of fleeting partners, and never could have expected his chance meeting with Brett to lead to a long-term commitment. These charts have been printed in double-ring wheels so you can easily see the planets in each person's houses.

Their charts show a number of contacts to angles. Alan's Moon and Saturn straddle Brett's Ascendant, while Pluto sits precisely on his seventh cusp. Alan's North Node, which will intensify anything it touches, is practically on Brett's IC.

We can interpret Alan's planets on Brett's angles as the planets having the strongest effect on Brett. Brett's mutable angles bring changes in self, relationship, and home life (he eventually moved in with Alan). The Moon and Saturn make him relate strongly to Alan's feelings and readily accept the limitations and commitment the relationship demands (let alone Alan being five years older). Pluto emphasizes his own seventh-house Pluto and manifests it immediately (it's a very close conjunction) in the shape of a relationship that completely transforms him.

It is an important similarity that Brett's Saturn sits precisely on Alan's Ascendant, completing the bond of commitment and the demand to accept what may not be perfect but that has the potential to last a long time. (Later you'll see why Saturn can make a relationship last and be good.) Brett's own Jupiter in his seventh house brings gainful changes from a partner, and also emphasizes his own romantic Neptune there.

Brett's first three houses all have planets of Alan's. The relationship has given Brett a sense of security, self-worth, and opportunity unprecedented in his life—not unexpected with both of Alan's luminaries there along with both Venus and Jupiter. Alan's Ascendant and Jupiter in Brett's third with Brett's own Neptune close to his Venus and Jupiter have led to travel and further study, neither of which had happened yet in Brett's life—a natal promise (Venus and Jupiter in the ninth promise travel) fulfilled by the planets from a partner's chart. Notice that Alan has his own third/ninth axis activated by Brett's planets of youth (the Moon and Mercury) closely conjoining it.

Brett became ill with flu soon after meeting Alan, and practicalities led to his new acquaintance, Alan, helping him by running errands to the drugstore. This in turn led to their brief acquaintanceship turning into a deeper relationship. No doubt Alan's malefic Mars and Uranus activating Brett's sixth had something to do with that (and shows how often even a trivial illness is an important function of our *karma*[1] unfolding, not just something going wrong).

Alan's fifth house is strongly intensified by Brett's Pluto and Uranus there, no doubt causing him to confront issues about his own romantic and sexual life—but also adding lots of excitement to the fun-filled fifth.

The other succedent houses also are highlighted. Brett's Sun in Alan's eighth brings resources from a partner as well as some lessons in letting go. Brett's Ascendant highlights Alan's eleventh-house cusp (as well as his Moon-Saturn conjunction), giving Alan an opportunity to pursue his ideals and activating the natal promise of love received.

Finding Patterns of Interaction

The information you have gleaned in the analysis so far is plenty for the clients to work with, but it describes only how they see each other, how their first impressions are different from reality, and the effect they have on each other. We now need to describe how the two individuals interact. This will give you (and them) an understanding of the interpersonal issues and how they actually are played out.

This is useful because it provides objectivity in an area where it is most needed. Usually we are so caught up in the games we play with each other that it becomes like a loop that we cannot get out of. Often the problem is one of how to express the problem or how to be understood properly.

Much of our behavior is automatic—when a certain emotional button is pushed, our reaction happens before we can control it. Many people have had the experience of "seeing" themselves react inappropriately yet were not able to stop it, or they realize imme-

---

1. Karma is a Sanskrit word meaning "action" that has been absorbed into many modern languages, including English. It describes the Vedic (later Hindu and Buddhist) philosophy whereby our experiences are a consequence of our actions in a previous incarnation. Fundamental to this idea is the notion that actions arise out of our attachment to things *and people* in the world—hence the importance of karma in understanding the spiritual implications of relationships.

diately *after* a bad reaction that it happened—a realization that comes too late to stop a chain of buttons from being pushed and eventually the game being played out to its usual ending. This creates patterns of behavior in the relationship and is one of the reasons that it is so difficult to overcome some relationship problems. With both people locked into the pattern, once the first button is pushed the cycle of behavior will unfold again.

Without some way of both partners becoming objective enough to see the process from the outside and *together* doing something about it, it is unlikely to change. This is where aspect analysis in synastry becomes so useful. You will be able to provide the objectivity by describing what is happening and, more importantly, contextualizing the pattern in the greater picture of the relationship. This provides the understanding of *why* the pattern is fallen into—and the key to changing it.

Measuring Important Interchart Aspects

The aspect grid showing the interchart aspects is different from the one you are used to from natal charts in some important ways:

- It shows the aspects from one person's set of planets to the full set of planets in the other person's chart. This makes the grid twice the size (meaning that it is square rather than triangular, as you can see in the example in chart 15).

- In each chart, each planet is checked for aspects against every planet in the second chart. In a natal aspectarian we identify only aspects from each planet to slower-moving planets, as all the aspects with faster-moving planets already would have been found when the faster planets were analyzed for aspects (so if we find an aspect from the Moon to the Sun, we don't need to check if there is one from the Sun to the Moon). In synastry, though, we are working with a second set of planets, so if the Moon of chart 1 aspects the Sun of chart 2, it does not mean that the Sun of chart 1 will aspect the Moon of chart 2, an altogether different situation. But this does mean that once we have checked all the aspects from chart 1 to chart 2, there is no need to then check those from chart 2 to chart 1.

- Orbs usually are different from what is used in natal practice. It is common for astrologers to use half the orb that usually is used in natal work, but some will use even smaller orbs than that—say three degrees for a major aspect and one or two degrees for a minor one.

- The most important aspects are the conjunction, sextile, square, trine, and opposition, as well as the minor aspects of the semisextile and inconjunct, which are especially useful in synastry.

Focusing on the Most Important Planets and Aspects

While all the planets and aspects have significance, too much information is not going to help your clients get a very clear picture. You need to establish a set of priorities. You also will learn to look out for particular aspects or pairs of planets that tend to recur in particular relationships. As you become more experienced at synastry, this will be very helpful in identifying typical issues and even discovering patterns that tend to occur in relationships that lead to marriage or divorce.

Planets in Relationships

The planets symbolize the same things no matter what you are doing in astrology, but you do need to adjust your emphasis and choice of keywords to help keep the analysis relevant and meaningful. It is helpful to think of the planets as behaving differently according to whether they are receiving the aspect or making it. Of course, in every aspect both charts are affected, but the distinction between giving and receiving is greater than in natal astrology because each chart is clearly in a different position in this aspect. For example, if my Jupiter aspects your Sun, for me it is Jupiter that receives the aspect from your Sun while for you it is the Sun receiving an aspect from Jupiter. For me, Jupiter is enlightened by the Sun. For you, the Sun is positively enhanced by Jupiter. Clearly, these have very different implications. Table 8 lists some of the keywords to get you started.

Table 8: Keywords for Planets in Aspect in Relationships	
Planet	**When Casting an Aspect**
Sun	Illuminates the matter, highlights issues of the receiving planet
Moon	Highlights feelings about issues of the receiving planet
Mercury	Makes a connection or communication, meeting of minds, argument
Venus	Improves, attracts us to, provides pleasure

Mars	Challenges, causes problems and conflict
Jupiter	Enhances, expands, brings good things and opportunities
Saturn	Limits, forces compromise
Uranus	Brings dramatic insight, forces changes
Neptune	Confuses, conceals, deceives
Pluto	Creates dramatic challenges, trauma, power lessons

Aspects in Relationships

The aspects have the same meaning in synastry as in all other areas of astrology.

- **Sextiles and trines** allow for easy understanding of each other, and the ability to interpolate goals, ways of doing things, or whatever the specific planets represent. You can emphasize these positive connections as a way to concentrate on what works well in the relationship. The couple will find it easy to cooperate in these areas, as well as to understand each other's approach. This also lets you identify planets that represent ways of working together to overcome problems identified by other, more difficult aspects. This is a practice most astrologers follow in their interpretation of natal charts too.

- **Conjunctions** can be challenging or inspiring. They may represent areas where the couple combine forces very successfully and feel very passionate about something. Each planet becomes highly activated and has a strong effect on the natal chart of its owner. The nature of the planets and houses involved is the best guide to the accurate interpretation of these aspects.

- **Oppositions** may be positive or negative aspects. Sometimes they are challenging because they indicate where one person's ways directly conflict with some other aspect of the partner's life. If it is the same planet in each chart, then it is in that specific area represented by the planet that the conflict occurs and can be readily understood. Opposite ways can be difficult to reconcile, but this aspect often allows the astrologer to make practical suggestions about what to work on. Planets in opposite signs share their quality of cardinal, fixed, or mutable (i.e., quadruplicity) and are in elements that are highly compatible, so there is a lot of potential for compromise. In other circumstances, reconciliation may not be the required approach and the opposition indicates an area in which an individual lacks something that the partner can provide. One of the most useful ways to approach the opposition is to view the planets as representing opposite viewpoints or methods that need to be *synthesized*. Oppositions show where a lot of work needs to be done, work that will tend to produce results.

- **Squares** are especially challenging in synastry because they represent types of conflict that are particularly difficult to resolve. Mostly, they show areas where the parties lock horns and fall into patterns of resistance. It may look like stubbornness, but the squares often reveal deeply hidden personal attitudes or behaviors that the individuals cling to out of insecurity, defensiveness, or some other feeling of vulnerability. They also can represent areas where the parties fail to understand each other or become the victim of each other's weaknesses. Squares, too, show where work must be done, but this is usually ongoing work that is not easily resolved and that requires a lot of compromises and adjustments to be made. Not all squares are all bad, of course; Venus and Jupiter often create shared pleasures through any aspect at all.

- **Inconjuncts** can be similar to oppositions, although the conflict they represent is less dramatic as well as less easy to resolve. Planets in an inconjunct (or quincunx) aspect have neither element nor quality in common, making the differences seem insurmountable. The only solution is for one of the partners to compromise significantly. You will need to help the individuals keep this in balance by ensuring that on the whole each of them makes as much compromise as the other—it is not unusual for these aspects to represent things that improve with time and effort.

- **Semisextiles** are not always used by astrologers, but in synastry work they can be useful. The semisextile in particular can reveal areas where partners simply fail to connect. Although this is sometimes seen as a mildly positive aspect, it certainly is not the case in a relationship. Adjacent signs share neither element nor quality—they have nothing in common and usually are very different. Planets in semisextile represent irreconcilable differences, especially since the individuals often fail to see the dynamics of the problem. But they don't represent conflict or difficulty, like the square—they can be seen as planets that treat each other politely but impersonally. The differences involved are not the kind that would affect the relationship as a whole. For practical purposes, it is only when the same planet from each chart has a semisextile with its partner in the other chart that it becomes of any concern (for more about this issue, see the discussion about Mercury later in this chapter).

- **Other aspects.** Kepler's theory of harmonics has led to the arsenal of aspects growing enormously, and also has allowed astrologers to conceptualize the influence of aspects in a different way. Many astrologers find particular aspects to be especially meaningful in natal work. If you have special aspects that you have found particularly useful and meaningful, you can explore them in synastry once you are comfortable with the basic method. Similarly, for the traditionally oriented, connections by antiscia and contra-antiscia, reception, and other traditional methods also may prove useful and provide room for your work as a relationship analyst to grow.

EXAMPLE: ASPECTS SHOW THE BASIC INTERACTION

Director Steven Spielberg (chart 2) has married twice. His first relationship with actress Amy Irving (chart 16) was notoriously bitter, while his second, with actress Kate Capshaw (chart 18), is a rare Hollywood success story.

At a glance, the charts of the wives (and even Spielberg) don't look that different (note the Cancer Ascendants, fourth-house Libra Moons, and below-ground hemisphere emphasis). Some of the issues persist in both relationships—see how Spielberg's Neptune conjoins both their Moons. But why are the two relationships so different?

Just look at the aspect grids. Spielberg and Irving's personal planets are linked primarily by squares interspersed with sextiles. Squares represent patterns of conflict that are difficult to change. The fact that the two Suns as well as one of the Sun-Moon pairs are square makes the problems even more challenging. Even with those sextiles to work with, this relationship will be tough.

The interaction with Capshaw is very different. Conjunctions and sextiles link their personal planets almost exclusively, and the luminaries have much easier aspects, which we will see is very relevant.

We haven't even analyzed the specific aspects yet. In real-life analysis, this initial look provides only an introduction to the couple, but it gives us a sense of how they will experience the relationship.

Planets in Aspect in Synastry

The most important foundation work in astrology is learning to combine planets in the different ways aspects allow them to interrelate. In predictive astrology you learn how a second set of planets also creates a whole new set of aspects when compared with the natal chart. In synastry work we do exactly the same thing.

Some connections between planets are especially important in synastry and should constitute the main focus of your work. You eventually will look at almost all the aspects in the synastry grid, but you must learn to prioritize your analysis of those that are especially important to the type of relationship you are working with.

It is also important to get into the habit of checking *reception* between planets to see how they relate to each other. Reception can be a little like an aspect. Usually, when one planet is in another planet's sign, the two planets have a fairly good relationship.

In the following pages we will look at the principles behind such aspects by focusing only on the key combinations for fast and accurate information that is most useful to the clients. This approach will help you learn to prioritize information as well as to gradually increase the depth of your analysis while still being able to start with the basics. Later, you can use your knowledge of aspects to explore combinations not discussed here.

1. The Luminaries

The most important aspects are those between the luminaries of one chart with the luminaries of the other. The ideal connection is between the Sun in one chart and the Moon in the other, since they represent the archetypal masculine and feminine principles. Irrespective of our gender or sexual orientation, these archetypal aspects of ourselves are fundamental to how we interact with others. The relationship between the luminaries is so important that you should always check the receptions, too, especially if there is no aspect between them.

- **Sun to Moon**. Connections between one person's Sun and the other's Moon are particularly important, no matter whose luminary it is or what the gender of the individuals: the luminaries are the essence of the personality and ideally relate to the essence of the other person. Sextiles, trines, and conjunctions are ideal, and provide the right balance of opposites mixed with similarities for the relationship to have a good chance of success. Squares and oppositions usually lead to the solar partner being insensitive to the other's feelings or attempting to dominate, but they still produce a strong bond as long as other positive connections exist.

- ***Sun to Sun***. These connections are felt very deeply, and are even partly responsible for attracting the couple to each other in the first place. But people often become fixated on the experience of this connection (because the Sun represents the ego) and may have difficulty in adapting and growing with the relationship as it changes. With time, these individuals will find it increasingly hard to maintain a relationship. Those with a positive solar connection will find it easy to get along when sharing activities and handling the outer world. The basic value systems are compatible, but deeper personal matters could be harder to understand. When the aspect between them is an opposition, trine, or sextile, they tend to make very strong friendships that can be lifelong relationships. Squares demand constant adjustment, but are still highly compatible because the two Suns share quadruplicity (quality.)

- ***Moon to Moon***. With a positive lunar connection, the private relationship may be deep and meaningful but the couple will have little success in the outer world, which may even become an obstacle to the relationship. Still, there is an ability to understand each other emotionally and instinctively. As long as there also are solar aspects, the lunar ones make strong connections between the partners. Squares and oppositions are more troubling, even though the quadruplicity is the same. Since the Moon operates at the level of instinct, these differences are hard to resolve and there can be an automatic fear of or aversion to something that is a challenge to one's feelings.

Usually these are not the only aspects formed by the luminaries, and their connections to other planets are extremely important and will provide room for growth and understanding. These aspects will be discussed under the relevant planet headings that follow. If there are no other aspects or receptions at all made by the luminaries, the individuals are likely to eventually feel that the relationship has become stagnant.

EXAMPLES: CONNECTIONS BETWEEN THE LUMINARIES

Brett and Alan (charts 14 and 15) have a full set of luminary connections. The Sun-Moon square creates a need to dominate, but since both Suns square the other's Moon, neither partner wins this contest. Alone, this could produce a very difficult relationship (although still a strong attraction), but each luminary also has a wide trine with the same luminary (itself) in the other chart. This ability to understand the other's inner and outer needs and shared value system produces high compatibility, matched by an ability to understand and appreciate the partner's feelings. (The connections between both Venuses and the other's luminary also help.)

This network of Sun-Moon connections, emphasized by the mutual Sun-Sun and Moon-Moon trines, leads to a strong bond that can help the Sun-Moon squares become positive and dynamic challenges since it keeps the two individuals on a level playing ground.

Luminary connections are the key features in relationships and rarely do not exist when people actually do become involved. Notice that Spielberg (chart 2) has squares from his Sun to Amy Irving's Sun and Moon, while he has sextiles to those of Kate Capshaw. His Moon has positive aspects to both of their Suns, but of course the conjunction to Capshaw's is powerful and lasting.

Joanne Woodward (chart 12) has conjunctions from her Sun and Moon to her husband's Moon, while even relationship-challenged Dan and Janice (charts 10 and 11) have the powerful Sun-Moon conjunction balanced by the square between their Suns. Even unsuccessfully married Brad Pitt and Jennifer Aniston (charts 30 and 31) have a conjunction from her Moon to his Sun and a sextile between their Suns, although they have too few personal connections and too many Saturn ones for the relationship to succeed easily.

Browse through all the example charts used in this book and in your own records and you will find a remarkable number of Sun-Moon connections.

---

2. *The Angles and Their Rulers*

The angles are always the most important cusps in a chart and often show more immediately significant developments than do planets. The angles describe the most immediate and practical facts of life: self, relationship, home, and work. They are the anchors into the real world. As we know from predictive work, this is why they are so sensitive to change.

More importantly, and certainly in the context of synastry, the angles are also the four components of identity out there in the world. They are aspects of identity that are sensitive to change and environmental influences, much more so than the archetypal, almost genetic forces that the planets represent.

If a relationship is to prove meaningful in somebody's life, a major reason is because it will represent some change or lead to some change. So we must expect to see connections between planets of each partner with the angles of the other partner. These links also allow us to see what kind of change to expect and where in life it can be expected.[2]

---

2. Remember that angles can be considered only if the birth time is known to be accurate.

When we find a number of angle-planet connections, especially with planets pertinent to the relationship, the relationship will have a strong impact on the partner whose angles receive the aspects.

In all cases, consider which angle is being aspected. This is what indicates how the influence is felt and where the changes occur. The planet casting the aspect naturally reveals which aspect of the self (in both people) is brought to prominence.

- *Angles to the Sun*. These are the most powerful long-lasting or deep connections. They indicate that the chart owner receiving aspects to the angles will be deeply affected by the other person, who in turn tends to have his or her personality potentials brought to the surface (as if his or her Sun became angular).

- *Angles to the Moon*. These connections are similar to solar ones, but the recipient will see him- or herself in a new light. The person may discover an emotional response in an area or a way that is unprecedented for him or her. Connections from another's Moon can also be disconcerting and may not have the implications of lastingness suggested by those from the Sun. The Moon's owner may become more emotionally aware than usual, but perhaps a little more self-centered in his or her needs (which often happens when the Moon is angular).

- *Angles to Venus*. These connections traditionally are associated with marriage or long-lasting romantic relationships. This is a good indicator for a strongly harmonious link. Both partners will find the relationship easy and fulfilling. The person with the recipient angles may feel that the partner brings harmony or balance to an aspect of his or her life, or fulfills a dream. Similarly, the partner whose Venus casts the aspect may feel that the relationship is an opportunity to manifest a dream. Remember to keep in mind that whenever we deal with Venus, we need to consider issues of romanticism and avoidance of conflict (see the discussion of this planet in chapter 4).

- *Angles to other planets*. All the connections made between planets and angles have significant impact, so they should be considered in the same way you already have looked at the more obvious relationship significators. (Discussions of the individual planets on the following pages will help you interpret these aspects.)

- *Rulers of the angles to the angles*. When we look at the planets, we are looking at the natural significators for various aspects of life. It is always equally important to look at the specific, personal significators for an individual. Examine the seventh-house ruler in each chart first, then the chart ruler, then the Midheaven and IC. If these planets make contact with the other person's angles, then there will be a powerful bond between them: consider which angle receives the aspect and which ruler makes it.

- ***Rulers of the angles to each other****.* If the ruler of an angle in one chart aspects the ruler of an angle in the other, this represents the same kind of angular contact. Pay particular attention when the ruler of the seventh aspects the ruler of the first or seventh in the other chart (indicating the likelihood of marriage or a long relationship).

- ***Angles to angles****.* Contact between two accurately timed and calculated charts' angles is significant, but may represent a connection that, while powerful at first, is not long-lasting or particularly deep. The couple will experience each other as apparently similar or compatible, but if unsupported by planetary contacts this is not enough to build a relationship on.

3. Mercury

Communication is probably the single most important quality in a relationship. Solving problems and capitalizing on good connections are not possible if communication isn't achievable. Mercury's connections with the partner's planets can show whether the partners are receptive to each other verbally as well as the extent to which they share mental attitudes and understanding.

When conflict occurs in a relationship, the effort (or failure) to talk about it often becomes a bigger obstacle than the original problem. We often say things we don't mean when we're angry, or our efforts to put feelings into words convey completely the wrong meaning. This leads to further conflict based on "you said that" or "I didn't mean that." In essence, emotional problems become transformed into semantic and comprehension problems, making it impossible to deal with the original issue and often magnifying beyond realistic proportions the sense that there is a real issue to be concerned about.

Occasionally, one partner may even deliberately take advantage of the other's lesser verbal skills by manipulating words to ensure that he or she wins an argument. It is important to gain a thorough understanding of each person's natal Mercury, as these issues often are reflected in the planet's natal aspects and dignity and recur from one relationship to the next.

To avoid these unnecessary complications, it is helpful to concentrate quite heavily on what each Mercury reveals to you, so that you can later help your clients develop strategies to accommodate communication problems rather than interpreting them as emotional problems.

- *Mercury to Mercury*. The fastest measure of communication and understanding is the aspect between the two Mercurys. If there is no aspect between them, there may be some issues around lack of understanding of each other, but positive aspects with other planets will provide the opportunities to resolve these. Positive contact between each partner's Mercury also can help overcome difficult solar contacts (or the lack of them). Negative aspects can dramatically enhance the types of problems just discussed in the general remarks about Mercury. The semisextile is particularly stressful in this regard, representing as it does the consistent failure to see eye to eye.

- *Mercury to Sun*. This usually is not an important connection, but can add useful information. A positive connection can overcome a lack of an aspect between the two Mercurys and give the ability to understand each other intellectually, while a negative connection could show arguments and battles of will.

- *Mercury to the Moon*. You learned about the relationship between emotions and the understanding or expressing of them in chapter 2. The same principles apply when checking these aspects between charts. The aspects now reveal whether each person can understand *the other's* feelings.

4. Venus

You already know how important Venus is in relationships, especially in romantic ones. If there are no important Venus aspects between two charts, you wouldn't even expect there to be a romantic relationship at all. Venus is the planet that describes the romantic feelings the couple have for each other. Apart from the aspects to the angles, the most significant Venus aspects are:

- *Venus to the Sun*. When one person's Venus aspects the partner's Sun, there are very strong romantic feelings between them. The person whose Sun it is may feel that the partner is his or her perfect match, and Venus's owner is able to express love in a way he or she may never have managed before. These aspects often occur in the charts of people who marry. They are favorable for all other kinds of relationships—even business. Even the challenging aspects rarely have a strongly negative impact, although they can have important consequences. Venus adversely aspected by a strong Sun may feel dominated or controlled, while the Sun's owner may feel that the relationship is stagnant.

- *Venus to the Moon*. A connection between these two emotional planets is common and desirable in romantic partnerships. Positive aspects between them make the relationship feel smooth and easy; the feelings between the partners are strong and readily expressed, and there is a sense of a deep, inner connection. It is easier for them to share their inner selves. With the negative aspects or dignities, the relationship can become indulgent, with each partner allowing his or her emotions and emotional interactions to dominate the relationship. There can be an overemphasis on the emotional and sensual aspects of the relationship.

• ***Venus to Venus***. As long as the two Venuses are not badly dignified, positive aspects between them contribute to harmonious living, strong mutual feelings of affection, and shared tastes and pleasures. A negative connection can show codependence or a tendency to avoid conflict and other serious issues.

• ***Venus to Mars***. You should expect to find strong connections between these planets when there is a physical relationship. This is the passion combination, and a harmonious aspect link makes for a strong sexual connection as well as the ability to understand each other's sexual needs and drives. It also can contribute to understanding in the area of goals, and is a good combination for working together toward a common goal. It's a great idea to suggest that your clients create shared goals to really get the most out of this aspect. It is usually the Mars partner who is inclined to take the initiative. Although these aspects are usually present in romantic relationships, they are not enough to cement a bond. When the connection is negative, there still is likely to be a magnetic attraction, but the partners' sex drives may operate on different schedules and the Mars partner may be experienced as too aggressive and selfish or the Venus partner as too passive or self-indulgent. Squares can show involvement in a romantic relationship when a platonic one would have been more appropriate.

5. Mars

Sex as pleasure is the domain of Venus, but in a relationship sexual issues relate almost as much to Mars, the source of the libido itself. Feeling passionate about the same things—and about each other—is a further key to relationship success.

In a permanent relationship, the main role of Mars is to describe how the individual goals interpolate or compete as well as the joint goals that the couple will pursue. If an individual's Mars receives difficult aspects from the partner, the partner will inhibit the person's pursuit of goals in the manner suggested by the planet and aspect involved.

Similarly, a partner may enhance the ability to achieve goals when there are positive contacts. In fact, such contacts are often key indicators for success in the relationship.

True success in relationships doesn't mean success only in love, sex, and living together; growth in other areas of life also should benefit. Positive connections show a person's Mars being activated by the partner. This may give the individual the inspiration or the push to pursue goals that, without this relationship, might never have been possible. This makes Mars connections critically important in all relationships. The ability to share goals is also a major contributor to success in relationships—in the long term the couple needs to develop goals for the relationship itself or else risk stagnation.

- *Mars to the Sun*. This connection is highly energizing and usually will prove beneficial to the relationship as long as there are outlets for the energy. It is a combination that is common in partnerships because Mars symbolizes the masculine archetype and is the planet responsible for "stimulation." Attraction or repulsion is the response to stimulation, a key relationship ingredient. Positive contact between these planets is experienced as inspiring and stimulating. The partners feel a greater sense of themselves, more powerful and more able to achieve personal goals thanks to the influence of this relationship. This combination can be interpreted similarly to Mars-Mars combinations, but the effects are longer lasting and more fundamental, as is always the case when a luminary is involved. The consequences of a negative contact have a similarly stronger effect on the solar partner, who may have his or her pride challenged but will not necessarily respond in an equally forceful manner. That is why this combination is often particularly challenging for the solar partner, who may even feel threatened by the other's strength.

- *Mars to the Moon*. This is an even more stimulating connection, especially when it comes to passion. Attraction and sexual response are based largely on our deepest feelings and instincts, and the aspects between Mars and the Moon bring them rushing to the surface. Any aspect between these planets creates some sexual tension and magnetism between the individuals. The conjunction can be quite challenging, creating a raw emotional energy that feeds the power of the Mars individual, who may become aggressive or domineering. As long as the partner is a strong individual, this could make sex unforgettable! The challenging aspects lead to high levels of tension and irritability—these are individuals who can really press each other's buttons.

- *Mars to Mars*. Positive connections show that each person's goal path is enhanced in the relationship. This couple can really fire each other up and create a lot of excitement in their relationship. They are able to work together not only to allow each of them to achieve success, but also to easily develop common goals. The conjunction can make it hard to remain objective (which is sometimes necessary to avoid competition) but also creates enormous passion sexually and otherwise. Negative connections can cause irritability, conflict, and destructive behavior. The passions still can be strong but often are out of sync or are used to play interpersonal power games. It is difficult to work together toward common goals, and battles of will are common and difficult to resolve. Use the other interchart aspects of Mars as well as natal Mars aspects to suggest strategies to lessen the impact of these challenging connections.

EXAMPLE: ASPECTS OF THE PERSONAL PLANETS

After meeting, Bruce (chart 20) and Louise (chart 1) quickly developed a comfortable relationship and settled down together. They have the connections typical of marriage: his Sun conjoins her Moon and his Moon opposes her Sun, so they relate to each other well. His Sun in her fifth brings out her need for children, while her Pluto in his fifth intensifies his own Plutonian aversion to fatherhood.

The lack of Moon-to-Moon contact makes emotional relating more difficult. Her Moon is on his Descendant, making him perceive her as an ideal embodiment of his partnership needs and causing her Moon (also conjunct his Sun and Neptune) to have strong, idealized emotional reactions to him.

Their chart rulers, Mercury and Venus, make a sextile. Their approach to the world is similar, with the same taste in furnishings, food, and clothes. Note the variety of easy contacts between each of their Venuses and the other planets, particularly her Venus with her Moon in his seventh house and his Venus sextile her Sun, creating all those romantic feelings that made this relationship so easy from the start.

His Mars does stir her up with the square to her Sun. His fixity drives her to unexpressed (square) anger. With the trines Mars makes with her Moon and Venus you might expect lots of passion, but actually the sexual side of their relationship is wanting. His Mars and her Moon and Venus are all debilitated. Being in each others' signs (in reception) limits the problems that these debilities cause, but there still will be some ill effects. They work well together in many ways, but the essence of those planets (passion!) just doesn't happen because their essential nature is detrimented.

He stirs her desire (note his planets in her fifth, although Neptune reveals there is a problem), but because of the fears raised by his own Pluto in the fifth, as soon as she desires sexual intimacy he becomes afraid to engage with her in that way. This would give us a lot to help the clients with since it probably provides a perspective they rarely see so objectively.

6. Jupiter

While the personal planets are undoubtedly the most important considerations for examining the personal life, Saturn and Jupiter represent our connection to the greater forces of spirit and karma. We should expect that if a relationship is to last, if it is to make a difference and have an effect on somebody's life, then it should go beyond the essential but trivial stuff of daily life. Even if these essential daily trivia alone are enough to make or break a relationship, the real concern of most clients is whether the relationship fits into their larger pattern of life, their spiritual and psychological growth. This is the function of these two important outer planets.

Jupiter represents gains that become apparent through the relationship, but more significantly it can be used to understand the quality of the growth. The union of minds through Mercury is as much a part of a successful relationship as the union of other aspects of life, but eventually even this must go beyond the level of conversation and intellect that planet symbolizes.

The mental connection at the level of philosophical and spiritual concerns is the business of Jupiter. Because it is such a beneficial planet, the negative aspects are not as challenging as those of other planets and may even contribute to fun and playfulness, essential ingredients for a happy relationship.

- *Jupiter to the Sun*. This connection allows the Sun person to expand and helps this individual fulfill his or her potential. The Jupiter partner will be experienced as a source of growth, gains, and fun. If it is a positive connection, the Sun person might think his or her luck has improved since the relationship began. Jupiter can help alleviate the negative effects of other aspects if it is strong and especially if it also aspects the troublesome planets. A weak Jupiter can produce wastefulness, procrastination, and the like. These may become a problem only if there are already issues around money and differences in how the two value and spend it.

- *Jupiter to the Moon*. These are the connections that help the couple experience the pleasure of the relationship. When positive aspects exist, they feel heightened emotions and have a great ability to have fun together and enjoy each other's company. There also can be feelings of deep, nonverbal mutual understanding. The negative aspects can create the tendency for emotional problems to magnify to unrealistic proportions. This can make the couple believe there are deep emotional problems when in fact the real problem is overreaction or oversensitivity to each other's ways of saying and doing things. Helping your clients understand these aspects can be extremely beneficial. If they know that they simply trigger a reaction in each other, then they can stop worrying about supposed hidden feelings and develop a strategy to contain these strong reactions. I have found that the best advice for such couples is to teach them not to "read into" what the partner says as if they were a literature exam but rather to just listen.

- *Jupiter to Venus*. Although these are not the most important contacts in synastry, they deserve a mention because they also relate strongly to the ability to have fun together, a key for lasting relationships. Aspects between the benefics are common in successful relationships and contribute to each person seeing the other in a positive way and as a source of gain and benefit. This is true for both the easy and challenging aspects, although sometimes the square or opposition may heighten the Venus partner's Venus issues (see chapter 4) or lead to extravagance or self-indulgence.

- *Jupiter to Mars* aspects may be significant if Jupiter emphasizes a difficult Mars. Positive connections between them allow the individuals to find common goals and ideals that they can share and pursue.

- *Jupiter to Jupiter*. These are the aspects that show the extent to which the partners are able to relate on philosophical and spiritual matters, the higher level of the mental connection. Positive aspects show an affinity of philosophies and the tendency for the relationship to cause growth at this level, unless one or both partners have a severely debilitated Jupiter. Such a Jupiter is unable to grasp abstract ideas or may develop strange notions about spiritual matters, making it unlikely they'll find philosophical compatibility even when the aspects are good. Challenging aspects also can indicate a failure to understand the other's worldview or a tendency for the perspectives to be very different. Although it is not usual for Jupiter incompatibilities to cause a relationship to fail, it is *not* unusual for people to develop irreconcilable spiritual differences that eventually can lead to a breakup. (Naturally, you would need to find other evidence of the same thing before you come to this conclusion.)

7. Saturn

Traditionally the most difficult of all the planets, Saturn has been seen as a threat to relationships, but this is a rather narrow view. Saturn represents things that are natural to relationships: limitations and restrictions, foundations, solidity, and compromise. It also represents responsibility and commitment—key ingredients for long-term success. It's interesting that Saturn is exalted in Venus's sign Libra, the traditional sign of romance and relationship. Clearly, it plays an important role in relationships.

Astrology is also a very important tool to understand karma. Karma is especially meaningful in the context of relationships because a basic premise of this worldview is that our relationships are not accidental or do not happen by chance. We have links with specific people for better or worse. This aspect of relationships will be discussed fully in chapter 6, but for now it is important to know that one of the main significators for *karmic* connections is Saturn.

- ***Saturn to the Sun***. These planets are incapable of forming a friendly relationship: each rules a sign in which the other is in detriment and each is exalted in a sign in which the other is fallen. This means that their connections by synastry will always be challenging. That does not mean they're bad, though. It is not unusual to find these aspects in the charts of married couples, especially where tradition plays a strong part in their lives or their style of marriage, or in couples who are more than a couple of years different in age. The positive aspects between Saturn and the Sun show the capacity for commitment and responsibility required for long relationships, although of course compromise and accepting limitations are required. Saturn can give the Sun a greater sense of security and stability, while the Sun can "lighten up" Saturn. Even though the individuals will feel some of the restrictiveness of this combination, there is likely to be a sense of a deep karmic connection and acceptance that this relationship is going to last a long time. The conjunction and the challenging aspects will make the commitments and responsibilities seem a burden. The solar partner may feel trapped or duty-bound, although there is often resignation to this feeling. If Saturn has poor essential dignity in such an aspect, the Sun partner may feel as though an overly authoritative or critical partner is draining his or her life and soul energy, while the Saturn person feels the need to be overly parental for the sake of the partner's best interests. Saturn may feel isolated, insecure, and "pushed" by the Sun. The challenges represented by this combination are difficult to change and ultimately need to be understood from a spiritual perspective if acceptance is going to happen.

- ***Saturn to the Moon***. These are similar to the solar connections, as the relationship between the planets is similar—each finds its detriment where the other rules. When they are in aspect to each other, the dutiful acceptance of undesirable restrictions is as much a feature as in the solar connection, but this combination carries the added burden of negative emotions. It is hard for such a relationship to be enjoyable. Saturn and the Moon combine to produce melancholy and depression so even the best aspects and dignities are a challenge to a happy relationship. While the positive connections will produce the typical responsibility and commitment of Saturn, the lunar partner is likely to feel held back and unable to express feelings. The challenging aspects can overpower the Moon person, who (unless the Moon is really strong and well placed) is unlikely to assert his or her needs at all and may become increasingly withdrawn or fearful. The Saturn partner may feel overwhelmed by the lunar person's emotions and may not understand why his or her helpful criticism is being rejected. Although it will be helpful to understand why this is so, the couple will need to do a lot of work to make the relationship manageable. (The question of how much work will be effective on Saturnian matters will be explored in the next chapter.)

• ***Saturn to Venus***. Even though there are some similarities to the Saturn-Moon relationship with respect to how the Venus partner may feel constrained, this is a much more promising connection. Saturn is exalted in Libra, a sign ruled by Venus, implying they have more in common than at first glance. Specifically, they are both fair and just when in good dignity, and this allows for a relationship to be built on a balanced and equitable foundation if they meet through positive aspects. This combination is the right kind of glue for the relationship—it produces loyalty, stability, and consistency. Still, fun and pleasure are severely toned down and this may prove overbearing to the Venus partner, while the Saturn partner may find his or her mate to be shallow or frivolous. The conjunction may be an important aspect for marriage, but like all Saturn-Venus connections, it often produces the difficult lessons typical of karmic bonds. These are much more apparent in the challenging aspects, and sometimes these kind of aspects make it unlikely that a relationship will form unless there are strong *karmic* lessons to be learned. When a relationship does form, the individuals will experience a lack of pleasure and very different styles of expressing love. The radically different styles of expressing affection will add to the confusion of each partner never being clear on how the other feels, and in keeping with the typical Saturn effect may lock the partners into a pattern of sacrifice, misunderstanding, and awkwardness that seems to repeat forever. It may seem as though breaking up is the only possible solution. Even when that is the case, challenging Saturn-Venus aspects often cause the partners to endure beyond all usefulness. Such relationships may become cold and distant or, more commonly, gradually transform into polite friendliness. The sense of loyalty and responsibility outweighs other important considerations, and they may stay together even after reaping any benefits the relationship may have originally offered.

- **Saturn to Mars**. The combination of the two malefics is very difficult. The couple experience a lot of frustration, worsened by a reluctance to communicate. Look for good Mercury connections to help them work around this. The Mars partner especially feels blocked, held back, and often angry, while the Saturn partner may feel that everything the other does "winds him or her up." Lack of sexual drive is a potential issue, especially if Venus also aspects Saturn.

- **Saturn to other planets and to Saturn**. The general effect of one partner's Saturn acting as an inhibiting force on the other partner is well established by looking at Saturn's effects on the luminaries and Venus, but because of the importance of these contacts as life lessons and karma they will be examined in greater detail in the next chapter.

EXAMPLE: ASPECTS OF JUPITER AND SATURN

Louise (chart 1) and Bruce (chart 20) also have strong Jupiter and Saturn connections. Their Saturns square each other's Suns, making them feel somewhat restricted by each other yet providing a very strong glue to hold them together, especially since those Saturns also sextile both Venuses and both have Saturn essentially dignified by being in a sign it rules. They can get stuck for a long time with limited personal growth if they don't make a big effort.

Fortunately, their Jupiters also aspect each other's Suns, and sextile each other. Although his philosophical viewpoint is earthy and hers is emotional, which they often feel makes them very different, they balance each other's views well and end up learning a lot from each other.

Louise and Bruce still have not married or had children, but their relationship continues and they still love each other and enjoy each other's company. Astrology can help them focus on where the sexual and emotional issues lie and help them look for solutions while understanding the limitations.

---

8. Uranus, Neptune, and Pluto

The outer planets have a powerful effect in our personal lives, and the aspects between one person's outer planets and another's personal ones will create changes that affect the practical, everyday aspects of these relationships. Such changes arise from much deeper impulses and often have far-reaching implications for the individuals, let alone for their relationship.

These deeper, even karmic aspects of the relationship are discussed in the next chapter.

Checklist: Key Areas of Comparison

When analyzing the aspects between the planets, we have made broad although comprehensive conclusions about the likely results of these interactions. We have followed the common approach of analyzing everything and developing a picture of the relationship from the interpretation as a whole. We have discovered that the personality is a description not only of who we are, but of how we relate to others.

Professional astrologers don't just describe—they spend much of their time giving advice or information about specific areas. In relationship work, this is one of the most important roles of the astrologer because the clients usually are looking for practical solutions to problems they are already aware of.

In chapter 3 we identified some of the key areas where individuals may differ and that are likely to affect relationships. Now you need to look at those issues more closely with the tools of interchart aspects.

Use this checklist to ensure that you have covered all those areas in greater detail.

- Ability to relate to each other as partners: aspects between the seventh-house rulers and planets, and from one person's seventh-house ruler to the Sun, Moon, and Ascendant ruler of the partner (the parts of the chart that describe identity and that you have analyzed at length).

- Ability to understand each other's feelings: aspects between Moon-Moon and Mercury-Moon; aspects from other planets to Mercury and the Moon; aspects from other planets to the Moon. For example, even if Moon-Mercury aspects are lacking, one person's Moon receiving a trine from the partner's Venus can show compassion and sensitivity and a willingness to accept the partner's feelings.

- Ability to communicate: aspects between Mercury-Mercury; aspects from other planets to Mercury. For example, if a challenging aspect is received from Mars, misunderstandings can easily happen and rapidly turn into anger and saying hurtful things, which can have longer-lasting consequences.

- Ability to relate sexually: aspects between Venus-Mars, Mars-Mars, and Venus-Venus. Consider the extent to which challenges involving Mars (or Venus) being blocked or opposed by a planet from the other chart might describe the effect on each other's sex drive. Also check aspects between each person's fifth-house ruler and planets in the fifth. For example, if the Moon in the fifth receives a trine from a strong Mars, passions can be inflamed. On the other hand, a lack of contact between Mars in the two charts, or between Mars and another significant planet, may indicate their libidos being out of sync.

- Similarity or compatibility in matters regarding children: Fifth-house analysis also applies to this critical issue. Keep in mind how the planets ruling and inhabiting this house also can show parenting style, as can the planets concerned with the fourth house. The condition of the Moon also can give information about children, although this planet tends to be more useful in analyzing relationships with children themselves.

- Ability to live together and maintain a home: aspects between the fourth-house rulers and residents. Also pay attention to one person's planets in the other's fourth house. For example, if one person has Saturn in the partner's fourth, the partner may feel as though dreary and restrictive Saturn just moved into his or her home, whereas if it were Venus the partner might feel more at home than ever.

- Similarity or compatibility of life goals: Look at aspects between the tenth-house rulers and planets, as well as the aspects between one person's tenth house and all the other's important planets. Goals are an angular issue in life, giving them high priority and the tendency to take up a lot time and energy in our lives. It is not unusual for relationship problems to arise when one person is perceived as giving too much time and energy to his or her work, or when there is a distinct imbalance in earning potential.

    TIP: The aspects between angular rulers across two charts will give a quick and accurate picture of the key struggles in this relationship.

- Value systems and attitude toward money: These can be identified through aspects of the second-house rulers and planets and those of the eighth, as well as an aspect from one person's second-house ruler to the other's eighth-house ruler. To a lesser extent, aspects from Jupiter in one chart to the planets of the other chart can show that the Jupiter person causes the other to benefit through gains the Jupiter person brings or to suffer due to the Jupiter person's wastefulness.

Keeping It in Balance

Don't make an issue out of these connections as if they were somehow extraordinary. You could give your clients a sense that their relationship is unnaturally powerful or difficult because the astrological language is usually so clear and direct or because your analysis has revealed deep issues that seem relevant to you. Keep this in mind when discussing the synastry with your clients. It is easy to convey the notion that their relationship is karmic, dramatic, even soap-operatic when this is a relationship that to them may seem somewhat challenging but on the whole is quite rewarding. This is particularly important when considering the connections with the more dramatic and karmic outer planets, and the deep and often scary life issues these planets represent.

In real life there are many other influences that work to contain the apparent extremes that the charts often describe. Relationships are systems that have built-in mechanisms that maintain them for good or ill. Most importantly, the level of commitment and compromise that one or both partners must engage in, as well as children, houses, and other manifestations of these commitments, usually lead to them tolerating much more challenge than you might expect by thinking about astrological symbolism.

What You've Learned So Far

By now you have learned a lot about synastry. You understand the essentials of why we are attracted to others and what personal characteristics are involved. You know how to do a quick, basic comparison as well as a much deeper and thorough one using the tools of planets, houses, and aspects.

At this stage you can start practicing with charts of people you know, those of famous couples, and even some of the client charts you may have been working with. Although there is a lot more to relationships and to synastry (and we will go deeper in the second half of this book), you will find a lot of meaningful information in the analysis you can do so far.

It is worth spending some time becoming more familiar with the material you have studied so far so that you are ready to go much deeper as we explore what else is involved in a relationship. Relationships are not just about love, sex, children, and values; they are the most fundamental way of learning about life, and about ourselves.

CHAPTER 6

LIFE ISSUES

Relationships are not just about the interactions we have with other people. They are not merely about pursuing our needs and expressing our sexuality, or the many other interpersonal matters we have examined in the last chapter. At their heart they are about the lessons and experiences of our souls. They have the capacity to teach us more about ourselves than many other experiences in our lives. In the process they also may cause us to reveal more about ourselves than any other circumstance ever will. It's no wonder that, traditionally, relationships are the main ingredient that makes up our karma.

In This Chapter

In this chapter you will explore how you can identify when another person triggers deep personal matters that might affect a relationship:

- Learn to identify spiritual lessons and issues that partners trigger.
- How hidden issues affect relationship experience.
- How outer-planet aspects challenge spiritual growth.
- What is the "seven-year itch," and how is it related to karma?
- What age differences mean and what issues they raise.
- Helping your clients understand their relationship and its challenges in a larger spiritual context.

Going Deeper

In most cases, the extent to which a relationship may bring these deeper *karmic* issues to light depends on how long the partnership has existed. As you have learned previously, it takes some time before we start getting beyond the Ascendant and Mercury and start discovering the real person.

Similarly, revealing more of ourselves is risky and often requires us to be willing to break down defenses we have built over a lifetime. This is why there are times when people have a strong and positive connection, they have everything going for them in the eyes of all around them, and yet the relationship doesn't last.

Fear of Rejection

Sometimes the challenge of exposing one's vulnerabilities is so threatening to the sense of self and the defense mechanisms that have been put in place over a lifetime that a person would sooner lose the relationship than risk the imagined consequences of exposure. To us, our own weaknesses seem to be our Achilles heel, so powerful that they can topple the entire self. We imagine that in the eyes of the partner they will be monstrous and will make him or her reject us.

Fear of rejection is one of the most powerful fears that can affect us. Rejection is a denial of who we are. When we have problems or issues that we want to conceal from others, it is also a reflection of our own inner belief that it is these troublesome aspects of the self that actually define us. We blow them out of proportion.

As time passes, we cannot help but relax our defenses. It takes an enormous amount of energy to preserve them, as well as a lot of focus to keep them in place at all times. Very few people can maintain this defensiveness by two or three years into a relationship. Eventually, when time has worn down this focus and energy, there is only one thing left to do: reject the person who threatens to find out who we really are. Ironically, the real threat lies in the one who fears he or she personally will be rejected.

The Natal Chart and Life Experience

The tendency to conceal those aspects of ourselves that we believe to be our true weaknesses is analyzed astrologically by starting with the second house, as you did in chapter 4. When it comes to comparing charts, you should be aware of any propensity toward poor self-worth and concealment because you already have analyzed each natal chart extensively.

Succedent Houses Show Core Issues

Having analyzed the natal chart, you are aware of the extent to which the planets inhabiting and ruling the succedent houses (2, 5, 8, 11) show issues related to self-worth and how that is related to the ability to love (see the discussion in chapter 4 on the connection between self-worth and love). Now you need to explore the same issues across two charts.

Although all aspects and planets in a chart describe the good and bad issues, the deeper, core relationship issues are contained largely in the succedent houses. Our analysis of these houses is aimed at determining how these issues are triggered in partnerships.

- Look at each succedent house ruler in turn and see what aspects it makes with the ruler of the same house in the other chart. Parties in a relationship may sometimes compete over their personal issues or they may deliberately use their problems as a way of manipulating or controlling the relationship—say by seeking sympathy or being weak. They may use the relationship to avoid their own problems by focusing on the partner's issues, or they may benefit from the partner's experience or insight—or just from the partnership itself—to deal with some of these problems. Avoidance, unconscious behavior, or surreptitious behavior is more likely to be found in a square. An opposition more often shows competition, while beneficial learning experiences show in the trines and sextiles. Be aware, though, that everyone's unique network of issues and their causes means that these aspects may vary. It is not adequate to draw meaning from the aspects alone—also consider the nature (and dignities) of the planet concerned.

- Look at the aspects from the ruler or inhabitant of one succedent house with *another* succedent house ruler or inhabitant in the other chart. Analyze these in the same way you did for the natal chart.

- Finally, look at the aspects that rulers and inhabitants of these houses receive from other planets, especially those that have strong accidental dignity in the partner's chart and therefore plenty of opportunity to express themselves.

- Saturn or outer planets (especially Pluto) in the *first* house make it difficult for someone to show his or her real self. Take note if the partner's planets trigger these planets.

- Sometimes a core issue may not even be coming from a succedent house ruler. Knowing the natal chart and talking to the client will tell you which planets or houses represent them.

EXAMPLES: ASPECTS INVOLVING SUCCEDENT HOUSES AND RULERS

We already have noted a number of fifth-house connections between the charts of Louise and Bruce (charts 1 and 20). Look at how they emphasize Louise's core succedent house issues described in chapter 4: her fifth-house ruler, Venus, is closely conjoined by his fifth-house ruler, Mercury, which also trines her second-house Mars, ruler of the eleventh. His Sun conjoins succedent house rulers Moon and Venus in the fifth, while eighth-house ruler Saturn, in the eighth, has its own core issues made immediate by the challenging square from his Sun and by the relationship planets Moon and Venus.

We can expect this relationship to cause Louise to constantly face the succedent house issues of children, love, power, and self-worth. The many positive aspects and planets involved help us identify and suggest positive ways to deal with these issues.

Dan and Janice (charts 10 and 11) have a relationship characterized by power struggles, with each trying to gain control (note how both have a challenging Pluto aspected by the other's Sun, bringing those Pluto issues to light. Her eighth-house ruler, Mars, and his, Jupiter, are strongly highlighted by personal aspects from each other's charts. But they have no aspect with each other. Why the struggle?

Her eighth-house ruler is in the sign in which his eighth-house ruler is detrimented, and his eighth-house ruler is in the sign in which *her* eighth-house ruler is detrimented. See how important dignity is to understand relationships between planets? This means that each of the planets sees the other as coming from the "place of the enemy," the place that they consider the weakest. Thus the planets "hate" each other and so they struggle for dominance.

Secretiveness and Denial

Now, we know that many of the core issues are the very things that the client is defensive about.[1] The relationship reading is the very last place you want to talk about these issues because the client's partner is the one person from whom he or she is likely to be concealing many personal issues. As issues arise in the consultation, though, you are in a position to help the clients understand the triggering process and ultimately—with clients who really want to work together to make a long-standing relationship improve—to help them find ways to reveal and deal with these issues so that they do not become stumbling blocks in the relationship.

The Twelfth House

Sometimes you are dealing with clients who are secretive by nature, which makes them prefer to keep their issues to themselves. Secretiveness also can describe people who keep secrets *from themselves*—sweeping things under the carpet or totally denying to themselves and to others that these issues exist. Occasionally, secretiveness refers to people who are likely to engage in activities behind their partner's back. This is the kind of secretiveness that can directly threaten a relationship. The twelfth house describes all of these.

Planets in the Twelfth

When key planets such as personal planets or important significators occupy the twelfth house, there are two basic consequences. Firstly, denial, secretiveness, or some other mechanism to conceal the matter from the self or other is likely to be in place, and secondly, there is a very real possibility that there will be new problems that arise out of the concealment.

This house is one of loss and sorrow, and shows that these planets rule areas of life that are likely to lead to loss. As the house concerned with these sad experiences, the twelfth produces problems in our lives (it is traditionally considered a malefic house) and so implies that concealment leads to problems. Of course, loss also can lead to great spiritual growth, so this house should be seen in a larger context.

---

1. It is useful for astrologers to understand the basic defense mechanisms that people use to avoid dealing with their problems all the time (the best-known one to laypeople is denial). Many introductory psychology texts cover this area. An excellent overview for astrologers is given in Noel Tyl's *Synthesis & Counseling in Astrology* (see appendix A for details).

Look at each client's chart to see which planets occupy this house. In the context of a relationship, the main planets to look out for are the key significators for relationship work: the luminaries, the personal planets, and the rulers of the seventh and the fifth. The planets here represent things that are not expressed in their true form, although they may be expressed in more roundabout ways.

It is a common error to believe that knowing about something is enough to understand and change it: a client with the Sun in the twelfth but Mercury in the first was happy to talk about his feelings all through a session, but did so to rationalize them and so feel that he was master over them. Yet he never delved into the meaning behind his problems and how they affect him and his life. Knowing is usually only the beginning of the long path to understanding and change.

- When one of the partners has the Sun in the twelfth, it is likely that other people don't really see this person for who he or she is, partly through the individual's own deliberate efforts to conceal this and also because he or she doesn't understand him- or herself very well. The younger the client is, the more likely it is that the person feels he or she has not yet discovered his or her own potential. When discussing the client's personal issues as well as relationship ones, you will need to bear this in mind.

- The Moon in the twelfth house can have similar implications but more usually shows a reluctance to reveal feelings or even to get in touch with them at all. Sometimes this is because of the fear of experiencing loss or sorrow, probably because it has been experienced before. It is not an uncommon problem for some people to avoid becoming deeply involved in a relationship because of the fear of loss. Your careful analysis of this Moon can be a great help for the couple to understand the problem and find safe, conscious ways to deal with emotional problems without the additional burden of secretiveness or avoidance.

- Even more significant is a primary relationship significator in this house. Venus, the natural significator for relationships, can fare well here because our private life is, after all, private, but that does not make it a good place to have Venus when you are involved in a relationship. There can be too much secretiveness. It is not unusual for people who have extramarital affairs to have Venus in this position, although of course merely having it here does not automatically make someone unfaithful!

- This also may be the case for a person who has the ruler of the fifth in the twelfth. In any event, these people are not inclined to talk about relationship matters at all, which makes your job a little harder.
- The ruler of the seventh in this house also makes for secretiveness about the partner, about relationships, and even toward the partner, but also can warn of loss of partners as a potential pattern.

Of course, not everyone with a twelfth-house Venus or fifth lord is likely to have an affair or experience a loss. Always keep the overriding rule in mind—you need more than one piece of evidence to draw any conclusions, and such conclusions must be balanced against other chart facts. With earthy, loyal individuals, it is unlikely that they are having secret relationships, but it is very possible that their discretion is leading them to keep silent about relationship issues and not get help or support from any quarter (even their partners).

To you as the astrologer, this position is a warning light that, one way or the other, discretion or secretiveness may be a threat to the relationship. You needn't create or stir up problems by suggesting that someone's having an affair, but it can be helpful to talk about secretiveness or a general reluctance to share feelings and how this can be an obstacle to relationship growth and other Venus-related matters—shared values, seeking pleasure, and self-worth.

EXAMPLE: SECRETIVENESS AND UNADDRESSED ISSUES

Alice (chart 22) complains that relationships reach a point where they end before they get serious. It becomes apparent that she considers most of her personal issues and private life none of her partner's business ("intimacy is about what is shared, not about me waving my dirty linen around"). She feels safer when keeping things secret.

Astrologers will note a lot of fear and secrecy related to her insecurities about relationships. Having the Moon in the twelfth is, of course, why she doesn't reveal her feelings, but note how the ruler of the seventh (Mars) is also in the twelfth, and it is also the ruler of her second house of self-worth. Her twelfth-house ruler, Mercury, sitting in detriment in the second house emphasizes the connection between secrecy and self-worth.

Saturn's opposition to her difficult twelfth-house planets was emphasized at her Saturn return, when four close relatives died in a period of five months. When Saturn, ruler of the fifth, reached her seventh-house cusp some two years later (and was in its own fall), her boyfriend died in an accident (ruler of the seventh conjunct Pluto and Uranus in the twelfth).

Alice went through a difficult five years after that, while Saturn transited her seventh and eighth houses, but with the help of astrology came to understand how secrecy and isolation are related and began work with a psychologist to find healthy ways to express the concerns of her troubled twelfth-house planets.

Triggers from the Partner's Chart

While all twelfth-house matters are potentially threatening to the well-being of a relationship, some relationships are likely to trigger issues related to this secretiveness just as transits can do. As always, you look for aspects from the partner's chart to the planets in the twelfth house of a particular chart.

It is not secretiveness itself that is triggered by the partner; in fact, it usually is exactly the opposite problem: hidden issues rise to the surface because of the partnership. Bearing in mind that many issues are in fact hidden from ourselves, the twelfth-house person may not recognize that these are his or her own issues that have come to the surface, and holds the partner responsible for the sudden appearance of these problems.

- When the partner's planets are in the individual's twelfth house, and especially when they make conjunctions with natal planets already there, the existing twelfth-house planets and the house as a whole are "woken up." The partner causes the individual to have to look at his or her hidden twelfth-house issues without any specific triggers. The individual may experience the relationship as intense and challenging.

- Positive aspects and aspects from positive planets help the experience seem positive. The awakening of these issues will come through rewarding experiences such as shared learning or a partner who helps the individual understand him- or herself in a way that helps the person grow.

- Negative contacts cause the person to experience the partner as forcing him or her to confront things the individual doesn't want to look at. Often, the partner also is seen as the *source* of the newly realized problem, or the partner is perceived as the one who actually has the issue. This is especially true when the triggering planet is the same as one in the twelfth or the ruler of the twelfth.

TIP: Remember to talk about twelfth-house matters with the greatest care. It sometimes is useful to suggest that the client see you privately for a few sessions or that the person consult a therapist to understand the issues better.

The Challenge to Grow

The real challenge in a relationship comes from the emotional and spiritual growth that is the inevitable outcome of having to engage with another person in such an intimate way. Most people rate such growth as one of the most important reasons to persist in a relationship even when it is a difficult one. Of course, there are those people who have no conscious desire to grow, who perhaps even desire the contrary, or who have peaceful relationships in which no such challenges seem to occur.

As usual, astrology can explain both of these conditions. In a nutshell, the challenge to grow is usually the result of contacts from one partner's outer planets to the personal planets of the other, especially to the all-important relationship significators we have identified.

The effect of contact between outer and personal planets is dramatic, even in a natal chart. Uranus, Neptune, and Pluto represent deep transpersonal forces that as individuals we experience only during dramatic changes in our lives (occurring at the transits of these planets). Individuals born with these contacts often seem more intense to others and may feel that they grapple with powerful issues that others are less aware of. On the other hand, they may personify some of the principles symbolized by those planets. For the most part, though, these planets remain remote generational forces that are usually more significant by their house placement than by anything else.

So you can imagine the effect when somebody else's Uranus suddenly makes an aspect with a personal planet that was dealing with personal matters until this time. Just as the twelfth-house trigger did, these contacts lead to individuals facing aspects of themselves that might otherwise remain remote, or being challenged to confront changes to how they see themselves and how certain areas of their lives are experienced.

For all intents and purposes, these outer planets are malefic, but since they operate at a level of consciousness beyond the personal, their apparently malefic effect can have profound and ultimately positive effects on the growth of consciousness. This is one of the reasons why contacts from one person's outer planets to the other's personal planets can make the relationship seem more intense, challenging, and exciting. It is as if the relationship provides access to states of being that otherwise cannot be reached. We feel like a different person because of the relationship. It is also why the absence of such contacts can make a relationship seem calm, peaceful, unchallenging, and even occasionally dull.

Effects of Outer Planets

One of the best ways to grasp the effect of an aspect from one person's transpersonal planets to the other's personal planets is to consider the outer planet to behave something like it does in transit. Transits of the outer planets are well known as being some of the most life changing there are. Similar to these transits, synastry contacts can have effects that last long after the relationship may have ended.

While the more personal planets show that we behave differently in relationships and show aspects of our character that otherwise are unseen, the outer planets describe lasting changes. This is where you can help your clients understand the real meaning and value of the relationship and start asking those difficult questions that everyone asks: What is the karma of this relationship? Why are we together? Ironically, it is often these very same aspects that make an individual want to flee the relationship either literally or by developing strong defense mechanisms like avoidance.

Aspects Between Outer Planets and Personal Planets

Like all other aspects involving the personal planets, these are felt the most intensely. Some effect of these aspects is discernible from the very beginning of the relationship, although with time the real meaning of such contacts will be seen.

Remember, aspects work both ways. Although we can compare the effects of these aspects to those of transits, the aspects work as they do in natal charts—each planet is having an effect on the other. While the personal planets' interactions often seem more like a combination of forces that each partner will experience similarly, the outer planet to personal planet contacts more often are experienced a little differently by each person.

The partner whose personal planets receive outer planet aspects will have the transpersonal quality make a strong impact on his or her life. The relationship is functioning at a deep level to bring some karma to the fore. It will make the individual face issues that he or she is unlikely to face on his or her own but that are unavoidable and inevitable because of this relationship. Perhaps all the more mundane aspects of the relationship—the emotional, sexual, and mental connections—are the binding forces that get the individual into a situation where the deeper issues will have to be faced.

The partner whose outer planet is involved will have the qualities of that planet in its natal house become highlighted in ways or through circumstances suggested by the nature of the personal planet with which it has an aspect.

- *Aspects to the Sun* cause deep and fundamental changes. They are long-lasting and change the way the solar individual sees him- or herself while enhancing the personal qualities of the outer planet by house position in its owner's chart.

- *Aspects to the Moon* cause strong emotional reactions and cause the lunar partner to respond in unexpected ways. These contacts often are felt as threatening or challenging, and the lunar individual can feel vulnerable and exposed.

- *Aspects to relationship significators (ruler of the seventh, Venus)* cause the individual to experience the relationship as very different and having a permanent effect on the way he or she handles all relationships. The specific nature of the effect also will depend on which personal planet is the relationship significator receiving the aspect, as illustrated in the next point.

- *Aspects to other personal planets* will trigger those personal planets' natal effects in a dramatic way, often with challenging consequences. These effects can resemble those of similar combinations in transits. For example, if Mars receives a challenging aspect from the partner's Uranus, it may provoke sudden rash and aggressive responses. A positive aspect also will be sudden and unsettling but in a more stimulating and exciting fashion.

- *Aspects between outer planets:* With individuals close in age, these aspects often exist within each natal chart and between charts because the outer planets are in similar positions for people of similar age. Always check if this is the case before you emphasize too much interpretation of these positions. When these aspects are formed, they show important *karmic* bonds that will be discussed more fully in the pages that follow.

How Each Outer Planet Takes Effect

When considering the outer planets in the checklist that follows, keep in mind which of the personal planets is involved when you consider the likely manifestation of effects. As always, you also should bear in mind the essential dignity of the personal planet to see how it tends to do things and the accidental dignity of the outer planet (the outer planets have no essential dignity) to see the extent to which that quality is expressed by the individual.

- *Aspects from Uranus*. The attraction to the partner initially may be experienced as "electric." The personal planet individual may see him- or herself and the world in a whole new way. These people may allow more eccentric or individualistic aspects of themselves to show. If they are willing to let go of their more traditional view of themselves, this relationship may be the most excitement or fun they can ever have. That also can become a problem—these relationships rarely feel settled and stable. Sometimes the contact is experienced as somewhat threatening since it may make the individual feel suddenly exposed. The karma of Uranus is the challenge to become an individual. The relationship may force these individuals to examine what is unique about themselves and where they need to have the courage to express that. They will be faced with having to change a lot about themselves and to learn to respond in a more intuitive, immediate way to the special challenges their partner creates. They may have to assert their uniqueness or even eccentricities no matter how this causes others to view them. Relationships challenge independence by their very nature. When Uranus is involved, such challenges become a key to the spiritual lessons concerned. Many people avoid relationships because of their need for independence, while others may become involved in relationships that give them independence but few of the shared comforts that make relationships satisfying (for example, a long-distance relationship). The challenge is to learn to find independence within the context of a relationship and not undermine the integrity of the relationship itself.

- *Aspects from Neptune*. Neptune seems to be more troublesome in relationships than in almost any other aspect of our lives (although it is one of the important transiting planets of the midlife crisis in the early forties). It is a subtle and insidious influence and initially may even have the opposite effect from the challenges it later provokes (appropriate for the planet of illusion). Initially, the recipient of the Neptune contact may believe the partner fulfills his or her romantic and spiritual ideals. These individuals often think they have found their "soul mate," leading to the dangerous assumption that since the relationship is "meant to be," it will somehow take care of itself. Such escape from reality is typical of this planet. Later on, this contact also may produce feelings of doubt, confusion, and uncertainty and make it very difficult for the individual to know where he or she stands in the relationship. Neptune always raises the challenges of proper boundaries, but the important karmic issues are those of romance versus reality. This relationship will force the individual to let go of beliefs and ideals about relationships and discover that life is not like a romance in a movie or a novel. Romanticism is an effort to escape from the mundanity or harshness of reality, and the consequences of not facing reality can be the hardest lessons in the relationship. The confrontation with reality also will go deeper, requiring the individual to examine his or her spiritual practices and beliefs in the light of this relationship.

- *Aspects from Pluto.* These contacts can create powerful, magnetic forces of attraction between people. For some, there is a Svengali effect, making the Pluto partner seem charismatic and powerful. Often this partner actually holds some kind of power and quite obviously has the capacity to cause change. Pluto brings change through the principle of letting go and leaping into the unknown. The partner receiving these aspects is challenged to confront his or her fears and issues about giving power to others. Like most lessons, this is likely to be learned through the challenges in the relationship, not through intellectual realization. The Pluto partner may represent the other person's darkest shadows and fears. This can generate very powerful karmic lessons about realizing that there are things we cannot change and must accept, that we do not have power over all aspects of our lives (least of all other people). This lesson can be embodied by the partner, who may have characteristics that are considered unacceptable, even dangerous, and that are often specifically the things we hate most: the partner who is perfect in every way but one, and that fatal flaw is the one most feared and despised by the other person. (In fact, it is not uncommon for abusive relationships to have strong, negative Pluto aspects with few redeeming features.) On the other hand, when the karma is accepted and the partners are willing to face the Plutonic shadows, these relationships can offer the opportunity for profound spiritual growth and personal change because Pluto's lesson of accepting what we cannot change and learning to let go is the most fundamental spiritual lesson of all.

EXAMPLE: OUTER PLANET ASPECTS CREATE DEEPER CHALLENGES

Maggie and Ken (charts 8 and 9) have challenging Neptune aspects that suggest perhaps they at first overlooked many of the issues that exist between them. His Neptune sits almost exactly on her Moon, while her Neptune squares his Venus from his twelfth house.

Maggie's parents had a troubled marriage, causing her to feel that she had to look after herself as a child. She attributes her affinity with older men to this experience, but continues to depend on herself for emotional support and fails to communicate her needs in her relationship. She responds to Ken as she did to adults in her early life. The Neptune "soul connection" combined with Ken's obviously Saturnian reserve, which she recognizes and accepts as being so similar to her own, means that she fails to realize there is an emotional "disconnect," since she doesn't recognize either of their emotional needs.

Ken, on the other hand, needs to express his affectionate Leo Moon but doesn't know how in this relationship. Apart from being loosely squared with *her* Moon (see the effects of this in the example of Anne and Raymond described in chapter 3), rendering it difficult to meet each other's needs, the square to his Venus from her Neptune makes him romanticize her but feel rather unsure of what she is feeling for him. This makes it harder for him to express his own feelings—and a circular problem is set up as she again fails to "read" his feelings and thinks he is unemotional.

Aspects Between Outer Planets

Aspects made between one outer planet and another are less pertinent to the everyday details of a relationship, but as a relationship becomes more committed and longer lasting these aspects also can be used to understand growth patterns and karmic lessons.

The majority of romantic relationships take place among people of a similar age. For that reason, each of the outer planets in a chart is usually very close to the position of the same planet in the partner's chart. Similarly, many of the aspects between the outer planets of one chart and those of the partner's chart are the same aspects made among those planets in either of those charts.

These simple astronomical facts should be kept in mind when analyzing these aspects. It is easy to unintentionally give the clients a sense that they are dealing with karmic issues of huge proportions when realistically these could be issues they have been familiar with for much of their lives, and possibly in pretty ordinary ways.

Astrologers consider these planets to be largely representative of the generational influences that help make up our personalities and experiences. This is why we are somewhat similar to our peers in attitudes and values. We already have discovered the importance of similar values in relationships. Our analysis of these planets concentrates on the extent of this similarity or the compatibility between such values.

Karma also has a role to play in the understanding of generational influences. We are born at the time and place that is most appropriate to our personal karma, so it follows that our social environment—this same peer group—functions to bring these lessons to the fore.

In my practice as an astrologer, I have encountered the commonly observed problem that if partners grow spiritually at different rates or in different directions, the relationship will begin to undergo enormous stress and often end in a breakup. When we undergo spiritual changes, we begin to seem like a different person from who we were when the relationship began and so the very ground that the relationship was built on begins to change. It's no surprise then that it can have such dire consequences.

Although this issue will be more appropriately discussed later when we look at the importance of transits and progressions in synastry, it also is evident in the sign placement of the outer planets. For this reason, one of the ways to analyze outer planet aspects is with the view to help the partners prioritize growth issues and find a context for them in the relationship where they will not prove threatening.

- *Outer planet natal aspects being repeated.* This is the most common situation and frequently occurs in people who are born within two or three years of each other. Although natal interpretation should not emphasize outer planet aspects precisely because they are generational (think of the decades of births with Neptune sextile Pluto), the recurrence of the aspect from one chart to the next indicates that the generational issues represented by the aspect become a personal issue in this relationship. This is especially true if the recurrence works in both charts (as it often will). It should not be overemphasized, but you can help your clients understand that this is an area where they can discuss their personal approach to issues that they share (and share with their peers) and perhaps how they can find a cooperative way to work on them together. It is very important that they should grasp the tendency to project these issues onto the partner (as is frequently the case with the outer planets). When a positive contact is reinforced this way, the partners should try to find shared activities and interests so they can begin to develop common ground at a deeper, karmic level. Even the challenging contacts, though, represent enough common ground for the partners to make a deliberate effort to interpolate and share their personal journeys, perhaps by going to lectures or worship together, sharing reading material, etc.

- *Outer planets in different signs.* If one of the outer planets is in a different sign in one person's chart than it is in the partner's chart, a karmic challenge exists that resembles the difference between their generational values. Usually this occurs when there is a significant age difference between them, although occasionally the difference is minimal if the planet is at the end of a sign in one chart and at the beginning of the next sign in the other chart. Partners with these positions will find themselves constantly challenged by the different way the partner's generation handles things. This can sometimes feel like a "generation gap," although occasionally it gives the partners new ways and means to express their personalities. Even still, a lot of compromise is required as it is unlikely that either of them is capable of doing things differently—these values are deeply ingrained not because they have been there since childhood (after all, the parental value system is not necessarily carried forward by the next generation) but because they are a function of how we assert our own individuality, which begins with identifying with our peers rather than our parents. But these sign differences are often evidence of deeper karmic challenges because of the patterns they tend to set up. To analyze these, we need to take another look at Saturn and then return to what the outer planets are doing.

Karma, Saturn, and the Seven-Year Cycle

Saturn is the most important significator for karmic connections. Its traditional role as lord of fate and the boundary between the worlds and its important role in mythological and religious culture always meant that it was studied to see where personal will ends and divine will supersedes all. Although this particular issue often is analyzed using Pluto's placement, Saturn's place as the force that manifests spirit into the physical world remains key to its interpretation. While all the planets represent karma, Saturn is the primary significator for karma, especially through the principles of limitations and lessons.

Some of Saturn's karmic connotations in synastry were explored in the last chapter. The relationship between the two Saturn placements in the partners' charts, though, is often the most important indicator of a relationship that will be important and long-lasting enough to describe deep karmic lessons. As is the case with almost everything about Saturn, most of these lessons will be learned through the Saturnian principles of limitation, responsibility, and acceptance. While it may be Neptune that makes it feel like the partner is a "soul mate," it is Saturn that explicitly indicates the need for lessons to be learned through each other.

The familiar seven-year cycle of the transiting Saturn making squares and oppositions to its natal position is one of the best-known principles in predictive and developmental astrology, showing the stages of challenge and growth in our lives. As we shall see in chapter 8, the same cycle is responsible for the "seven-year itch," a phenomenon whereby change is *sought after* every seven years, observed in most things but especially relationships.

In synastry, the same phenomenon occurs in the relationship between the two Saturns. When partners are seven years or a multiple of seven years apart, there are built-in limitations in the relationship that will bring the lessons to light and force the partners to deal with them out in the open (without having to wait seven years for them to come to light, as other couples may do). This is a relationship full of challenges but with plenty of Saturnian "glue" to give the couple the ability to stay together and sort it all out.

In this checklist, age differences and aspects have been combined. Age difference alone usually will put the two Saturns in signs that have a basic aspectual relationship, and this is strongly emphasized when an actual aspect exists between the two.

- *Saturn in the same or adjacent signs, similar age*. Couples who are fairly close in age—up to around three years apart—usually will have this placement. In the same sign, it is only relevant when conjunct, emphasizing the similarity of basic limitation and authority issues common in peer groups. In adjacent signs and in semisextile, it indicates a tendency to deal with problems somewhat differently. This is not an especially challenging position.

- *Saturns in sextile or trine, age difference a multiple of five*. The couple are able to interpolate the different ways of dealing with limitations and other problems in order to reach a mutually satisfactory outcome. Sometimes these couples deal with separate, personal karmic issues without allowing them to impinge on the relationship. Their different ways of dealing with problems often will offer the partners fresh insight, although there still will be some difficulty in letting go of old, useless methods and accepting the other's advice.

- *Saturns in square or opposition, age difference a multiple of seven*. With this classic karmic relationship, the partners have to constantly learn to adjust to each other's way of handling things. There is a constant need for compromise. Both may feel that their own issues are constantly put before them and may find that the relationship constantly challenges them with new problems. Some couples will find these relationships exhausting, while others will find them difficult but full of growth. These relationships are often long-lasting, but never easy. The square requires the partners to adjust to outer conditions through joint compromise rather than through one person getting his or her way; the opposition requires them to pool their resources and devise an entirely new strategy to deal with problems.

- *Saturn in the same sign, age difference around twenty-eight years*. This is a powerful indicator of a karmic bond. Despite an age difference of more than a generation and many other outer planet differences, these partners find each other remarkably similar. They experience similar issues and challenges and often have a similar approach to dealing with them. Their karma is so strongly linked it is almost tangible to them, producing a strong force of attraction overcoming the natural obstacles of the unlikelihood of the relationship as well as the strong social disapproval that often follows in its wake. These are souls so similar that they each offer the other the unique experiences of their generation in a manner that allows them both to overcome obstacles that may otherwise have seemed insurmountable. Make no mistake, there are many difficulties and challenges (as there always are when Saturn is involved), but these relationships usually surpass the odds against them and allow the individuals to experience personal spiritual growth easily and in parallel with the partner. The "different path" issues discussed earlier are comparatively rare; even when the age difference engenders a seemingly different approach to spiritual growth, the partners are on compatible paths or they are tolerant of the other's way.

Using Uranus and Neptune to Enhance Your Understanding

The tendency for age differences to be close to multiples of seven when there is a strong karmic link is not surprising when you understand Saturn's cycles, but a full understanding of the dynamics is incomplete without analyzing how the outer planets provide additional information through their own seven-year cycles.

Uranus and Neptune take seven and fourteen years, respectively, to move through a single sign of the zodiac. This means that partners with an age difference that is a multiple of seven may well have aspects between the two Uranuses or Neptunes in their charts. Given the slow and erratic orbits of these planets, the same aspects can occur even when the age difference is greater or less than that, but you should note the particular emphasis of karmic bonds when both Saturn and one or both of these planets are aspecting their counterparts in the other chart.

- ***Uranus semisextile Uranus, age difference seven years.*** *May occur with Saturn square Saturn.* This is a challenging aspect. There is a different approach to asserting the individuality that is awkwardly incompatible with that of the partner, making it more difficult to understand how and why the partner is different. It is not enough to be seriously challenging, although the difficulty in pinning down the difference can enhance the problem and the feeling of incompatibility. The lesson is to learn to respect the other's way of expressing individuality. If the Saturns also square each other, then this aspect makes compromise especially difficult and the characteristics just described under the Saturn square become very challenging.

- ***Uranus sextile Uranus, age difference fourteen years.*** *May occur with Saturn opposite Saturn and Neptune semisextile Neptune.* This aspect also reveals a different approach to asserting individuality and independence, but it is a difference that adds interest and stimulation to the relationship. It reveals a deep soul connection that gives the ability to delight in each other's company despite the apparently large age difference. If the Saturn opposition is present, this aspect can make it easier to resolve the differences and challenges that Saturn represents. The presence of the Neptune semisextile Neptune can lead to the partners underplaying the differences between them and potentially avoiding problems and never resolving them.

- ***Uranus square Uranus, age difference twenty-one years.*** *May occur with Saturn square Saturn and Neptune semisquare Neptune.* This is an extremely challenging configuration. The younger person may think that the partner is too parental and will feel a strong urge to rebel and break the rules. The way that each expresses his or her individuality and personal goals clashes with the other. If it occurs with the Saturn square, it dramatically enhances the challenges and makes it very unlikely the relationship will ever be easy or comfortable. The presence of the Neptune semisquare can lead to a failure of the couple to recognize the problems, an avoidance of the issues, or a persistent difficulty in grasping the problem or finding solutions to it—all of which exacerbate the perceived differences and the likelihood of the relationship becoming more difficult over time.

• ***Uranus trine Uranus, age difference twenty-eight years****. May occur with Saturn conjunct Saturn and Neptune sextile Neptune.* These couples typically revel in their differences. They are fascinated by the partner's unique qualities and ways of expressing individuality and may even feel a renewed sense of their own. This configuration can add fun and excitement because they both get exposed to new things through each other. The older partner often feels reinvigorated by the relationship. If this configuration occurs with the Saturn conjunction, it enhances the sense that obstacles can be overcome and that differences can be constructive. It also helps make that conjunction easier than one would expect it to be. When the Neptune sextile also occurs, it contributes to the conscious sense of soul connection and the often-described feeling that they have known each other for much longer than is actually the case.

• ***Larger age differences****.* You won't often encounter couples who are more than twenty-eight years apart in age, but when you do what works best is to consider the Saturn conjunction of twenty-eight years already established in their relationship (along with all its implications) as if it is "within" the relationship. Then, consider how many years more than twenty-eight years apart they are, consider this to be the age difference, and add that information to what you already have. For example, if a couple are thirty-five years apart in age, you would consider them to have the strong bonds of the Saturn conjunction but there will be additional challenges described by the Saturn square (and Uranus semisextile) that actually exists in the chart. However, this will be less challenging than the usual Saturn square because of the bond provided by the complete Saturn cycle contained within this relationship.

EXAMPLES: OUTER PLANET ASPECTS CREATE POWERFUL CONNECTIONS

Remember to calculate the aspects; age doesn't tell you everything. The elliptical orbits of the planets mean that these ages are only approximate. Maggie and Ken (charts 8 and 9) have outer planet connections that help them deal with their age difference and help the relationship work despite the troubles the personal planets have. With the twelve-year age difference, they have a sextile between their Uranuses.

South Africa's former president Nelson Mandela (chart 23) married his third wife, Graca Machel (chart 24), at age eighty. She was shortly to celebrate her fifty-second birthday. As many couples experience when there is a large age difference between them, critics searched for some ulterior motive or deeper meaning to the relationship. While the two obviously had a lot in common—from the lifelong struggle against oppression that they each had conquered to their profound concern for children's issues—they suffered the usual suspicions such age differences engender. Was she after his wealth and influence? Was he a weak old man being taken advantage of by a younger woman?

Astrologers could have had no such concerns. Their synastry reveals the profound connections typical of this age difference and the true soul-mate connection between them. The two Saturns are conjunct in Leo (detriment), which gives them a sense of the shared difficult past and the sometimes odious burdens of responsibility their positions demand.

Their Uranuses are trine in air and their Neptunes have a warm sextile between them. These combinations allow them to express their ideals as well as their spiritual goals in a way that is individualistic yet in harmony with that of their spouse.

Their sense of the "magic" in this connection is evident in their obvious love (they are always seen holding hands, laughing together, helping each other) and even their willingness to go ahead with the relationship despite knowing it would be controversial (Mandela's former wife Winnie was still a powerful, popular public figure, and Machel was a foreigner and the former first lady of a Marxist regime).

They must have had a strong sense of the karma of Saturn. Both suffered tragically at the hands of the same Saturnian establishment (the government of apartheid South Africa that imprisoned Mandela was complicit in the death of Machel's first husband, Mozambican president Samora Machel). Perhaps they also experienced their passionate concern for children as a shared destiny. With the unique resources each offered (his children's fund, her experience as a special United Nations consultant on refugee children), they probably realized that by joining forces they were a formidable partnership.

As important as these karmic connections are, they are not enough to make a relationship succeed, especially with a large age difference. We still expect to see many of the personal connections we have discovered in previous chapters. Not surprisingly, many of those are present, especially the ones associated with marriage: Sun square Sun, Sun sextile Moon, and both Suns sextile the partner's Venus. Age difference or not, we can be surprised neither at the marriage nor at its success.

Other Outer Planet Connections

Although all the planets represent the karmic forces at play in our lives, the outer planets have the additional ring of things that are beyond our control. For many, the feeling that fate lends a hand to events in our lives is very strongly felt in the circumstances leading up to the beginning of a relationship. Even when two people decide they don't want to get involved, somehow love finds them.

How the outer planets are connected to these fatalistic events will be discussed in chapter 8.

CHAPTER 7

CHARTS OF THE RELATIONSHIP

Once you have a good foundation in the methods of comparing charts and analyzing the interaction between them and between the individuals they represent, it is time to take the interaction to the next level. The relationship is not just an interaction; it is an entity in its own right.

In This Chapter

Relationships seem to make people behave very differently, as if the relationship is an entity of its own. This chapter will show you:

- How to create a composite chart for a relationship.
- How to interpret the composite chart.
- Alternative methods of creating relationship charts.
- Why these methods have problems, and why they don't all work.
- How to create and interpret the marriage chart.

What Defines a Bond?

We are surrounded by people in every aspect of our lives. Some of them are casual acquaintances, others become important partners on our journey in life, and still others produce conflict and difficulty. Synastry implies that our charts are constantly interacting with those of all these other people, like molecules bouncing around, and that the astrologer is like a lab scientist who can, at any given moment, isolate two of these bustling human molecules to see how they are interacting. At what point do we say these two molecules have bonded to form some kind of relationship?

Much of astrology depends on the "moment" being considered significant. The traditional way to define a relationship depends on establishing the moment that the relationship began. This is sometimes considered to be the time the couple met, or the time that they committed themselves to a relationship. We will explore some valuable astrological techniques that can be used to analyze a relationship this way.

Many couples, though, have no clear recollection of precisely when such a meeting actually happened, and in many cases it is difficult to pin down the moment a relationship began because the process is usually gradual. Many relationships lack a beginning point because the individuals may already have been friends or acquaintances before their relationship became romantic. There are countless other complicating circumstances that make this method of timing problematical and even somewhat arbitrary.

This has led astrologers to seek an alternative approach: to find a way to produce a chart of the relationship from the charts of the individuals, a new chart that will stand on its own regardless of precisely when the couple met. Rather than using a time and confining the chart to an arbitrary moment, astrologers have sought to *combine* charts mathematically and thereby create a third chart that will describe the relationship itself.

Combining Charts

What is generally considered to be the original method of combining charts was devised by John Townley and published in his 1973 book *Composite Charts*.[1] Townley used the long-established principle of midpoints as the foundation of his method. Using this approach, the position of each of the planets in the new composite chart is established by finding the midpoint between the position of that planet in each of the two individual charts. The resulting position is said to be the composite of the energies of the natal planets, and the chart itself is referred to as the "composite chart."

---

1. Townley's book has been expanded and revised in a modern Llewellyn edition (see appendix A).

Thus, if partner A has the Sun at 10° Aries and partner B has the Sun at 20° Cancer, then the Sun in the composite chart will lie exactly halfway between those two positions along the shortest arc, at 0° Gemini. This procedure is used to find the positions of all the planets, and their sign position is thus established.

To find the house cusps of the composite charts, the midpoints of all the house cusps are found. This often produces the problem that the resulting house cusps do not seem to follow the correct sequence in the zodiac because some of the midpoints end up at the opposite end of the zodiac from what is expected. Townley suggests that the Ascendant or Midheaven be used as the starting point and then, if necessary, some of the cusps be modified by 180° so they follow in the correct sequence. (Since midpoints represent axes of influence similar to house cusps themselves, this adjustment does not effectively change the notion of a midpoint between the original cusps.)

Townley's method also requires Mercury or Venus to occasionally be similarly adjusted so that they end up near the Sun, as would be expected if the chart represented real planetary positions as in a natal chart. The end result is a chart that looks like any natal chart, except that the combination of planetary positions never existed in reality (and probably never could).

An Alternative Method

Another well-known astrologer, Ronald Davison, devised an alternative way of calculating the new combined chart, basing his idea not on midpoints but on his own theories of time.

In his work on prediction, Davison explored the extent to which symbolic points in time may relate to future trends, developing the method of converse directions, which suggests that just as the number of days after a birth can be used to represent the number of years after birth (in standard day-for-a-year secondary progressions), so can the number of days *before* birth be used in the same way.

Following on from this, Davison proposed that a point in time exactly halfway between the births of the two individuals in a partnership represents the special moment that describes their relationship. Similarly, the point in space exactly halfway between the latitude and longitude of the two individuals' births is said to represent the location of the relationship. Having found a date, time, and place in this manner, a chart can be drawn up in the usual fashion. Similarly to Townley's approach, this chart (which Davison called the "relationship chart") represents some kind of a midpoint, in this case the midpoint in time and space.

Advantages and Disadvantages of These Methods

The two methods often produce similar positions for the outer planets, although the inner planets and the house cusps typically are very different. As with a number of other astrological techniques, astrologers find themselves in the position of having to choose the method that seems to make the most sense to them, an approach that is admittedly a weakness because it relies excessively on the intuition of the astrologer rather than the inherent merits of the method.

The primary advantage in Davison's approach is that, since the chart is drawn from a date, time, and place, this can be progressed like any other chart. This is not possible with Townley's composite, since no "birth" details exist, although as with a Davison relationship chart the composite can receive transits. In fact, work with midpoints has established that transits to midpoints have great predictive validity.[2] Unfortunately, the question of whether midpoints between two different charts have as much validity as midpoints between actual positions in the sky cannot be easily resolved.

The most typical criticism leveled at the Davison chart is that there is no real or symbolic way in which this chart is actually linked to the people involved in the relationship, or their relationship itself. It is, in fact, a somewhat random chart, and for many astrologers it is an excessive stretch of the imagination to presume it is somehow linked to the relationship of people who have no connection to this chart by time, place, or any other circumstances.

On the other hand, the composite chart is clearly constructed out of the charts of the parties to the relationship and draws on an already established method in astrology that has been generally accepted as valid. More importantly, since the composite method is essentially a space composite, the midpoint positions actually do exist in space and are receiving transits, illustrating the validity of the chart. In contrast, the Davison relationship chart is a midpoint in time, representing a point in the past that cannot be construed to be relevant to a relationship that is happening in the present. (The natal chart is not in the past—it describes the beginning for an individual who still exists in the present. The Davison rela-

---

2. See Reinhold Ebertin's work in *The Combination of Stellar Influences* (Tempe, AZ: American Federation of Astrologers, 1994), which remains one of the most important and influential works on midpoints.

tionship chart has no direct connection to anything outside of its unique moment in time, and the transits it receives do not relate to transits received by the couple's natal charts.)

Helping Clients Understand the Composite Chart

Most astrologers find Townley's composite method consistently reliable, and it remains one of the most important modern contributions to astrology. What makes it especially valuable to the analysis of a relationship is that it seems to become more descriptive and more accurate the longer a relationship lasts and the more transits it receives. In long-lasting relationships where the dates of inception are in the distant and irrelevant past, this is an especially valuable characteristic.

From the clients' perspective, it is particularly constructive to describe the composite chart as the third entity in the relationship. The notion that the relationship is an entity in itself, with its own needs, experiences, cycles, and ways of expressing itself, removes the burden of responsibility that so often is carried by one or both partners. People feel responsible for meeting each other's needs and finding some way to ensure that a partner will meet his or her own needs, often leading to the vague notion that perhaps somebody exists "out there" who would be a better match.

The problem with this belief is the idea that it is somebody else's responsibility at all. While relationships do involve having some of our needs met, the burden of expectation creates unrealistic beliefs that often lead to disappointment. On the other hand, if the clients understand that the relationship has needs of its own, which each of the partners has some obligation to meet, then this fresh perspective helps them see the relationship in similar terms as in the composite chart. This makes the chart an especially valuable tool to help them work with the relationship more objectively rather than falling into the trap of becoming too concerned with subjective needs and disappointments, which inevitably leads to the exchange of blame.

This means you need to be totally direct with the clients about this chart. Discussing the following points is a valuable way to introduce the chart:

• While the clients' own charts describe their individual needs that apply to all relationships, the composite chart relates to this specific relationship.

- The natal chart describes needs that it is our own responsibility to meet, while the composite chart describes those that it is appropriate to expect this relationship to address.

- Understanding the relationship as a third entity helps clients to not confuse their own issues with what is best for the relationship, and removes a lot of blame.

- Knowing that the relationship is a separate entity helps clients retain the integrity of their own life goals while remaining part of a partnership.

- The composite chart describes the relationship on equal terms for both individuals and does not emphasize one's influence over the other (which often feels like blame).

Working with the Composite

The composite chart is very similar to a natal chart, except that it describes the entity of the relationship itself. The skills you use when describing a natal chart will be applied to the composite chart, although the emphasis will be a little different,

- ***Identify the house emphasis.*** Just as in any chart, houses are the most personal features of a chart and describe the areas in which this relationship tends to play itself out. When a house is emphasized, it often describes the most dominant features of the relationship, especially when the Sun is one of the planets that emphasize it. The presence of the Moon, Venus, and ruler of the seventh also add weight to an emphasis of planets in a house.

- ***Pay attention to the house of the Sun.*** As you would expect, the Sun describes the identity of the relationship. The house that it is in shows where the focus of the relationship lies. A marriage that has the Sun in the tenth house is more focused on goals, while one with the Sun in the fifth might be more focused on children or sex. This simple detail often can go a long way to explain basic problems in the relationship—is the focus on things that are appropriate to the kind of relationship this is? For example, when the Sun is in the first house, there is a tendency for the couple to be more concerned about how the relationship looks to the world than the real issues of how the partners relate to each other. This is a common source of problems and explains why we are sometimes so surprised when the "perfect couple" suddenly get divorced.

- *Identify aspects similar to those in the natal charts.* While all the aspects in the composite are important, those that exist between planets that also are aspected in one or both of the natal charts are especially important. In fact, if both natal charts have an aspect between the same two planets, then a similar aspect will almost certainly exist in the composite. This is valuable in understanding how relationships highlight and modify our personal issues. Most importantly, it shows how our relationships can create new problems or solutions in matters that exist in our individual lives.

- *Identify new aspects.* Aspects that are unrelated to positions in the natal charts provide opportunities for the couple to work on new goals together, but can also be valuable in showing why things that were never a problem before suddenly have emerged as problematical in this specific relationship.

- *Examine conjunctions to one of the natal charts.* When a composite position is conjunct something in one of the natal charts, this emphasizes the natal issues of the planet in the individual's chart. It shows that this relationship will bring the issue to the fore. It may show how the relationship strengthens a particular issue or characteristic, and will sometimes show why in some ways this relationship may be better (or worse) for one party than it is for the other.

EXAMPLE: EMPHASIS IN THE COMPOSITE CHART

Chart 25 is the composite of Louise (chart 1) and Bruce (chart 20). It provides an accurate summary of their relationship: the Sun is in the fifth, and the chart ruler, Venus, is in the seventh, clearly showing a romantic relationship akin to marriage. Venus also rules the fifth, so between Venus and the Sun the focus on children and sex in this relationship is very evident.

The composite identifies these as challenges. The Sun is closely square a tight Moon-Saturn conjunction in the difficult eighth house of power and endings. Both individuals have easy Sun-Saturn configurations natally and are naturally responsible and capable of handling compromise, so they must feel quite stuck when compromise feels like an obstacle. They each have mildly challenging Sun-Moon configurations—need and desire a little out of sync—but that suddenly has become a real clash in the composite chart's square, and the conflict between need and desire must be addressed for any progress to be made.

As astrologers, we would concentrate on the emphasized eighth house, also identifying how the couple can emphasize the "partner's resources" aspect of this house,
and use the positive aspects of the Moon and Venus to identify ways for the couple
to find pleasure together and work toward a better expression of their sexuality.

Emphasizing Aspect over Sign

Even professional astrologers are sometimes tempted by the simple categories of the
twelve signs, especially since laypeople have a basic understanding of them. When these
laypeople are your clients, there is also a strong pressure to meet some of their most basic
expectations.

Popular astrology's obsession with zodiac signs creates the impression that there are
compatible and incompatible Sun signs for the partner, and once you have taken the pains
to explain that the relationship is rather like an entity with its own chart, the same temptation arises as the need to tell the clients "your relationship is a Taurus!"

Putting across the composite information in this way does little to help the clients understand the relationship and probably leads to misunderstandings and oversimplifications.
While identifying the relationship as an entity allows you to make sense of such notions
as the relationship having *needs* of its own, it is somewhat of a stretch to suggest it has a
personality of its own.

Neither Townley nor Davison addresses the troublesome logical issues that arise when
you describe composite planets in terms of the sign they are in. (Townley actually offers interpretations for the composite planets in the signs.) The essence of the problem is evident
in the fact that the sign that occurs at the midpoint of two other signs usually does not in
any way relate to the other signs.

For example, in the relationship between a Pisces Sun individual and one with a Taurus Sun, the composite Sun is in Aries. As individuals, these partners are both likely to be
more reticent to assert their ego and identity, perhaps even rather insecure about it. Yet the
composite seems to suggest that in this relationship they suddenly are highly energetic,
challenging, goal-oriented, and rather insensitive to the people around them. Is it really
likely that passive, sensitive individuals suddenly will become highly energized and somewhat aggressive when put together?

What is really important is that the composite positions represent midpoints. Midpoint
theory suggests that this position therefore is the point where both natal Suns are equally

influential. Townley describes it as being like the "shore," where the influence of the one begins to take over from the influence of the other. Whichever way you look at this, it is difficult to presume that the zodiacal sign is relevant, since it relates to neither of the original natal planets and implies that the "shore" is thoroughly dissimilar to the things that constitute it.

We regularly over-interpret sign meanings. When midpoints are used elsewhere in astrology, the zodiacal sign generally is not taken into account and the dignities of the original planetary positions (not of the composite) are used.[3] The composite planet is not actually at that zodiacal position, so therefore it cannot have dignity. Midpoints, like aspects, emphasize the relationship between two bodies. When they are transited, they imply that both original bodies are receiving aspects at the same time. When their aspects are measured, they in fact describe simultaneous aspects to both original bodies.

This means that the aspects of the composite planets are their most significant characteristic. When a composite planet receives a transiting aspect, both original planets are being simultaneously aspected and are likely to respond according to their natal dignity. Thus individuals are responding differently to a development in their shared life, as we would expect. As much as a relationship is an entity in itself, the two people involved do not experience it the same way.

When working with clients, I suggest you avoid the temptation to interpret meaning or dignity from the zodiacal sign and instead develop the habit of referring back to the natal positions in the individual charts to establish the reaction to changes that are described by transiting aspects to composite planets.

EXAMPLES: ASPECTS MODIFY THE COMPOSITE CHART

Chart 26 is the composite for Dan (chart 10) and Janice (chart 11). Earlier analysis of the synastry revealed power struggles in this relationship. The composite shows that this will be played out in the third house, through arguments, problems of communication, and misunderstandings.

Their individual third houses are challenged by malefics in them. Both luminaries are in the composite third, along with Mars and Jupiter for emphasis. Four planets in one house are too much for comfort, especially with Mars there. The

---

3. Ebertin originally didn't consider sign or even house in his midpoint work, although later he revisited the issue of sign and explored the use of the signs in a limited fashion.

natal charts show that Dan's Mars is better dignified, dominating the arguments with aggressive force, while Janice's Virgoan Mars will attempt to dominate with argument and words.

Notice how the composite Mars conjoins Janice's strong Venus, intensifying the passion and the power struggles and making Dan a potent force of attraction. Their marriage lasted over fifteen years, although the arguments persisted the whole time. Composite Jupiter is also on her Moon, adding to the clear fact that it is she who is so strongly affected by these arguments.

Chart 27 shows how aspects in the charts of Brett (chart 14) and Alan (chart 15) are modified by the relationship. Alan's Mars opposite Saturn brings out the potential of Brett's out-of-orb opposition between those planets—there it is in the composite for both to share. Brett will feel potentially frustrating limitations here he has not experienced before, while Alan's naturally over-influential Saturn is somewhat enhanced.

But it seems that the enhanced Saturn ends up signifying compromise and commitment: both have no real Sun-Saturn natal connections (Alan has the semisextile, which makes it difficult for him to accept Saturn, and Brett has no aspect, but they are in signs that are inconjunct). In the composite, however, the planets have a close sextile, and compromise and commitment prove possible and constructive.

Combining Multiple Charts

When exploring combining charts on your computer, you may have noticed a whole variety of other methods that are available, or it may just have occurred to you that you can analyze a group or a family by adding everyone's charts into the combination. In fact, computers have made the mathematical part of astrology so easy that innovators have come up with all sorts of ways of manipulating and transforming numbers.

We need to be cautious with these methods because for each "transformation" that we subject a real planetary position to, we lose the connection between the planet and the reality it represents. Group composites are a good example of this problem: although ordinary composites represent the midpoints between planets and therefore "the place where the set of transiting cycles … affecting one chart's planet begins to wane and the others begin to wax by comparison,"[4] the group composite represents the *average* positions of a planet over a number of charts. This average actually has no relation to anything, least of all the positions of the planets in the natal charts. It is at best an obscure statistic, but its value in describing the group energy has no foundation in reality.

Marriage Charts

Using too many charts becomes confusing and also diffuses the value of the information you find. The one chart that might provide a valuable addition to your arsenal on some occasions is the chart of a marriage or commitment.

This chart can help you find why and how a relationship might seem to change after the partners get married, or why the practicalities of marriage might overwhelm the relationship and obscure the good connection between the couple. Occasionally, it might do the opposite and show why a couple, despite having little in common, may be able to make a marriage work.

Use this chart when the partners have issues about the practical difficulties of managing their marriage or to help them deal with how these daily details have overshadowed their relationship. These couples may complain that things are not what they used to be or that everything changed the moment they got married.

The marriage chart is the chart drawn for the moment a wedding ceremony begins. (Some astrologers draw the chart for the moment at which the marriage becomes legal or the vows are accepted.) Sometimes these are in fact electional charts that have been used in advance of the wedding to select the best time for the marriage to take place. This strategy often allows the astrologer to help underemphasize problems in the relationship and give greater focus to potential strong points, although this is usually much easier said than done and there may even be new difficulties described by the marriage chart.

Although electional astrology can be very helpful, it cannot change the karma between the couple and the way their personalities interact. It can, though, create a new common ground (the marriage) within which the couple can work to make the relationship as good as possible.

It must be remembered that this is not a chart of the relationship between the couple; it is a chart of the marriage itself. A marriage may be difficult although the underlying

4. John Townley, *Composite Charts* (St. Paul, MN: Llewellyn Publications, 2000), p. 28.

relationship is not—marriage involves many legal and social responsibilities, new financial issues, often the enormous job of bringing up children, and countless other pressures, goals, and opportunities. These are what the marriage chart describes.

What to Analyze in the Marriage Chart

For a thorough grounding in this area, it is best to study a book on electional astrology (see appendix A). The key points to concentrate on are:

- The relationship between the Sun (male) and the Moon (female) is very significant and often has the strongest influence no matter what else is in the chart. This contact is used to explore the relationship between the two parties. These significators also hold in gay relationships, where again you can determine (by discussion and observation) which of the luminaries represents each partner.

- The relationship between the first-house ruler and the seventh-house ruler also describes the couple. In many cases, you can quickly establish which of these planets represents which partner by briefly describing each ruling planet in human terms.

- Venus is the natural significator of marriage, so its dignity and aspects are critical to understanding the opportunity to experience and express love and harmony in a marriage, or the extent to which the marriage is based on these things. Helping the couple give expression to the Venus placement can be very helpful in providing a pleasurable outlet that reminds them of their feelings for each other and why they got married in the first place. This can even save a marriage that is drowning under the weight of everyday mundane challenges.

- The first house represents the relationship itself and how it is seen in the world.

- Each of the houses is used in the conventional way, but instead of describing the aspects of an individual life they refer to those things in the shared life. Thus, the second house refers to the financial affairs of the marriage, the fourth is the couple's shared home, the seventh is their interaction with other people, the tenth is their shared goals, etc.

- The remaining planets have their usual uses and implications.

It is best not to rely too heavily on the marriage chart, but rather to help the couple understand their roles and to use it in comparison with the synastry and composite analysis to help them understand how the pressures of marriage itself change the relationship.

EXAMPLES: MARRIAGE CHARTS, GOOD AND BAD

Joanne Woodward (chart 12) and Paul Newman (chart 13) may differ in many ways, but their marriage works famously. Their marriage chart (chart 28) reveals a powerful Sun, Moon, and Venus.

The Sun and Venus are conjunct and trine the Moon, a strong factor for love and harmony despite the opposition they have with Uranus. That opposition, and the sixth-house location of the conjunction, do inflict some problems—each partner is very individualistic and pursues his or her own interests. Some may consider that incompatible, but the harmonious trine makes it perfectly suitable to them, and the cadent house position of Uranus makes it a much weaker challenge.

It isn't all easy; remember, the marriage chart always reveals compromises and new challenges. Venus's squares with Jupiter and Neptune enhance the potential for fun and romance, although Neptune must have caused a good deal of illusion and disillusionment in the early years. Pluto in the first house square the Moon would also be challenging. They must have had to let go of a lot of preconceptions, but in doing so became a powerful union and a symbol for independence and individuality within a marriage.

The marriage of Brad Pitt and Jennifer Aniston (chart 29) has some similarities astrologically, but lasted a brief four years.

The Sun, Moon, and Venus are all in the seventh house of marriage, unsurprisingly, but the Sun and Moon are both in their own dignities—each feels like the boss. Individual needs will not easily be compromised, especially since no aspect or dignity exists between them. Venus has left the conjunction to the Sun and is opposed by Uranus. Unlike Woodward and Newman's similar aspect, this one is in powerful angular houses, making the need for independence and individuality highly emphasized.

The marriage chart is fairly similar to the chart of the long-lasting marriage of their Hollywood seniors, so why didn't the marriage last? Remember, in a marriage chart the condition of the luminaries is the final arbiter: here, the Moon is conjunct a fallen Mars, and the Sun is opposed by Neptune, both again emphasized by angularity. Although this Moon is the seventh-house ruler and has a sextile with first-house ruler Saturn, showing the lasting love and friendship the couple have, the odds are against these luminaries: they are both close enough to the node to start feeling the effects of the solar eclipse a day later.[5] Eclipses represent a bad relationship between the luminaries and will inevitably lead to problems, just as the eclipse on the wedding day of Prince Charles and Diana Spencer did.

Moving Forward into the Present ... and the Future

Although the marriage chart can show the important foundation on which the relationship is built, it usually does not seal the fate of the individuals, who have the opportunity to face and deal with the issues as they arise over time.

The synastry and composite charts remain the best ways to understand the relationship, and the transiting, progressed, and other cycles these charts undergo form the ultimate description of how the couple's shared life will be experienced.

---

5. When the Sun, Moon, and node are within 18.5° of one another, an eclipse will occur. In this chart, the three fall within about 14°.

CHAPTER 8
BEGINNINGS
AND ENDINGS

Synastry is a powerful tool to understand the dynamics of a relationship, and for the most part it offers more than enough information for a couple (or occasionally an individual) to work with.

There are, however, much more pressing concerns that are at the forefront of most clients' minds. Clients often are concerned with when a relationship is going to "happen" or whether their current relationship is going to last.

In This Chapter

Prediction is at the heart of the astrologer's job. This chapter looks at how it works in relationships.

- Learn to find signs of a relationship beginning.
- How to use progressions and transits specifically for relationships.
- When changes will happen, and when the relationship could end.
- What changes will happen, and how to find the patterns for future change.
- How marriage charts and composites work in prediction.
- A full case history of the doomed relationship of O.J. Simpson and Nicole Brown Simpson.

When Does a Relationship Begin?

Astrologers quickly learn that some predictions are much easier to make than others, and discerning when a relationship is likely to start is among the most difficult calls to make. This is especially vexing considering how often people want to find out exactly that.

A significant part of the problem is that the beginning of a relationship is often hard to define. Is it when we meet the person? The first kiss? A declaration of commitment? All of these are often imprecise and fleeting moments. In the early stages of getting to know someone, there are many times when we make meaningful connections, experience intense feelings, or make some kind of commitment. How could we know which of the experiences leads to a relationship actually forming? Additionally, there are many people we have such experiences with, who may turn out to form one of any number of different kinds of relationship with us. In short, we can't even define what begins a relationship, let alone identify when that beginning occurs.

If we cannot define what something is, then it follows that our capacity to predict it is severely limited. In retrospect, however, often we can look back on what was happening in a chart when a relationship began and use the information we find to discover more about the relationship, including some of the information about how likely it is that the relationship will last for a long time. Of course, sometimes the indications are clear and reliable enough to make a prediction, and you need to be able to recognize the typical indicators when they do appear.

Progressions Show Lasting Changes

As with all events, both transits and progressions singly or in combination are capable of describing the beginning of a relationship. Since the beginning point itself is rather vague and often prolonged (after how many dates do we call it a relationship?), it is more reliable to base the judgment on a progression, as the influence of progressions can extend to many months and even as much as a year. Although this makes timing the prediction more challenging, a combination of progressed aspects and transits, as well as the all-important progressed Moon, can help sharpen your focus.

Remember with progressions that they work three ways: a planet may progress to a new position and make new aspects, a natal planet may receive new aspects from a progressed planet, or two planets may progress and form a new aspect with each other.

- *Progressions involving the angles.* Since the angles measure things that have an impact on our lives, they often are involved when a relationship begins that will be lasting and even lead to marriage. While any angle can be involved, the Ascendant/Descendant is particularly important since it is the "me/you" axis. Aspects with the Sun, Moon, or Venus usually indicate the start of important relationships.

- *Progressions involving Venus or the ruler of the seventh.* The ruler of the seventh is the personal significator for marriage, and Venus is the universal one. As the natural significator for marriage, Venus very often is involved at all the key times in a relationship, right through to the ending. For either of these planets, aspects with the luminaries and the angles are powerful and reliable predictors of a relationship beginning or leading to a marriage. Very similar aspects may exist at the time of a divorce, so it is important to always consider other aspects before making a prediction.

- *Progressions involving the Sun.* We already have examined the extent to which relationships are an identity issue. This means that the Sun is likely to be involved when the potential relationship is going to have any impact on the sense of self, identity, how others respond, and most of the critical needs the Sun implies (see chapter 2). Progressions of the Sun typically indicate very important years in life that can help redefine the sense of self. New aspects of the self come to light, and others see the individual differently. A possible reason for or result of this shifted sense of self could be the appearance of a relationship. Although the Sun's aspects with any planet could lead to this, it is particularly the case with Sun-Venus aspects. The conjunction, trine, and sextile are the most important progressed aspects, although challenging aspects still can show a relationship because they indicate change. Progressions involving the Sun and one of the angles are also strong indicators of a relationship (although you must consider the likelihood that the progression also may involve the specific concerns of the angle if it is not the seventh- or first-house cusp).

- *Progressions involving the Moon.* The natal Moon receiving progressions also can be a good indicator, although it should be considered only if there are other indications that this is a relationship development and not one of the many emotional changes we frequently experience. The progressed Moon can play a very significant role in highlighting what is significant during a time of change or by timing just when a progression is likely to manifest. If it aspects a planet that is involved in another progression, the month that the Moon's aspect is exact is often when the progression involving the same planet is at its peak.

EXAMPLES: PROGRESSIONS AT THE TIME OF MEETING

Joanne Woodward (chart 12) and Paul Newman (chart 13) both have the Moon ruling their seventh house. They met when her progressed Moon was conjunct her natal Moon and his progressed Moon was conjunct his fourth-house cusp.

Brad Pitt (chart 30) has the seventh ruled by Mercury. At the time of his marriage, his natal Mercury received a solar arc semisquare from Venus[1] and his progressed Mercury was sextile the progressed Venus. His wife, Jennifer Aniston (chart 31), had the progressed Moon conjunct her fourth-house Sun and exactly sextile her seventh-house cusp.

Transits Time the Changes

Many astrologers feel more comfortable making predictions from transits because they are easier to time, although it is not so easy to know exactly what changes they describe and whether these are significant or temporary ones, even though key chart points may be involved. When predicting a meeting or relationship beginning, it is best to rely on a combination of transits and progressions.

Transits also seem to set the tone for the future of the relationship, which makes them very useful to analyze retrospectively even once a relationship is already well under way. Relationships seem to be typical of the transits that formed them for years to come (although gradually other influences become increasingly apparent as time goes on). We will see later that the very same transits that show the beginning of a relationship can show its end—once again displaying the tendency of the significant planets to characterize the relationship as a whole.

- *Points receiving transits*. Transits to the Ascendant/Descendant axis are by far the most reliable to make predictions from. They unfailingly show changes in relationship status (depending on the current situation the individual is in) according to the nature of the planet that aspects them. Transits to Venus are also highly reliable, while

---

1. In solar arc progressions, semisquares are considered equal in strength to all the "change" aspects (those that are multiples of 45°).

those to the ruler of the seventh are good to support directions that may imply but not specify relationships, such as those involving the luminaries. The MC/IC axis also has a significant bearing on relationships, especially those likely to have a long or lasting effect on the individual. While you should not rely on transits to this axis alone to make such a prediction, they will add significant weight to other factors suggesting a possible relationship.

- *Transits from Jupiter.* In all situations Jupiter can indicate a positive development, but Jupiter transits are not always long-lasting or even deeply significant. Use these transits as one of a number of factors—they show the emotional experience such as joy or excitement that might explain the effect of changes. Occasionally these transits indicate meeting a wealthy person, a teacher figure, or someone who will bring gains to the individual's life.

- *Transits from Saturn.* Although these transits are slow to show their effect and therefore not the best for timing, many long-term relationships begin with some influence of Saturn. These relationships may start slowly or subtly, and Saturn often represents a person older than the individual.

  Challenging aspects may indicate relationships begun under difficult circumstances. In fact, obstacles may characterize the relationship, although relationships begun under Saturn can last a long time even when they are difficult. Saturn is the chief indicator for karmic conditions, and these relationships are often part of an inevitable lesson that the individuals need to undergo.

- *Transits from Uranus.* Uranus transits can be a good indicator for relationships because they so often take us by surprise. When relationships begin under Uranus's influence, they can dramatically change the course of our lives and also can seem uncharacteristic and surprising to others.

  Uranus may represent a very different type of person from oneself or from what is expected. These relationships may have a quality that feels as if some external force has lent a hand to this beginning. Relationships begun under Uranus are usually very exciting and stimulating. It is not uncommon for these relationships to end as suddenly and surprisingly as they began if there are no other factors indicating the relationship's longevity.

- *Transits from Neptune.* Since Neptune is so often connected to romanticism, it is also a common sign at the beginning of some relationships. These relationships are characterized by feelings of extreme romanticism and often the belief that a fantasy has become real. Many people feel they have finally met their "soul mate" and that destiny has finally answered their prayers. The strong feelings of unreality are often confusing although usually exciting. Unfortunately, much of the situation is illusory and will eventually lead to disappointment or worse when reality dawns again. The slowness of Neptune transits can make that dawning a few years down the line, leading to a great sense of loss when it finally happens.

Although all these outer planets are very capable of malefic effects, Neptune seems to be especially challenging for relationships at any point in their progress. It is wise to encourage the client to go slowly and carefully—the stronger Neptune's influence at the beginning, the more certain you can be that there will be an unfortunate ending. Even the easier aspects are challenging because they can create delightful fantasies or feelings of "connectedness" that turn out to be illusions. These transits usually don't lead to serious disaster, but can produce early disappointment.

- *Transits from Pluto.* Like Uranus, Pluto is appropriate to the exciting yet fatalistic feelings often accompanying the start of a relationship. It shows that the relationship will have a profoundly transformative effect as well as challenge us at the deepest levels to let go of attitudes, beliefs, or experiences from the past. These transits may indicate very deep karmic connections and reasons for the relationship. The newly met partner may be powerful and challenging but often is also charming or magnetic. Sometimes relationships under Pluto transits begin traumatically or at the least dramatically. There can be battles of will that will characterize the relationship in the future, and the relationship itself can come to represent lessons of power and control. Like all things involving Pluto, there will be challenging lessons of letting go and yielding to forces greater than oneself. Although this may seem desirable at the start of a relationship, it can come to feel quite threatening. Pluto relationships can be very long-lasting, although they are always challenging.

- *Solar return charts.* Whenever you work with transits, you can get a very good sense of the "themes" for the year you are examining by drawing a solar return chart for the client, which is essentially the chart of the transits at the moment of the individual's true solar birthday. We will use these in a later example in this chapter.

EXAMPLE: PROGRESSIONS SHOWING A DEEP CONNECTION AT MEETING

Author Richard Bach (chart 32) enchanted the world with his romantic tale of meeting and finally marrying his wife Leslie Parrish. His books describing their relationship, *One* and *The Bridge Across Forever*, helped establish the contemporary definition of a "soul mate," a label he very firmly attached to her, and gave thousands of readers the hope that serendipitous meetings leading to eternal romance were just around the corner.

Bach says that when they first met, he was unaware of their deep connection and didn't even experience any particular degree of attraction to her (chart 33). Are there any signs in the astrology of that 1973 meeting?

Certainly, an astrologer has good evidence for a sudden, unexpected, yet meaningful connection: Bach's progressed Ascendant is conjunct his Uranus, while the transiting Uranus is conjunct his Ascendant. He has progressed Venus (his chart ruler) trine progressed Jupiter, while the progressed Moon conjoins that Jupiter and trines Venus. In the months before it completes those aspects, that same Moon squares his Neptune, and not long after it squares his Saturn, portending the deep and soulful connection between them but also perhaps hinting at darker difficulties to come.

Given Uranus's strong role on both occasions, would we expect the relationship to last? Venus is a promising sign, so clearly present on both occasions especially in "classical" form at the marriage itself, and in light of Bach's deeply spiritual worldview and tendency to attach deeper meaning to things as well as his celebrated unconventionality (in fact, the hero of his acclaimed book *Illusions: Adventures of a Reluctant Messiah* might be the ultimate personification of Uranus). Still, we may not expect the relationship to last based on the evidence of its beginnings.

Will It Last?

One of the more valuable ways to analyze the conditions at the time people meet is to assess whether the new friendship has much likelihood of lasting and becoming more serious or whether it is a temporary situation that probably will not lead to anything significant. The issue also is raised at other times in a relationship, particularly when there seem to be insurmountable problems to face.

Analyzing this issue at the start of a relationship is really a way of trying to determine how powerful and effective the astrological conditions are at the time of meeting, and whether there is enough synastry between the charts to keep it going. Later on, while the same analysis can hold the key to the answer, it is also helpful to look at upcoming transits that may change things.

- *Transits with no future.* It is difficult to judge whether transits are merely transitory. You should always expect that beginnings under Uranus could go any way at any time (it is common for relationship events that happen under Uranus-to-Venus transits to end as suddenly as they began). Transits from Jupiter can also be short-lived, causing the attraction between the individuals to fade as soon as the initial aspect is gone and especially if Jupiter has transited into another house. Follow the rule that if the transits and progressions at meeting or relationship beginning change relatively quickly, and there are no synastry aspects to back them up, then there is not much likelihood of the relationship lasting. Relationships begun under transits of Neptune are unrealistic and over-romanticized and rarely last, although it can take a while for reality to set in.

- *Few synastric connections.* Even when transits are not lasting, the relationship between the two charts is the best judge of lastingness. Fast-changing circumstances may bring together people who have powerful interchart aspects. These will be activated by the meeting and remain the best indicator of how likely it is that the relationship will last. The fewer connections there are between the personal planets of the two charts, the less chance the relationship has of lasting. If the Sun is not involved in the synastric connections, the relationship probably won't last—certainly, if neither of the luminaries connects to any of the other's planets, there is little chance of it going anywhere.

- *Directions to the other person's chart.* Some relationships begin when the planets of one parson's chart have progressed to a position where they form synastric connections with the other person's natal or progressed planets. Since you already have calculated the transits and progressions for each individual in order to assess what "caused" the meeting to happen, it is a simple step to check the aspects between the progressed charts. (Luckily we have computers to make this job quick and painless!) What you are looking out for is the fact that when the directions that have brought them together come to an end, the attraction or circumstances that brought them together also may end.

EXAMPLES: TRANSITS IN INDIVIDUAL CHARTS AT THE MARRIAGE

Even though Brad Pitt and Jennifer Aniston had appropriate progressions in their charts at the time of their marriage, the transits were less pleasant. Pitt had transiting Pluto precisely on his Ascendant (opposing the seventh), while Aniston had transiting Saturn in its detriment on her eighth-house cusp opposing her Mars-Neptune conjunction (Mars rules her seventh) and squaring her Sun. Saturn can make things last, but this is a little too much Saturn.

Preparing and Delineating Directed Charts

Create three new aspect grids, one for the interaspects between the two progressed charts and one each for each progressed chart to the other natal chart. Use orbs of only one degree, which will allow you to focus on new connections between the charts and to identify which connections may be causing a relationship to begin and which may not last very long.

- Progressed Sun aspects last from one to three years.

- Progressions of Venus and Mercury are even shorter-lived (often less than a year).

- Mars progressions may last as long as those of the Sun, although Mars also can indicate a difficult relationship with lots of conflict, a factor that can end a relationship.

- The progressed Moon aspects last for only one to three months. If these aspects seem to be responsible, then you can be reasonably sure it is a temporary situation.

- Progressions from personal planets to outer planets may create links that last much longer than the aspects between the charts.

- Aspects between outer planets are likely to be the same as those that exist in the synastry between the natal charts, but sometimes you will find differences that themselves can be enlightening. For example, planets that have natal synastry aspects may not have aspects between them any longer, explaining why the natal effects you have described may not seem relevant to the clients.

Directions of Marriage Charts

The charts of the relationship itself also can be directed using astrological methods. Although these often give interesting and even useful information, most astrologers have found that the directions to these charts are considerably more subtle than those of the individual charts, and for that reason may represent a whole bunch of extra information that is likely to make your work harder rather than offer any special clarity. As with all such techniques in astrology, keep these results in reserve. If you can't find anything in the regular charts that explains what the partners are experiencing, then you are sure to find the information in the transits to one of these charts.

EXAMPLE: TRANSITS AND PROGRESSIONS IN A MARRIAGE CHART

The marriage chart of Brad Pitt and Jennifer Aniston (chart 29) had Saturn in detriment in Cancer conjunct the seventh-house cusp and Moon at the end of 2004 when their relationship came to an end. At the same time, the progressed seventh cusp was conjunct the marriage chart's Mars.

Making Composites from Progressed Charts

Although it seems logical that creating a new composite from the progressed charts would provide information about that year in the life of the clients, in practice this is stretching astrological symbolism to the point where it stops making sense. Since composites represent a midpoint that derives its strength from the fact that it represents the point where the natal influences meet and simultaneously receive transits, doing the same to the progressed chart will result in a chart that doesn't represent anything real and is purely theoretical in construction. These midpoints do not represent a point where planets are receiving equal influence of anything.

Composite charts are still useful in predictive work, though. See "Directions Involving Composite Charts" later in this chapter.

When Will Changes Happen?

Understanding the astrology of how a relationship begins sometimes is useful, but it is not particularly beneficial to clients who are already involved in a relationship. These clients usually are very interested in knowing the future of the relationship.

Although it often is useful to treat the relationship as if it were a separate entity, so that the individuals are able to gain greater objectivity and learn to see the distinction between their own needs and those of their relationship, this separation also can be misleading. It is not really accurate to suggest that a relationship has a future of its own distinct from the individuals who constitute it.

For this reason, the best way to understand the future path of the relationship is by looking at the transits and progressions of each of the clients and using the information gleaned from both to construct a single picture of the relationship. People in a relationship or living together naturally have an effect on each other's path. Working with these charts will create the most complete and accurate picture of the future, as well as give a depth of information that cannot be found from any single chart.

There are, of course, many other changes that happen in a relationship other than beginnings and endings. Sometimes, you can help the clients understand the challenges they will face by understanding how issues that exist in the natal and relationship charts can affect the relationship even when they are not specifically relationship issues.

What Changes Will Happen?

While transits and progressions will give us a great deal of information, the natal chart will provide the guidelines to interpreting these directions. In chapter 2 you learned that the natal chart shows the promise of what to expect in life, and we have seen through various examples that the patterns of our relationships throughout our lives can be discerned from characteristics of the natal chart irrespective of the specific relationships that we become engaged in.

But the idea of "promise" goes further than this: it means that when transits or progressions "trigger" the natal positions, this promise will unfold. The traditional use of transits also shows that when the directed planets repeat the same or similar aspects as they have in an individual's natal chart, this can act as a trigger to the natal promise even when there are no direct aspects to the natal chart.

In our use of synastry and composite charts, we are of course making the same assumption: we expect the relationship to unfold in the way that these charts describe the dynamics between the two individuals. Similarly, we can expect that *when directions repeat conditions shown in the synastry or composite charts, the promise of that condition in the relationship will be triggered and manifest in the relationship.* This is a very important principle that will help you understand what developments will occur in the course of the relationship and what kind of changes you can expect to happen. It also gives the composite chart another important role, since it is the chart that most closely fills the role of a natal chart for a relationship.

EXAMPLE, PART I: NATAL, SYNASTRY, AND COMPOSITE ASPECTS PROMISING CHANGE

In this example we will use the charts of family members to illustrate how you can use the same principles you already have learned in relationships other than those of romantic couples.

Penny (chart 35) has had a very good relationship with her daughter Hayley (chart 36) all the way into Hayley's adult life. Now in her early sixties, Penny naturally expects these years to be enriched by the pleasures of a mature mother-daughter bond of love and friendship as well as the unique joys of being grandmother to Hayley's three children.

Her natal chart does not have any alarming warnings involving the ruler of her fifth house of children, Saturn, although its conjunction to Uranus may well signify that the relationship should not be expected to remain consistently the same throughout life. What the astrologer should note, however, is the Moon-Neptune conjunction in the first strongly emphasized by the North Node. Since the Moon is an important planet for all relationships, we should be concerned that she is capable of being deceived and deceiving herself or simply of sweeping problems under the carpet. In fact, we will regularly see Moon-Neptune configurations in charts that promise relationship difficulties.

In Penny's case, it naturally relates to issues in her marriage, as the Moon is an important significator for these relationships. We certainly would expect some problems in her marriage with her Mars closely conjunct the seventh-house cusp and yet in the sign Pisces, another indication of hidden or avoided issues.

The Moon has other implications, though: it often is used to describe relationships with women; in the case of a mother, this certainly includes her daughter. So this Moon is an alert to us that everything is not quite what it seems (to Penny) in the relationship with Hayley.

Hayley's Moon is considerably better off, placed in its own sign and conjunct the very positive planet Jupiter, ruler of her seventh, in the sign of its exaltation. In a natal reading we may not be overly concerned about its applying squares to both Venus and Mars. If we were doing a relationship analysis for this mother-daughter pair, however, we would need to give that T-square a little more of our attention: Venus and Mars are the rulers of her parental axis, an axis that is dramatically emphasized by the fact that Venus, ruler of the fourth (the father), is in the tenth house (of the mother), and similarly Mars, the tenth-house ruler, is in the fourth—and they both are conjunct the nodes, overemphasizing their positions.

While the fact that Venus and Mars are both in their own sign could be considered a positive indication, it also must be borne in mind that while they may be in each other's house (they are married after all), they are each following their own agendas (in their own sign), in opposition to each other and in the sign of each other's detriment. We must expect that at some point Hayley's relationship with her parents will reach an obstacle, possibly related to this "detrimental" relationship those parents have with each other.

As is often the case in parent-child relationships, there are many positive aspects from mother Penny's outer planets and Jupiter to Hayley's personal planets. This is simply because one of the important roles of a parent is to teach a child morals, ethics, how to relate to society, and similar things associated with the outer planets. Look a bit closer, though, and we can see there are personal issues that may become a problem later on.

Hayley's Sun has challenging aspects with Penny's personal planets, opposing the Moon, squaring Mercury, and squaring Venus—the three planets most important to the everyday dynamics of a relationship (the synastry grid is not shown, but you can easily see these aspects just by looking at the two charts). While communication is not the major issue (their Mercurys are in a trine), clearly Hayley's sense of self and identity (her Sun) will not feel able to express itself. In childhood this probably will not be very apparent, but as identity grows when adulthood comes around, this will become increasingly frustrating to Hayley. Since Penny's Neptune-Moon and North Node conjunction is opposite her Sun, it may take a while before it becomes obvious that this is a problem as her identity may struggle to come to the fore in the shadow of her mother (Penny's destructive South Node is on Hayley's Sun). The alert astrologer will have an alarm bell ringing when he or she realizes that it is that very Moon-Neptune of Penny's that is the source of problems with her female relationships. Now the promise seems to be that her connection with Hayley will become just such a relationship.

The composite chart (chart 37) gives a final clue: Much of the analysis will show the positive aspects that describe their seemingly happy relationship right into Hayley's adulthood, and the Moon even takes part in a weak grand trine (out-of-sign aspects weaken a grand trine because the pattern's characteristic elemental emphasis is not present). However, the Moon is conjunct Pluto: the close aspect of a difficult outer planet to a luminary will make the power of that outer planet very obvious and personal in this relationship.

Pluto is usually a very destructive influence, and in any relationship it would not serve well to have it so close to the all-important Moon. This is especially the case in a mother-daughter relationship, a relationship among women that therefore makes the Moon, key symbol of the feminine, an even more important planet in the composite chart. Its angular position promises that this aspect will become manifest in the lifetime of this relationship—an aspect that implies destructiveness through the coming to light (Moon) of hidden things (Pluto).[2] In part 2 of this example we will see how the directions finally triggered this unhappy promise.

———————————————

EXAMPLE, PART 2: RELATIONSHIP PROMISE FULFILLED BY DIRECTIONS

Penny and Hayley's relationship began to deteriorate in the early months of 2004. Hayley had been seeing a therapist and was working on the blockages surrounding memories of her early childhood.

During these months, Hayley's progressed Moon had begun to square her natal Pluto (chart 38). It reached the exact square in April and would simultaneously begin to square her natal Uranus. The progressed Moon has the effect of throwing light (and therefore focus) onto the affairs of the planets it aspects. Not only would it stir up this otherwise latent conjunction of Uranus and Pluto (outer planet aspects are generally impersonal, and in this chart they are further deemphasized by being in a cadent house), but it also would evoke the Moon-Pluto conjunction of the composite chart with her mother.

———————————————

2. The Moon, and therefore this conjunction, is also conjunct the fixed star Regulus, a star associated with a great rise followed by a terrible fall. This emphasizes the promised change in the nature of the relationship.

When we found that aspect in the composite chart, we suspected that sooner or later the hidden aspects of this relationship would come to light. It was at this time in her therapy that Hayley began to uncover memories of being sexually abused by her father at a young age. By this time, her parents had long since divorced, and her father had distanced himself from the family by moving to another country.

Naturally, given these conditions, Hayley's first attempt to confront her childhood issues would be by confronting her mother—not only because she had maintained a relationship with Penny and had access only to this parent, but more critically because she blamed her mother for not doing anything about it and allowing her father to perpetuate his crimes against her.

There are a number of other directions in Hayley's chart that emphasize the importance of this discovery. Jupiter has progressed to the exact conjunction with her Moon, while the transiting Jupiter is becoming exactly conjunct her natal Pluto—thus both the key planets Moon and Pluto are being simultaneously emphasized by Jupiter the expander. It will be only a few more months until the transiting Saturn conjoins Hayley's Moon while the progressed Moon squares her natal Saturn, showing that this matter is going to become a lot more serious before it can be resolved. That conjunction from a detrimented Saturn (in Cancer) also carries implications of the past arriving unavoidably in the present, as well as feelings of sadness or depression, emotional difficulty, and even separation from the mother (the Moon is a key mother significator in a chart).

Even more to the point, the solar arc of Pluto starts applying to within one degree of the square to Hayley's natal Moon (solar arcs not shown). This is a dramatic emphasis of the key relationship configuration as well as an illustration of the importance of using solar arcs to get the full picture of progressions. The astrologer should have little doubt that these themes of the composite chart will now come to the fore.

The solar return chart (chart 39) also should be used as a guide to what is important about the transits of the year ahead. It is no surprise that Hayley's solar return for 2004 has the detrimented Saturn in an angular house (the first), Pluto conjunct an angle (the seventh)—and the Moon in a tight square with Pluto. Mars is the ruler of the tenth house of the mother, and is both detrimented and in the twelfth house of loss. Such a relentless repetition of symbols leaves little doubt that the manifestation of these configurations and their situation in the relationship analysis cannot be averted.[3]

To get the full picture of the promise of the relationship being fulfilled, we must of course also look at the directions in the mother's chart.

Penny was completely taken by surprise by her daughter's allegations when Hayley confronted her shortly after her birthday in June 2004. After the confrontation, Hayley cut all ties with her mother and prevented her from having any contact with her grandchildren. Penny felt devastated and alone, at once wracked by guilt for not having known about her ex-husband's deeds and allowing her daughter to be hurt in that way, as well as confused as to whether it could even be true, given that she had seen absolutely no sign of it in the home. Given Penny's natal Moon-Neptune conjunction, we are not at all surprised at this reaction.

Novice astrologers often are tempted to interpret the dramatic aspects of Pluto such as those seen in this case as a description of the physical abuse itself. Because of the nature of this particular crime and the fact that it usually has been perpetrated in the distant past, it is rare for actual physical proof of the abuse to exist. As astrologers, we are not in the position to judge whether indeed the abuse actually took place, as tempting as it is to believe that astrology is capable of revealing everything. The astrological conditions we discover can be equally indicative of emotional issues or trauma as they are of real traumatic events. Our job is not to judge whether the experiences are real experiences or inner, emotional ones, but to help the client, Penny, understand the dynamics of her damaged relationship with her daughter. We should attempt to guide her toward ways to accept what has happened in that relationship and to move toward healing it by revealing the essential problems she has in her relationships and why she has been taken so by surprise.

Penny's solar return (chart 40) immediately sets the scene for the conditions we have come to understand as the promise of this relationship, which was revealed in the synastry and composite analyses. The Moon is tightly conjunct Pluto, and the conjunction is dramatically angular in the first house and conjunct the Ascendant. It also opposes the Sun, which naturally is a very important symbol for the year in a solar return.

---

3. Analysis of matters involving her father, alleged perpetrator of the abuse, are not included here because she has no relationship with her father and birth details of the father are unknown.

There are many other difficulties revealed by this solar return. The fifth-house (children) ruler is Jupiter, detrimented in Gemini and influentially placed in the angular tenth house. It opposes Uranus, which is in the fourth, a sign of domestic upheaval, and the traditional malefic planets Mars and Saturn are conjunct in Cancer, a sign in which they are both debilitated, and in the eighth house, another house promising difficulties. Certainly this is going to be a painful year for Penny.

Examining the transits to Penny's chart at this time reveals more of this troubling picture (chart 41). Pluto is exactly conjunct her fourth-house cusp, clearly indicating the coming to light of deeply hidden traumatic secrets as well as the trauma related to domestic matters. The difficult Saturn-Mars conjunction is tightly opposing her fifth-house cusp, and the detrimented Jupiter is on her Ascendant, shortly to conjoin and emphasize (for the worse, since it's detrimented) her difficult natal Moon-Neptune-node conjunction. As we saw in Hayley's chart, Pluto is emphasized at the same time, here by the solar arc Jupiter in a conjunction to her natal Pluto.

The Moon-Pluto theme repeats itself over and over. At the time of the confrontation, Penny's progressed Moon is exactly opposing her natal Pluto, and the solar arc Pluto (not shown) is almost perfectly conjunct her natal Moon. Not only are the promised themes of the relationship reflected in these directions, but they also show in both partners' charts at the same time.

For the astrologer, this is a clear and certain indication that the time has come for these promised themes to play themselves out. We are able to understand what changes to expect because we already have determined from the relationship analysis alone that this relationship eventually will be challenged by secrets coming to light.

This example is not isolated. As you will see in the complete analysis of another difficult and traumatic case at the end of the chapter and as you will discover in your own work, the repetition of synastry and composite themes in directions is a reliable way to understand and predict later developments in a relationship.

Giving a Joint Predictive Reading

While sometimes the thought of combining transits, progressions, solar arcs, and other favorite techniques into a single reading is daunting enough, the task of doing it with twice the information may seem impossible. In fact, it turns out to be even easier than a single reading and entails no special preparation. Here's a simple strategy:

1. Determine whether either of the clients is experiencing major transit changes during the period in question. High priority must be given to life-change transits at critical years, such as the Saturn return or Uranus opposition.

2. If this is the case, start with that client and explain the time ahead in your usual fashion. With both clients in front of you, make it clear the extent to which such life-changing events affect all areas of life, including the relationship.

3. Then read the second client's chart using what you have learned from the first chart as a basic time structure, since the events of the life change are going to dominate the life of the client. Deliberately link the events and the timing.

4. Pay special attention to the extent to which the second chart reinforces or contradicts the timing and type of changes shown in the first chart. Fortunately, since the clients actually do share a life, you are likely to find reinforcement, but in any event this similarity or difference will become a good source of information about what kind of time lies ahead and how this is likely to affect the relationship. Can the second person be sympathetic to the partner's changes, or is the timing too different? Do the second person's transits reveal that he or she is being affected (adversely or otherwise) by the partner's changes?

5. If neither of the charts is showing special changes, simply begin with the one that looks busier, and then when you get to the second chart you still will find that the first chart has given you a structure to work with as well as plenty of information to compare.

6. For the last part of the session, use the information you have gleaned from both charts and their synastry to create a strategy for the time ahead. The synastry reading has helped you understand where the couple can work together well and what type of common goals they can establish. By encouraging them to do so on a yearly basis, with the help of the charts, you will help them deal with many of the bigger changes that invariably must come.

Important Directions in Individual Charts

All the progressions and transits we have identified that can show the beginning of a relationship also can show changes in an individual chart that affect an existing relationship. Working with two charts, you often will find similar transits or major transits occurring in both charts at the same time. In order of priority, these are the ones that will cause changes in both the partners' lives, even if they are showing in only one of the charts:

- *"Midlife crisis" transits.* The major midlife transit is the opposition of Uranus to its natal position, responsible for the major overhaul that takes place for a few years around the early 40s. It can be linked with divorce if a relationship is already in trouble, especially if the natal Uranus is in the first or seventh house, but at the very least there are profound personal changes that inevitably affect the relationship. The squares of transiting Neptune and Pluto to their natal positions often occur around the same period and heighten the change and uncertainty. Most astrologers find that the majority of breakups (and unexpected new relationships) happen during this time.

- *The Saturn return.* This life crisis regularly leads to the end of a relationship. This is often a relationship that has existed since the early 20s or even the teenage years, and the Saturn return represents a time when the individual eventually will move on to more mature and committed relationships. On the other hand, it also can be present at the start of a long-term relationship or a marriage.

- *Outer planet transits to Venus.* These are remarkably reliable in their indication of change happening in a relationship. Always check what's happening in the partner's chart; you'll be surprised how often you find transits to Venus or one of the changes listed here.

- *Directions involving the angles.* These are always the most important changes in any reading when the birth time is known to be accurate, and you can be sure that they will affect a relationship. Transits of planets over the cusps of the seventh, fourth, first, and tenth houses (in that order) dramatically affect the status of a relationship.

- *Directions involving the seventh-house ruler or other angle rulers.* These may be less dramatic but eventually will affect the relationship. Compared with directions to the cusp itself, these may seem like personal changes affecting a relationship rather than changes to the relationship itself.

- *Other relevant planets.* As with all predictive readings, you also will consider how other aspects and other significators (such as the ruler of the fifth for matters concerning the couple's children) may be relevant to this particular partnership.

EXAMPLE: DIRECTIONS AT THE TIME OF A MARRIAGE

The circumstances that began Richard Bach and Leslie Parrish's relationship (chart 33) help us understand its future. We would expect Uranus to characterize any future relationship that developed. Bach and Parrish actually married some four years later just as he experienced the midlife configurations of Uranus opposite itself and Neptune squaring itself, further emphasizing the themes of these planets.

There were also much more traditional relationship configurations present, helping us be more sure of what kind of event would occur: progressed Venus was conjunct his progressed Midheaven, while the progressed Moon opposed (and highlighted) his natal Sun-Venus conjunction and, soon after, the Midheaven. At the same time, transiting Jupiter was conjunct that Sun-Venus conjunction, and transiting Pluto sat right on his Ascendant.

There are powerful themes of karmic connections and the deep effect this relationship would have on Bach, as well as enough of the standard relationship configurations to enable the astrologer to make a reasonable prediction at the time of the meeting and of the marriage. Knowing that he already was divorced and single when he met Parrish, we would expect the Uranus configurations to bring a new relationship, and knowing that he was involved in a good relationship when the configurations of 1977 rolled by, we would likely predict a marriage for them (although we would discuss the possibility of an ending given that Uranus and Pluto were so prominent).

Directions Involving Composite Charts

John Townley, the astrologer who devised the composite chart, suggests that one of the reasons such charts work is because they are sensitive to transits. As the composite planets receive transits over and over again, thus representing both charts becoming more energized by the same transits at the same time, the value of the midpoint is strengthened and its relevance to the relationship increases.

Transits have proved to be the only valuable way of directing these charts. Although Davison's relationship chart method allows for progressions to be calculated, since the chart has a date associated with it, these progressions make no symbolic sense at all. Townley points out that since nothing was "born" at the time and date of the chart, progressions cannot be said to represent anything. Experimentation in my own practice has shown this criticism to be valid.

Strategies for Using Transits to Composites

As with any other chart used in astrology, it is possible to measure transits using the full array of astrological aspects. With composites, you prioritize conjunctions. The directions to the natal charts remain the primary source of predictive information. For that reason, you should develop a strategy for using the transits:

- First, delineate and interpret the transits and progressions to the natal charts thoroughly.

- Then concentrate on transiting planets *conjunct* planets in the composite chart. These are by far the strongest transits in composite work.

- Finally, go on to examine the remaining aspects, and identify those that give valuable or important information. As in all transit readings, the specific concerns and questions of the clients will help you identify transits that provide useful information.

- Take special note when one or both of the individual charts' planets are receiving transits when the same planet in the composite chart also is receiving transits from the same transiting planet. These are also very strong influences and can show when an event in the shared life has a strong or special significance to one of the partners. If there is a close aspect in the *synastry* chart between the same planet from each individual chart (e.g., the two Suns), then they are likely to receive transits at the same time and the composite planet also will receive a transit. *These will be the most important and reliable predictors of change in the relationship.*

EXAMPLE: DIRECTIONS AT THE END OF A MARRIAGE

The composite chart of Brad Pitt and Jennifer Aniston (chart 34) has Venus, ruler of the seventh, conjoined by Uranus at the end of 2004. Saturn, causing so much stress to the marriage chart, is opposite the Sun.

———————————————————————————

When Will It End?

Predicting the end of a relationship is something many modern astrologers are reluctant to do, and there are many situations in which it would be counterproductive to do so. But sometimes it is important to be able to help someone who is in the process of an ending, or who is seriously considering whether to continue a relationship.

The complexity of the fact that three different sets of transit and progression cycles are describing the path ahead makes it challenging to make predictions about whether a relationship will end. In fact, there are so many deep personal issues wrapped up in how we handle a relationship that astrological trends simply do not provide enough information to base a judgment on. There are many instances of people staying in relationships that are difficult or that have long passed their natural end. Very often, ending a relationship involves so much upheaval in everyday life and in deep psychological roots that individuals gladly stay with the bad situation rather than change it.

You need to understand your clients very well to be able to make such predictions. All predictive work is more successful when you have worked with clients' charts before, as you begin to understand how they respond to different planets as well as how those deeper personal issues affect those responses.

Another issue common to all prediction but especially important in relationship work is people's tendency to hope that fate will take over and end a difficult situation all by itself, so they can avoid the difficulties of having to take charge of the situation or even do what is demanded of them. Be careful not to encourage this line of thinking by making it sound like a relationship event is a simple prediction.

Ironically perhaps, with experience you'll find that changes in relationship that lead to endings can become easy to spot and quickly become relatively easy to predict, but you always need to take into account the deeper issues mentioned above. Always be sure to find corroborative information in both parties' charts before you come to any conclusions, and always discuss the clients' own expectations and wishes to provide a better context for your predictions.

Generally, astrology follows the principle that the more frequently something of the same meaning occurs at any time, the more certain you can be of the outcome. However, you never can be totally sure—there are simply too many possible ways a planet can manifest. Although you should share the meaning of the directions honestly, pointing out perhaps that astrologers often *expect* a relationship to end under these circumstances, you also should make it clear that since we don't know the final outcome, the clients must proceed with their intentions, using the chart as a guide to what they are up against.

These are the astrological conditions you should pay special attention to:

- ***Both parties have challenging aspects to Venus or the seventh-house cusp.*** This usually bodes a real relationship crisis and is a common condition when a relationship ends. Considering which planets the significators are receiving aspects from and comparing the timing in the two charts will give you a lot of material to work with to give your clients the best opportunity to work through the crisis.

- ***Major life cycle changes.*** While the Uranus opposition in one chart can be enough to indicate the end of a relationship, if there are also critical life cycle changes in the partner at the same time, or if the partner is simultaneously dealing with directions affecting Venus, the seventh house, or the fourth house, there is a good chance that the charts are describing an ending.

- ***The "seven-year itch."*** This clichéd way of describing the periodic relationship crisis is useful because your clients are aware of it. Of course, the reality of this situation is that approximately every seven years, Saturn squares itself. Seven years into a relationship Saturn will square the position it was at when the relationship began. This is rather like the challenges for growth that come every seven years in our own lives. Typically with Saturn, the partners feel stagnation and boredom at this time. The challenge of Saturn is to remove another "layer" of complacency and take the relationship to a new level. This means adding new goals, sharing new activities, adding new responsibilities—everything that comes with the challenge of growing up. You can make the cliché into a real, practical matter and time it precisely. By helping the clients understand the principle of Saturn and how it operates in their relationship (looking at the synastry and composite charts), you can help them avoid the unconscious reaction to this configuration that typically leads to infidelity, a breakup, or some other inappropriate way of dealing with boredom and help them devise an appropriate challenge and strategy to take the relationship to a new place.

- ***Other aspects.*** Naturally, any other of the change-producing aspects discussed in this chapter (see "Transits Time the Changes") are capable of bringing the relationship to an end. Follow the principle of looking at both charts simultaneously to determine the effects of the aspects.

EXAMPLES: DIRECTIONS SHOWING DIVORCE

Bach and Parrish divorced after nearly twenty-one years, long enough to have defied the expectations raised by prominent Uranus and Pluto. Even still, the astrological circumstances at the end of the marriage seem to complete the patterns at the start. In the last months of their marriage, the progressed Moon opposes (and highlights) Uranus, which in transit is reaching the point square to where it was when they married, and square to Bach's own Uranus. Venus and Jupiter, so positive in the early days, now progress to a square as Venus progresses into Bach's twelfth house of loss and sorrow. As it does so, it becomes conjunct to Neptune, suggesting perhaps it is the romantic illusion and the bond of soul mates that is being lost.

Perhaps to make the point clear once and for all, transiting Saturn hits the Descendant, a very typical relationship-ending sign, while progressed Mars is squaring the eighth-house natal Uranus. But the ending appears to have been amicable (and followed soon after by his third marriage) with the seemingly out-of-place progressed Sun in sextile to Venus—a combination frequently found when the "war" that ends a relationship is finally over and peace returns.

Saturn is again prominent at the end of Pitt and Aniston's marriage in January 2005. She has it sitting squarely on her Midheaven and squaring its natal conjunction with the seventh-house cusp. That natal conjunction is dramatically highlighted by a conjunction from the progressed Moon. To add final emphasis, transiting Pluto is conjunct her natal Moon.

Husband Pitt has his natal Moon-Venus conjunction opposed by the transiting Saturn. Progressed Venus is beginning to apply to an opposition to natal Pluto, while the solar arc progressed Ascendant is conjunct natal Venus (see "Progressions involving Venus or the ruler of the seventh" on page 129). With the midlife transits of Uranus and Neptune only months away and Aniston's chart with such strong directions, the marital crisis is almost certain.

As an astrologer you will need to decide how much to concentrate on prediction. Fundamentally, the purpose of relationship analysis is to help people understand and manage their relationships in the present. Everything else—like prediction—is additional information, but is secondary to the task of understanding the relationship and helping the clients guide it along its best possible path while learning the lessons that change demands.

We have examined all the techniques that will be useful in the analysis of a relationship; now we need to put them all together in a consultation. For our last example before we do so, we see how a thorough analysis of both the relationship and the directions can give us a sense of the unfolding of a relationship.

EXAMPLE: CASE HISTORY OF O.J. SIMPSON AND
NICOLE BROWN SIMPSON

The notorious case of the violent marriage of O.J. and Nicole Brown Simpson and its terrible ending is an extreme example of a relationship gone bad. It is very likely that you never will have to deal with such a relationship, but it can be very instructive to study the details of such a case so that you can learn how to read warning signs for relationships that may turn violent.

This case also will give you a good sense of how to follow patterns through from the relationship charts to the directed charts, whatever such patterns may be, in order to see the big picture of the relationship over time. It is a powerful example of the validity of astrological analysis and the implications for how astrology may be used to pick up danger signs early on and perhaps prevent a client from becoming embroiled in a very difficult relationship.

Many relationships end in divorce, but as with Bach and Parrish this does not mean that they were bad relationships. In such cases, especially where the end of the relationship is many years or decades in the future, it is unnecessary and even destructive to make predictions about the end of the relationship.

However, there are some relationships that seem ill-fated from the very beginning. The techniques of synastry may well be useful in identifying relationships that not only are difficult but may bring more misery than reward for the individuals concerned. Although all relationships have their good and bad times, a basic principle of astrology is that if there is an overwhelming number of indications that say the same thing, then the outcome is more or less certain. This is how the principle of karma is understood to be readable in astrological charts, especially in relationships, since our attachments are one of the primary areas where such karma plays itself out.

It will require careful and diplomatic counseling to help a member of such a relationship to understand the challenges that face him or her, but with the help of the charts and the transits and progressions that will unfold, we may be able to identify critical periods in the relationship and empower the person to make better choices at the time. As astrologers, we also can learn about "negative" relationship dynamics in order to better understand the less consequential but very real problems that face many couples.

O.J. Simpson and Nicole Brown Simpson, Part 1—Natal Synastry

O.J. Simpson (chart 4) and his former wife, Nicole Brown Simpson (chart 42), are a notorious case of relationship dynamics that are so difficult they eventually ended in tragedy, with Brown and a friend savagely murdered and all the evidence pointing to her ex-husband, Simpson, who was caught fleeing in his car. Although Simpson was later (and controversially) found not guilty of his ex-wife's murder by a criminal court, a civil court later found him responsible for her death.

Nicole's death was the sad end to a series of violent episodes in their relationship, episodes that are documented because of charges laid against Simpson by his then wife. Clearly, the relationship was troubled from its earliest days.

In this example, we will put together all we have learned to analyze the charts in the systematic way outlined in chapter 5. We will add our knowledge of transits and progressions to follow through with the "promise" of the synastry to identify when the problems indicated in the synastry analysis become manifest in their relationship.

The elements of attraction are clear in the synastry between the two charts (chart 43): Nicole's Sun sextiles O.J.'s Moon, the traditional indicator of the ability to relate at an inner level, although O.J.'s Sun squares Nicole's Moon, suggesting insensitivity to her feelings and that he will attempt to dominate her. The fact that his Sun is also conjunct her Venus may prevent her from seeing the danger in the domination—with her Venus in the fifth house illuminated by the glare of his powerful persona she just may believe he is the incarnation of her romantic ideal. Deeper connections symbolized by Sun-Sun and Moon-Moon aspects are notably lacking in this relationship.

Connections between each of their angles and planets in the other's charts do little to help make a deeper, more meaningful connection. Nicole's Sun and Jupiter (ruling two of her angles, Midheaven and Ascendant) square O.J.'s Ascendant/Descendant axis, forming a difficult grand cross. Once again, this shows him being deeply affected by her, but again in a challenging way that could threaten his proud, dominant personality (his Ascendant is in Leo). His Moon squares her Ascendant/Descendant axis. Nicole will see herself in a disconcerting new light, while he tends to become more self-centered in his needs. Once again, the luminaries are involved in difficult, change-resistant connections.

We learned in chapter 5 that planet-angle connections may anticipate what kind of changes the relationship will experience. O.J.'s Mars (ruler of his fourth house) ominously throws a square to her Ascendant/Descendant axis. This Mars, unmitigated by any positive aspects to her angles at all and reinforced by the complete domination of squares in these connections, is an indication that changes won't come easily and may be accompanied by verbal abuse (his Mars is in Gemini) or even physical violence. (It's an interesting contrast to her Mars sextiling his Ascendant in the only positive angular connection they have, implying that his goals can be furthered by her. As with the Sun-Moon connection, he gains while she is dominated.)

The rulers of their seventh houses are also in a power struggle. His Saturn, detrimented in Leo, squares her Mercury. We already have observed the implicit warning given by his poorly placed Saturn, ruler of the seventh, and its conjunction with Pluto. You also will observe that Nicole has Pluto conjunct her seventh-house cusp.

The rulers of their Ascendants (his Sun and her Jupiter) have a much more positive relationship, and perhaps if there were more positive connections to work with, this would prove beneficial to the relationship—but in this case, since we can see that the angular connections are very challenging, it is likely to be responsible for why they would appear to be a perfect couple. While the Ascendant is important for a marriage, it is also the angle that represents how we are seen in the world.

This singular positive connection between the Ascendant rulers in the midst of all the squares may help us identify the common scenario of the appearance of the relationship in the world belying the actual differences between the parties.

Other Mercury connections in this relationship exist, and in a counseling situation we would try to encourage the partners to emphasize these. While there are no deep communication connections represented by Mercury-Mercury or Mercury-Moon connections, each of their Mercurys sextiles the other's Sun. Their ability to understand the other's essential personality—at least at an intellectual level—may help them tolerate things that they experience as problems with their partner. Of course, this will require a lot of work, work that may be difficult to do when so few critical positive connections (luminaries and angles) exist. As astrologers counseling this couple, we also would try to make use of the other positive aspects from Mercury and the Sun to other planets to help them develop this understanding further.

This lack of deep connections also is seen in the failure of the Venuses to form any aspect to each other. Certainly, the Sun (O.J.)-Venus (Nicole) conjunction we have already seen shows that they could experience the relationship as very romantic, but romance is anything but a deep bond. The remaining Venus connections are overwhelming in their ability to bring problems out of this unrealistic romantic view: his Neptune squares her Venus, clearly showing that her perception of him as an ideal partner is illusionary, while the square from her Moon to his Venus speaks of the emphasis on the emotional and the sensual and the tendency of both of them to indulge and emphasize their own feelings at the expense of their partner's.

Sadly, the opposition from her Saturn to his Venus will increase his perception that his feelings are not being acknowledged or reciprocated and may heighten the anger and jealousy that would soon fuel his violence toward her (his Sun conjoining her Venus is also conjunct her Mars: while he embodies the ideal male "warrior" to her, as is not unexpected for a sports star, this combination emphasizes the fact that her fallen Mars in the fifth house will bring violence in her relationships).

Certainly, this Mars is one of the most important reasons for the attraction between them. Each partner's Mars trines the other's Moon, raising the passion and excitement in this relationship. For many relationships this is a highly desirable ingredient, but in the absence of more meaningful connections it is an alert to the astrologer and the couple that work needs to be done to forge longer-lasting bonds than sexual passion.

The aspects of Jupiter do provide some potential for a more philosophical and spiritual connection, but at this stage it should be apparent that such a connection would be better suited to a friendship between these two rather than an intimate connection, especially since the philosophical agreement of Jupiters mutually aspecting each other does not exist here. We already have explored the trine from her Jupiter to his Sun, and its remaining trines to his Moon and Mercury promise that she could be a great teacher for him—but would this be possible in a person such as O.J., who we already have seen is plagued by issues of pride and domination? In addition, the trine of his Jupiter to her Mars only serves to emphasize the difficulty her Mars is in (fall), for as we learned in chapter 5 even the trine may simply be an emphasis on whatever is already there rather than a positive influence of some kind. Still, in reading the charts for them we also would try to stress the possibility of using these positive Jupiter aspects as opportunities to learn from each other in a constructive way.

The potential for the relationship to last is evident in the sextile aspects of O.J.'s Saturn to Nicole's Moon. In a reading, we would try to emphasize this potential, although we would have to bear in mind that Saturn and the luminaries are natural enemies, and so the lastingness may be based on being "stuck." O.J.'s Saturn is detrimented after all, and may create attachment based on its own difficult position and the natural Cancerian possessiveness that in these challenged conditions becomes jealousy. These problems are further emphasized by the opposition of Nicole's Saturn—a Saturn with strong dignity—to his Venus and the Sun. Nevertheless, true to Saturn's promise, the relationship was long-lasting: they were together for fifteen years (married for seven of them).

Of the outer planet connections in these charts, the most revealing come from Neptune—the square of his Neptune to her Venus and the conjunction to her Moon. You will learn more about the meaningfulness of Neptune connections in the next chapter, but already you will not be surprised to learn that those meaningful ones that relate to learning the greater life lessons together do not exist in this relationship.

Venus and the Moon, as we already have discovered, are among the most important planets when analyzing relationships—perhaps even more so for a woman, who will express much of her femininity through them. In Nicole's case, these important planets are in the houses of relationship—the fifth and the seventh—and in mutual reception with each other. Clearly, she has a strong need for romantic, loving, and deeply emotional connections, and she will express these deep feelings to those she loves.

In such conditions, the challenging aspects from O.J.'s Neptune are especially dangerous. Neptune sows confusion and, while creating the illusion of romance, renders her unable to act (think of running underwater) and, also like the ocean, gradually wears away at things until no more is left. It is difficult for someone to respond to Neptune with firm, positive action, and even as she became aware of the illusions she will have been paralyzed to act for a long time, trapping her in a miserable marriage. In fact, knowing the difficulties often caused by the outer planet connections and transits, these aspects from Neptune to important personal planets should set off warning bells. As you have seen in the example of mother-daughter pair Penny and Hayley, if directions of Neptune aspect Nicole's Venus or Moon at some point in the future, these are likely to bring out these problematical issues and potentially threaten the relationship. We soon shall see that this is exactly what happened.

Many of the challenges that will become more evident later in their relationship are evident in the composite chart (chart 44). The conjunction of the Sun to Mars and Mercury in the first house alerts us to the problems of verbal battles and potential physical violence, since this position gives this triple conjunction quite an emphasis in their lives. In addition, that Mars as well as Venus are opposing the Moon, which is detrimented and in an angular house—the seventh house of marriage. These factors, in combination with the synastry we have examined, give us little hope that they can have an easy relationship.

It must have taken enormous strength and courage for her to get out of the marriage, and O.J. must have tried every wily Neptunian trick to prevent her from doing so—perhaps contributing to his enormous bitterness after the divorce.

The benefit of hindsight allows us to examine the years after the divorce and see Nicole's tragic fate unfold through the directions. From this, we can learn to identify what types of directions may exist at a time when a person is seriously threatened by his or her partner (let's not forget the terrible prevalence of domestic abuse); we can help a person see the potential for verbal or physical abuse; and perhaps most importantly, when a case of abuse does happen we can look forward to see the likelihood of similar or worse situations arising again.

O.J. Simpson and Nicole Brown Simpson, Part 2—Directions

The first sign that the relationship was doomed came on New Year's Day of 1989. O.J. severely beat Nicole, who called the police, and he later was convicted and sentenced to community service. The directions to both of their charts and the composite chart at this time strongly highlight the natal synastry patterns and clearly demonstrate how those patterns can be the promise of things to come.

Nicole was busy experiencing her Saturn return at that time (chart 45), within one degree of being exact at the time of the beating. Saturn returns often bring difficult lessons that initiate us into adulthood. In her case, Saturn squares her seventh-house Moon at the same time, reinforcing the natal Moon-Saturn square and of course bringing to light the issues that may have been difficult for Nicole to see in this marriage, since that Moon is conjoined by O.J.'s Neptune.

It should be pointed out that with the dignified Saturn that Nicole has (in its own sign), she did finally learn the lesson at this time. Although it is likely that abuse occurred before this time, it is to her great credit that she filed for divorce (three years later) before another incident would occur. Unfortunately, the divorce would not be enough to stop O.J.

The particularly telling aspect at this time is the fact that the transiting Neptune was square to her Moon and opposing her Venus, reinforcing the challenges from O.J.'s Neptune to these same planets. Remember that these are her two key relationship planets. As if to underline the point, the transiting Moon, rarely examined because of its hasty motion, is moving into its deep fall while shortly to conjoin her Neptune.

The nodes are underused in astrology, but can be very useful indicators when something is being emphasized. In particular, conjunctions of the South Node either natally or in transit emphasize things in a destructive, Saturnian manner. At the time of the beating, the transiting South Node sat on Nicole's seventh-house cusp, warning of destruction coming from her marriage or her husband, while her own South Node had been crossed over by Mars, strongly aggressive in its native home of Aries, only two weeks earlier. No doubt it was a tense and edgy holiday season for Nicole that had culminated in O.J.'s act of violence, further borne out by the fact that Pluto had been sitting opposite her seventh-house ruler Mercury, on and off over the previous two years, fulfilling the warning of O.J.'s square to her Mercury.

Some of the same patterns can be seen in Nicole's solar arcs (not shown). Most telling, her solar arc Moon was conjunct her natal Venus, yet again alerting the astrologer to the dangerous significance of the connection between those two planets in the natal synastry. The solar arc South Node was conjunct her seventh-house ruler Mercury, again warning the astrologer of the importance of the similar transit at the time.

It is immediately apparent that the directions of the time bring to the surface many of the concerns we discovered when examining the synastry, and could become a clear warning to the alert astrologer. We should expect to see some of the same reinforcements in O.J.'s chart to be certain that he is the source of these issues even though the evidence from her chart is so clear that it is the seventh house—her husband—that is the source of her woes.

In O.J.'s natal chart, one of the conditions that shows the astrologer that his wife would suffer at his hands in some way is the seventh-house ruler Saturn debilitated by its position in Leo, in the twelfth house, and conjunct Pluto (see chapter 4).

At the time he first beat Nicole (chart 46), his natal Pluto (and this conjunction) is being squared by the transiting Pluto while the transiting Saturn opposes his Venus, the significator for romantic life and for key women in his life. In itself that tells us of some danger to her, but remembering that Nicole's Saturn opposes his Venus, this also reinforces his "issues" with her that he experiences from that synastry connection.

At the same time, transiting Neptune is square to his natal Neptune, drawing our attention to the fact that the natal Neptune is the source of many of the problems Nicole experiences in this relationship.[4] His progressed Moon had conjoined his natal Neptune only a few months earlier, once again repeating the fated pairing of those two planets and throwing light on his Neptune issues. (The progressed Moon is helpful in shining a spotlight on where issues lie at any particular time. In the context of our reading of this chart, the Neptune issues are those related to the synastry with Nicole as already discussed.)

Finally, his natal Mars, already emphasized by its conjunction with the North Node, had recently been conjoined by the transiting Jupiter that had now retrograded to the exact position of Nicole's Sun, as if carrying the emphasized Mars energy (aggression, etc.) to her.[5]

In the last chapter we learned that one of the important uses of the composite chart is to identify significant transits affecting both partners simultaneously. In O.J. and Nicole's composite chart, we saw the Sun-Mars conjunction opposed by the Moon, already a hint of possible violence in the relationship; at the time of the beating incident, the conjunction of transiting Saturn and Uranus was on the composite Moon and opposing Mars. A Uranus-Mars opposition alone would be cause for concern to the astrologer, often signifying accidents or violence as it does, but in the context of all the directions we already have seen this is a sign of clear and present danger.

There can be little doubt at this point that the conditions in the synastry comparison can be a good guide to the astrologer to which types of directions might produce the problems indicated in that synastry. In many cases, this may help to prevent further disasters. Sometimes, however, the karma of the chart may be too strong for the astrological warning to be enough—and unfortunately it is a rare occasion when the astrology and the astrologer are clear enough to read sufficiently into these warnings to suggest to the client even more radical steps to protect his or her safety.

---

4. The often simultaneous squares of Pluto and Neptune to their natal places are part of the complex of transits that occur during the midlife crisis period and often bring deeper issues to the surface. For more about these cycles, see my book *Cycles of Life* (St. Paul, MN: Llewellyn Publications, 2004).

5. Users of the fixed stars also will note that the transiting Jupiter and Nicole's Sun are on the extremely negative fixed star Caput Algol, one that can symbolize death. It must be cautioned, however, that using the fixed stars in this way requires experience and a lot of support from other aspects—there are of course many Taureans with this Sun position who experience no effects of this star whatsoever.

Who could have known that divorce was not enough? Although Nicole divorced O.J. in 1992, he would continue to be a threat to her. We can learn more from the events that would unfold not long after the divorce.

On October 25, 1993, Nicole called 911 saying that O.J. was at her house threatening to beat her up. We can safely assume that if she made that call, the threat must have been very real—no doubt he was behaving extremely aggressively and she feared for her life. Once again the charts reveal how the indications in the synastry comparison are triggered and furthered by the directions at the time.

In Nicole's chart we again see the effects of a challenging Saturn, now squaring her Sun from the difficult twelfth house (chart 47). At the same time, her progressed Moon is in the sign of its detriment, Capricorn, almost exactly opposite her fallen Mars. We have seen how this debilitated Mars in her fifth and the transiting Mars already have come up in her altercations with O.J., reflecting the synastric conjunction of his Cancerian Sun to this Mars.

As if to emphasize the danger Mars represents to her, the transiting Mars at the time of this threat is again in its own sign of Scorpio (it was in Aries at the time of the prior incident), transiting her dangerous eighth house and just approaching the opposition to her Sun, while the transiting Jupiter squares the debilitated natal Mars, emphasizing its difficult implications to her romantic life. As if that wasn't a clear enough sign as to just what Mars is threatening, the transiting Mercury, ruler of the seventh, is in a close conjunction with that Mars and the transiting Pluto only a few degrees away.

The fact that this Mars opposition is still becoming exact at the time, and Uranus is beginning to oppose her natal Mars—two violent transits that have not yet reached their full strength—also would act as a warning to the astrologer that the threatening incident is not the last. Once again, we would have the opportunity to warn her that she needs to take serious steps to reduce the likelihood of the natal potentials turning into a really violent episode. Again, this hindsight cannot help Nicole now, but is a valuable lesson for the astrologer: when exceptionally difficult conditions exist in the synastry, and prior events have shown how the triggers to the difficult synastry manifested, the approach of further serious triggers to the same planets is an opportunity to provide the client with valuable cautions ahead of time.

This is especially so when we bear in mind the natal promise of O.J.'s chart: even without comparing his chart to his wife's, we identified the Saturn-Pluto conjunction as a real threat to any partner of his, since Saturn is the detrimented and badly placed (twelfth house) ruler of his house of marriage. Now (chart 48), after the divorce but unable to contain his rage and jealousy, the transiting Saturn is powerful in its own sign of Aquarius and sitting squarely on his seventh-house cusp, while the transiting Pluto, in conjunction with the transiting Mercury (Nicole's seventh-house ruler) and Mars, is precisely square to his seventh-house cusp (and of course his Ascendant). It doesn't take any further investigation to realize the seriousness of this threat.

Saturn and Neptune have proved to be key players in the unfolding of the ill-fated relationship; at the time of this threat, the transiting Jupiter has just passed over their conjunction in the fifth house of the composite chart, throwing emphasis on this aspect of their relationship. Apart from merely being key players, of course, the close conjunction of these planets in the composite suggests a struggle between appearance and reality, between the illusion of romance (Neptune in the fifth) and the obstacles against love and pleasure (Saturn in the fifth).

The threat, of course, is less dramatic than the actual beating that took place some years earlier, but it turned out to be a prelude to the final act of the relationship, the murder of Nicole that happened some eight months later. Although all the evidence pointed to O.J., not the least of which was his presence at the scene and his flight from the scene, the somewhat soap-operatic trial had little chance of exposing the truth of what really happened, and it eventually would be a civil trial that determined O.J.'s responsibility for the events of June 12, 1994.

The warning signs in O.J.'s chart, as we already have observed, occur when his Saturn-Pluto conjunction is activated. Jupiter was beginning to square it at this time, while the progressed Moon highlighted this threat to his relationships by squaring its own natal position in his seventh house (chart 49). Of course, it is also the ruler of his twelfth house and of the detrimented Saturn, so this particular progression of his Moon carries the promise of whatever danger to his partner exists because of Saturn's poor placement as ruler of the seventh. Greater clarity is provided by the fact that this progressed Moon is on his fifth-house cusp at the time, almost exactly opposed to the natal Uranus, both highlighting it as the progressed Moon always does and creating an aspect that represents restless and unpredictable emotional outbursts.

Uranus by its nature carries the warning of unpredictable, rash, impulsive, and even aggressive behavior, just like Mars, with which it often has been compared. (In some parts of the world, the glyph for Uranus is almost identical to that of Mars.) Mars itself reinforces this, now detrimented in Taurus and closely squaring the Saturn-Pluto conjunction.

But of course it is Nicole's chart that paints the fuller picture (chart 50), as ultimately she is the victim of the extremely challenging synastry patterns that we explored earlier. The threat to her life is now explicit in her chart, given the build-up we have seen from the synastry through the events of the previous years.

Transiting Pluto has moved into a tight opposition with her natal Sun, and because it is conjunct the transiting North Node at the same time, it reemphasizes the conjunction of the transiting destructive South Node to her Sun, which became exact between the time O.J. threatened her life the previous October and the time of her murder. While Pluto will not always produce such dramatic results, there are very few of its transits to major significators like the Sun that do not produce traumas and endings of one kind or another. In this case, the fact that the detrimented transiting Mars is moving into a conjunction with the South Node that is sitting on Nicole's Sun certainly brings additional Mars energy into the picture, resulting in quite an onslaught for the Sun.

Knowing the role of Pluto and its conjunction to Saturn in O.J.'s chart, it also is not surprising to see that the transiting Saturn (recently opposing her Pluto) has just conjoined Nicole's Ascendant.

Nicole's natal Mars, as usual, is not untouched by the unfolding drama of the transiting planets. Uranus has just completed the opposition to Mars and is still close enough to be having an effect, and Neptune is exactly in opposition. Neptune already has proved itself as a dangerous planet to her relationship life. Her natal Uranus also has been activated by the solar arc conjunction of Venus. Bearing in mind Venus's important role for relationships in general and for Nicole in particular (see part 1 of this example), its combination with Uranus suggests a sudden, dramatic, and potentially dangerous change in her personal life.

However, it is the Moon's conjunction to O.J.'s Neptune that has sat silently and ominously through the years of abuse. Just as the Moon received a square from the transiting Neptune at the time of the 1989 beating, which reemphasized that critical threat from an outer planet to a luminary, so at the time of Nicole's murder was her progressed Moon in a tight square to natal Neptune from its position on her twelfth-house (loss) cusp.

The same planets have become especially emphasized in the composite chart. Transiting Saturn has just entered its tenth house, becoming stronger by accidental dignity just as it has done in Nicole's chart, and more significantly the transiting Neptune now tightly squares itself and Saturn in the composite fifth, once again emphasizing this treacherous combination.

The unfolding of the directions over the years is a testament to the importance of synastry analysis not only to reveal the dynamics of the relationship itself, but also to identify the key players in the relationship so that the unfolding circumstances of the relationship can be more accurately predicted. While few astrologers may have had the ability to put these factors together ahead of time, there is no doubt that the story of this tragic relationship was waiting in the charts for anyone who had the courage and experience to see it. This is the lesson that lies in these charts for all astrologers, one that at some point may save another individual or couple from the destructive events that can emerge when a relationship goes wrong.

There is one more symbol that lingers at the end of this rich and even profound unfolding of the language of astrology, a symbol that has no astrological explanation and yet haunts the mind of the astrologer after all the analyses have been completed and laid aside. The composite chart of Nicole and O.J. has the Sun at 21 degrees Gemini, the position the transiting Sun occupies on the 12th of June every year, and of course the position it occupied on that fateful June 12th in 1994.

CHAPTER 9

THE CONSULTATION

Most people who study astrology do so because they want to help other people. Whatever approach the individual astrologer may take, the bottom line is that the information found in the charts is useful in some way to the owners of the charts, and the astrologer has the responsibility to convey this information to the clients.

Entire books have been written on the dynamics of the consultation, and there are a lot of considerations that the astrologer needs to take into account that make this an important part of the modern astrologer's training. Our concern in the present volume is not to cover all of these issues but rather to prepare for the special issues that arise when you are dealing with more than one person at a time.

In This Chapter

- Learn about the ethical issues in relationship consultations.
- Knowing how to decide what information to give.
- Legal issues.
- Strategies for preparing for and timing the consultation.
- How to give constructive advice.

Ethical Issues

Although all astrology requires consideration of what ethics to adopt, synastry addresses even more sensitive issues and potentially even legal ones. By their very nature, ethical issues rarely are absolutely clear, and you will need to use your own judgment to decide how they apply to your work. You also should keep in mind that some of these issues may be legal issues in your part of the world. The practice of astrology itself may even be a legal issue where you live. Be sure to educate yourself on the extent to which the law applies to you.

The Right to Privacy

What do you do when only one party in a partnership comes for a relationship analysis?

In the age of information, the right to privacy seems more important than ever. In synastry work, you often will be presented with a situation in which somebody brings you the chart details of another person and asks you for a relationship analysis. Do you have the right to look at the chart of someone who is not present and who may not even be aware that an astrologer is looking at it? After all, as an astrologer you know that you can learn an awful lot about someone by looking at his or her chart, details that would almost certainly be considered personal or private.

Ironically, since many people don't really take astrology seriously, they would never consider this an invasion of privacy. What's more, the only information you have been given is the birth data—information that is considered to be in the public domain just about anywhere in the world. Birth records of every person are available to anyone willing to go to the slight effort needed to acquire them. Legally, it is very unlikely you will break any laws by telling your client about his or her partner based only on this data.

You should establish a personal ethic around this issue. After all, *you* know how much personal information is available just from birth data. To make this decision, you need to decide what is the role of an astrologer.

In earlier times, the astrologer was seen primarily as a diviner and was expected to give information that nobody else could. Even today, this often is the role cast by the client seeking to find out about a newly met romantic or business partner. If you see yourself in this role and are comfortable with the ethical issue, then you have the precedent of centuries of astrologers. But if you are like most modern astrologers, you see yourself somewhere between diviner and counselor.

The approach that I take and that is followed by many astrologers nowadays is this:

1. If the absent party gives his or her full permission to me by telephone or e-mail (or any other communication), then I will go ahead and use the person's natal chart, as well as construct relationship charts using it.

2. If I have no such unequivocal permission, I will confine myself to the chart of the person who is present, and not construct a special relationship chart. I will use the natal chart of the person sitting with me to derive information about the people he or she has relationships with. *Derived houses* are a very powerful way to examine how others fit into the individual's life.[1] There is so much information in a natal chart and there is such a tendency for people to follow patterns and to reflect their own relationship issues in their choice of partners that there is more than enough useful material to help the client handle his or her relationship a lot more successfully—and no invasion of privacy is required.

How Much Information to Give?

At what point in a relationship is it best to consult an astrologer? Should it be at first meeting, when one needs to know if it's worth pursuing any further? Perhaps it's best to come once the relationship has been established a little while, when one needs to check if the partnership is going anywhere permanent. Or is synastry really useful only to sort out the complex problems that eventually develop?

At any time in the development of a relationship, the clients doubtlessly will benefit from looking at the charts, but at which point in their history they come does make a difference to the astrologer.

Clients who want the astrologer to divine the potentials of a just-met partner have very high expectations. Despite their intentions to find out more, they usually are hoping the astrologer will tell them that they have at last met their perfect match. Even the more experienced client who knows the naivety of such expectations can harbor this wish.

There are many situations that require the astrologer to have courage. The average predictive reading puts you in a situation in which you may have to talk about bad things that

1. If you are unfamiliar with using derived houses, consult any horary textbook or the encyclopedic *Planets in Transit* by Robert Hand (Atglen, PA: Whitford Press, 2001).

could happen. Even in this situation, though, there are fewer beliefs about the future that you stand to demolish, because people generally accept that the future is unknown.

This is not the case in a synastry reading. We have so many of our beliefs and expectations tied into our relationships that we automatically start projecting them onto the new partnership that seems to be developing. It is this edifice of personal psychology—in addition to simple hopes—that the astrologer may have to dismantle.

You will need to establish a method for dealing with consultations when people come at these very early stages. Since this branch of astrology entails giving such practical advice, you must prepare in advance for situations in which you will have to help people understand that the reality may be different from their hopes. You may have to be blunt. You also have to decide where your own ethics fit in: Is it appropriate to destroy hopes and dreams before the individuals have had an opportunity to engage in the necessary experience? On the other hand, is it unethical to allow your clients to persist in vain beliefs when you have all the data on the page to save them the pain?

There is no single solution to this dilemma, and like the other ethical ones you face, you will need to decide where you stand. The same factors will be brought into play in making such a decision—what is the role of the astrologer?

The situation is even more difficult when you are dealing with an established relationship that is going through a crisis. It is not unusual for the crisis to boil down to the question of whether to stay in the relationship or not. Now you are expected to help the clients make a decision that could fundamentally alter the course of their relationship and perhaps their lives. The advice you give may have implications that also affect you, the astrologer.

Advice and the Law

There are many places where the practice of astrology is governed by the law (often making it illegal). In some cases, there may not be specific laws about astrology but there are laws about setting oneself up as a professional advice-giver, especially when laying claim to special training or talents to do so. Many states consider the job an astrologer does to be similar to that of a psychologist and so a special license is required (not to mention a degree in psychology), whereas others simply classify divination as an illegal activity.

These issues affect everything you do as an astrologer, but most astrologers remain unpersecuted by these laws. This can change with synastry. Most states allow a third person to be named in a divorce suit as someone who contributed to the breakdown of a marriage. Since divorce often is acrimonious, and since very few states are benevolent toward astrologers, an angry jilted spouse may very well hold you responsible for advising his or her partner to end the marriage and name you as a respondent in the divorce suit.

While this scenario is unlikely, and while you certainly do not want to have to censor yourself and do a disservice to the client by misleading him or her that a troubled relationship is healthy or can easily be saved, this is another area where you need to be aware of the issues, understand your position, and determine your approach. Find out how the law affects astrologers where you live, and associate yourself with local astrological organizations, which often have a member or team who has done the investigative work and can be of help.

Preparing for the Consultation

Every astrologer has his or her own way of preparing for a consultation, and many professional or experienced astrologers like to do minimal preparation partly because astrology is a language they understand well and can read off a chart without too much advance work, but also because there are many occasions when too much preparation gets in the way of a good reading.

Relationship readings require a little extra work, though, whatever your level of expertise. Even if you are able to read a chart with minimal advance work, there simply are too many charts in one relationship consultation for this to be practical and for you to offer a comprehensive service to your client. Not only is it cumbersome to shuffle up and down through the stack of charts every time one of the parties asks a question or as you seek to clarify a point, but if your work is to be accurate you need to have studied all the charts so that you can determine what is relevant and important.

Selecting Information

In a relationship reading there is a lot more information you have to deal with than usual: not only do you need to manage it all, but you need to prioritize what will fit into a consultation rather than trying to interpret absolutely everything. There is only so much that your clients can take in during one session. Keeping in mind the specific reason they have come and questions they may have raised, you need to establish:

- What is likely to be accurate and relevant?
- What is the most useful or meaningful information?
- What is the most urgent information?
- What is likely to be subtle, only potential, or not particularly relevant?

As far as possible you need to use astrology to make these decisions rather than rely on your own opinion about what is important to the clients. Also, if you are properly prepared, you will be able to respond to the clients' own definition of what is important in their lives as the session unfolds and they raise issues you may not have thought important but that are represented in the charts.

To start, you need to go through the natal charts slowly and carefully. For each of these charts:

- Note the dominant aspect patterns and the planets that dominate by means of dignity and involvement in many aspects.

- Pay special attention to themes repeating themselves through different astrological indicators. Some of these are obvious—for example, a planet that has an aspect with Saturn and is in a sign ruled by Saturn has two Saturn connections. Others are only repetitive in meaning—for example, someone may have Neptune squaring Venus as well as Pisces on the seventh-house cusp, both related to a tendency to make sacrifices in relationships.

When considering the significance of an astrological indicator, consider how often the same theme has repeated, as in the point above, and then apply a simple and very useful principle: *once is a possibility, twice is a probability, and three times is a certainty*. Of course, this is only a rule of thumb, not an absolute scientific principle, but it certainly helps prioritize the information in hand.

Once you have examined the natal charts this way, move on to the progressions and transits for each person, keeping the order of priorities in mind:

- Directions related to the key life changes of the Saturn return or "midlife crisis" tend to dominate.

- Directions of planets over the angles almost always manifest clearly as events or changes in life.

- Directions involving the various significators for relationships in general and this type of relationship in particular.

- Take note of directions that reinforce things you already have found in the natal charts. Anything similar in the directions can be added to how many times the same thing already has come up natally and can make them extremely important.

- Directions involving the planets you have identified as dominant in the chart.

Finally, move on to the relationship analysis:

- Study the planets in each partner's houses and the aspects between the charts.

- Consider to what extent interaction with the other chart causes planets to have greater influence. For example, a planet that has little essential dignity or few aspects in the natal chart may end up in an angular house aspecting many other planets when placed in the wheel around the partner's chart.

Collating Information

Before you move on to include the synastry and composite charts, you should find a way to collate all the information so you can easily see what's most relevant and to discover the underlying themes and patterns. If you get a good grasp of those, you will have an anchor for your reading. When you get distracted by the "flow" and by the clients' questions and comments leading you off in other directions, you always will be able to return to this anchor.

Most astrologers have their own ways of collating information to make it easy to see these themes and patterns and to be able to link disparate pieces of information together, especially since reliable interpretation depends on a number of different chart factors pointing toward the same thing. I have found it easiest to use mind maps, which allow me to group relevant things together.

Looking at all the analysis you have now done:

- Read through your notes or outline and identify themes that keep cropping up. Those that occur in one or more of the natal charts as well as in the synastry analysis are the strongest ones.

- Similarly, identify planets or chart features that are repeated or reinforced by other things in the charts.

- Remember, you are not going to concentrate only on the repeated or emphasized aspects of the charts. All the delineation work you have done as you stepped through the method of chart analysis in this book will not only provide you with much of the information you need for collating, but also will raise issues that will be relevant whether or not they are repeated over and over again.

- Read through the information you have collated, and try to find positive features that can be used to counterweigh and provide constructive advice for the challenges that show in the delineation. This helps ensure that the bulk of your advice will be based on the actual dynamics of the relationship and your knowledge of astrology rather than your personal take on human relations.

• Make a new list or outline covering the newly collated information.

Develop a Strategy for Timing the Session

Why do you need a clear strategy for your relationship reading when the best readings are when the astrologer is not over-prepared? Because one of the most notably different features of relationship readings is the extent to which the clients will contribute and interact with you and each other.

All astrologers have had the awkward experience of dealing with reticent clients. Sometimes it's because they are "testing" you or astrology itself, but often it's merely that they're uncertain of what's going to happen and what they are supposed to do.

Relationship readings are never like that. Here you have two people who know each other well and who already are comfortable interacting with each other. The psychology of a relationship changes dramatically when another party is present, usually resulting in the interaction between them becoming more animated.

There also is the experience they have of hearing characteristics of each other and about the relationship itself suddenly being spoken out loud by a stranger. That sparks a lot of interaction between them and also is (inadvertently) a great icebreaker. Couples take delight in hearing someone else mention the same issues they themselves have raised with their partner (especially criticisms or personal habits), and that starts to raise the energy in your office.

The result is that within a relatively short space of time this consultation is more vocal and lively than you are accustomed to from natal readings. It won't take long before you are drawn into the dynamics of their interaction, sometimes as referee or peacemaker, and sometimes as a somewhat helpless outsider with a powerful tool (astrology) that you can barely find a way to use.

Clearly, a relationship reading can "run away" from you. Each time you raise a new issue from your list you have delineated, the conversation is likely to veer off in one of the many directions created by the relationship and consultation dynamics. This is why you need to be better prepared than usual, and prepared to take control of the situation rather than allowing the clients to run the show.

By now you have about a page outlining the material you are going to cover in your session. Organize this list more or less in the sequence you are going to work through the material, and consider how much time you are going to spend on each part of the reading. Although that will act only as a guideline, the purpose is to give you the chance to ensure that you manage to cover the important points. By watching the passing time and keeping an eye on what your notes say you need to cover, you will be able to see when you need to assert yourself and take control so that you can move on to the next relevant issue.

Let Astrology Be Your Guide

One of the best ways to plan your session and concentrate on what's useful and relevant is to draw up a chart for the consultation itself.[2] Although the delineation you have done so far remains your most important guide, and the input from your clients is an equally important one, the testimony of astrology itself is more objective and more appropriate so it should be figured into the total picture.

Consultation charts give you an immediate sense of what is relevant. They are a great way to make use of the astrology of the moment and have an incredible ability to accurately describe what is relevant right now in the relationship (or whatever charts you are analyzing). For all your astrological work, it will be worth learning more about consultation charts (see appendix A for recommendations).

Spend a Moment on Yourself

The role you occupy in a relationship reading goes beyond being an astrologer; there is also the element of the referee. Since the parties are likely to engage in their usual interpersonal ways of communication plus a whole bunch more brought up by the situation, it may be useful to spend a moment considering where you stand in the matter.

For this purpose, you should always do a quick check to see if any of the clients' planets are conjunct your own, or whether a heavily populated sign in their charts means that they have many planets in one of your houses. Be aware that they may trigger a response in you, and your own biases or issues may influence your reading of their charts.

Your planets in their houses show what you are likely to have empathy for, where you are perceived as an authority, or where you lack empathy and understanding. Perhaps your

---

2. This chart is drawn for the time and place of the consultation with the clients. Although it is drawn in advance, it should be adjusted if the clients arrive earlier or later than expected.

own relationship issues may be "stirred" by them having significant planets in your relationship houses and you end up giving "advice" that is better suited to you than to them.

While these are not matters of highest priority while giving a reading, and are usually subtle enough to fall into the background, the emotional atmosphere that can accompany a relationship analysis brings up the most unexpected reactions in everyone sitting in the room!

It is not unusual to feel more sympathy for one partner than the other, a condition that is not conducive to a balanced reading or fair advice. This also can help you understand that one or both of the partners may be easily "set off" by things you say. Again, this will create a bias and potentially a situation that is difficult to manage.

Always keep your true role in mind. You are not a friend, a therapist, or even a mediator. Your first job is astrologer, someone who can objectively describe the nature of the relationship in astrological terms. The last thing you want is for either of your clients to feel jilted because you are taking sides with the other one. In this way you could end up doing more damage than anything else.

Your Role as Astrological Counselor

Our personal lives encompass the most private aspects of our lives. Although any natal session raises private issues, secrets, and other things we don't want anyone else to know, the situation in a relationship reading is a lot more delicate.

Firstly, people are a lot more sensitive about their relationships and what happens in them than they are about almost any other aspect of their lives. There are lots of personal insecurities, past experiences, and fears caught up in our choice of partners and how we live out our relationships. There often are issues like shame, secrecy, fear of judgment, self-esteem, and countless others that seem more apparent in this aspect of our lives.

Counseling regarding these matters is not your concern—that is mostly the work of the client's therapist. Your role is primarily to uncover information and present it in an understandable and useful way to the client. The delicacy in raising issues such as these (apart from the distinct possibility that the client will be embarrassed by hearing such things from a stranger, often unexpectedly) is enhanced because there is another person sitting in the room—and not just any other person, but the partner: the one person to whom the client doesn't want this exposed.

It is good practice to develop a disciplined and consistent approach to your readings, especially these highly sensitive ones. Not only will this enhance your reputation as an astrologer, but more importantly it will convey a feeling of safety to the clients as well as help them to see you for what you are—a trained, professional expert who is there to help them. These are the basic skills you will need to do that:

- **Be present.** The situation of having two people, various charts and sheets of paper, and a whole lot of preparation often means that you can get so caught up in your "script" and covering the points you have listed as important that you may not be paying enough attention to the feedback you are getting. Notice how things are affecting your clients. Use verbal clues and body language to be sensitive to the way your clients are responding to information. This will help you see what's relevant, what is a "no-go" area, what needs great sensitivity in discussion, etc.

- **Be neutral.** As an astrologer you will hear astonishing admissions as well as surprising facts about people's lives, but no more so than when analyzing relationships. Since relationships are so personal, covering such deeply private things as one's sex life, you will hear secrets and you will discover lifestyles you never imagined existed, and that may well be outside of your definition of "normal" or "acceptable." You are a professional: your job is not to judge people morally or otherwise. No matter what your feelings, you need to be compassionate and convey to the client that it is safe to talk about such matters without judgment. Don't allow your own beliefs and prejudices to become part of the reading.

- **Be sensitive.** Most relationship readings are not the first time you have encountered one or both of the partners. You probably will have discussed at least one of the natal charts at length with its owner, perhaps even had a session to analyze transits and progressions. This has given you insight into what is going on in that client's life and what kind of issues the person is facing. Your awareness of these things should inform the reading you now are doing. You can avoid making unrealistic suggestions or anything else that might make the client feel awkward, or worse, feel that he or she is not understood or empathized with.

- **Be discreet.** The same prior readings also mean that you know things about somebody's life that the partner may not be aware of. Be careful not to accidentally (or intentionally) reveal information. Never assume that the person has shared everything with the partner. Sometimes you will need to use intuition as your guide here. Ensure that you are present and sensitive to what is happening in your office, what your clients are saying, and even what you yourself are saying. Intuition will help you decide when to reserve the discussion of some personal natal point that may not be appropriate to discuss right now. In general, the synastry and composite information is safe ground because it affects both people and they clearly are willing to know more; personal, individual traits or behaviors need your sensitivity.

- *Be professional.* All of these considerations require you to maintain the standards of any professional. Those who work with people are the ones who have the greatest responsibility to ensure that they are handling their clients with respect and sensitivity. The most important aspect of professionalism, however, is the fact that as a professional you are trained to use a specific skill for which your clients are paying you. That means that you need to ensure that the advice you give is always based on sound astrology. Personal opinions and homegrown psychology are not appropriate to your session. Try to back up everything you say and every piece of advice with what is going on in the chart. Most important, don't make choices or decisions for your clients—let your sound *astrological* advice be their guide.

The Relationship Goes "Live"

One of the ongoing issues that astrologers face is the extent to which their work depends on intangibles. We make a whole lot of statements and predictions that we may never have verified. Some clients are very interactive, which is helpful and often shows the validity of our work. Many aren't, and we have to proceed with the trust that we are providing relevant and useful information.

Relationship work is different. The couple sitting in front of you is the relationship gone live. They will interact with each other and with you, giving you plenty of opportunity to verify the implications of the charts as well as identify practical advice that is of immediate relevance. More than in most of the astrological readings you will ever do, synastry is living astrology.

There are some basic things to look out for, which you should learn to recognize. This will help you ensure that you are able to see past all the interpersonal games and countless other subtle and not so subtle things that pass between people who know each other well. It also will help you see where you stand as the astrologer so that you don't get too drawn into those dynamics.

Covering up. People behave very differently in front of others. This is especially true for couples. Remember, relationships encompass many of our insecurities, especially our fear of being judged: for example, most people are very sensitive to what others think of their choice of partner. We spend a lot of our energy maintaining a particular image of the relationship and concealing those things that we suspect are problematical and that could lead to judgment by others.

Having delineated the charts, you should be aware of each partner's individual insecurities and what each tends to conceal. The Ascendant, planets in that house, and the house ruler will give you a sense of how each person wants to convey him- or herself. The twelfth house and the challenging aspects to the personal planets from difficult planets will help you understand what each client conceals and why.

As a couple, the shared deceptions are represented by the same factors in the composite chart. In particular, a strong first house or even just the Sun in that house shows a partnership that tends to be more concerned with the image they portray than with sorting out what issues they may face at home.

In general, you can expect that anything in the synastry that is challenging is likely to be somewhat concealed. Be sensitive to things that are very personal, such as sex life. During the first ten minutes or so of the consultation you should be careful not to raise these personal issues. Spend that time describing more general features of the relationship as well as those first-house things that they have projected into the world. This will help them see the validity of your work as well as unconsciously prepare them for more personal things to follow.

Role-play. Not all the "acting" in a relationship is for other people's benefit. People often find security in their relationship by settling into a particular role. This is often a way to deal with conflict or problems: each partner has a "script" that makes things more predictable and ensures who will respond in which way when a crisis arises.

Unfortunately, many of these roles and scripts help negative behaviors become patterns and help the covering up become part of the way of dealing with things. The result is that the real core of the relationship—how these people actually relate to each other—is not brought into play in the dynamics of relating. Sometimes, abusive relationships can persist precisely because of the tendency for couples to slip into their respective roles and so endlessly play out the same destructive drama.

You need to be very careful when dealing with a couple that is playing out this script in your office. Tell your clients that your office is a place where they must temporarily leave behind their everyday experience of the relationship while they get the chance to view it more objectively.

Naturally, you should use the synastry to understand how this role-play may unfold. Receptions between planets can be especially useful to determine who takes on which role or who takes the upper hand. Remember, a planet always defers to the planets that rule it by sign and exaltation, and resists the planets that rule its detriment or fall.

Notice when the couple is engaging in role-play and gently redirect them by asking a question or raising a related but different issue. This defeats the script and helps you steer the conversation to a mutual discussion rather than the scripted, automatic behavior they are used to. If you think the best strategy is to actually "expose" the role-play, you should confine that to the "safer" issues, although generally unless you are a licensed therapist it may be best to steer clear of that approach. People may not react positively to someone exposing the script.

Pointing fingers. When you do start getting more personal, you will trigger the defenses that most people have to protect them from seeing themselves or their lives too negatively. In a partnership, the most basic way to do that is through *projection*, seeing the problem as the partner's rather than one's own.

As you raise issues during the session, both the partners will tend to think that the other is more responsible for what you are describing than they themselves are. It is important to constantly remind them that in a partnership, both people are responsible for half of what's going on.

More importantly, the synastry grid and the double wheels give you a very clear picture of who is doing what to whom. Most of the time you need only see the partners' planets in each other's houses to get the picture; when planets interact, your consideration of their aspects and respective dignities, and whether they have any reception with each other, will describe the situation fully. It may require a lot of tact (and no small amount of courage) to describe this clearly to the clients, but in my experience they usually concede to the accuracy of the astrology. From that point on, the reading will be smoother and easier.

Be careful not to take this too far: you don't want to make one partner feel that he or she is responsible for all that ails the relationship. Balance the reading so that you are alternately talking about how each of the partners contributes to some of the issues, and so that you discuss positive and constructive interaspects with equal emphasis.

Drawing you in. Much of what happens in a relationship becomes part of the pattern of the relationship itself. One of the reasons it is so difficult to change bad patterns is because our way of adapting to them creates a pattern in itself. For example, if a person is criticized by the partner, he or she may not have a way to deal with it constructively, so the person may make a sarcastic statement in return. It's not long before criticism is dealt with by means of sarcasm, and the likelihood is that trust and love will become eroded. Even still, the familiar pattern becomes the easiest way to deal with it. The criticized partner feels weak and the situation is unpleasant, but this person also feels safe from an unknown, potentially threatening reaction from the partner because the outcome is known.

Now, the clients find a third person in the room—you. Suddenly it is safe to react more strongly because it is unlikely the critical partner will get threatening in front of a stranger (or even a friend for that matter). The result is that insults and accusations are traded more readily, and the couple use the astrological session as a safe space to release pent-up feelings rather than benefit from the greater objectivity the charts are offering. It is a well-known phenomenon that couples in a conflict-ridden relationship bring up all the personal, unpleasant details in front of friends and strangers as a way of seeking support (it usually embarrasses and alienates the friends, of course).

Worse, and more challenging to the astrologer, is that in such situations one or both of the partners are very likely to try to rope you in to the mudslinging match and take their side. They do this initially by telling you things about their partner, right in front of the person, that they wouldn't dare say when they are alone together. They ask you to agree or confirm this accusation. They define who is the victim and who is the perpetrator and expect you to go along with that definition.

It is important to maintain your objectivity and neutrality. If one partner perceives that you are favoring the other, you could end up doing more damage to the relationship, your practice, and astrology in general than you might realize, because the real consequences are felt only when the couple return home. Become alert to people who try to take advantage of your sensitivity and compassion.

Learn to deflect attempts to rope you in by responding that astrology sees every interaction as a two-way street. With a persistent partner trying to get you to take his or her side, it may even be useful to use synastry and raise an issue about what that person does to contribute to conflict. Return to the charts all the time, making it clear to the clients that you will use the charts, rather than anything they are claiming, as a guide. Never take sides or be pressed into agreement—learn to keep yourself separate and not get drawn in. Rely on the astrology, not your feelings (or the clients'), and keep things balanced by creating the clear and accurate impression that it takes two people to play the game of relating.

Giving Constructive Advice

By now you may feel a little daunted by the prospect of the psychological warfare that may be taking place in your office. As if having three or more charts to work with wasn't enough of a juggling act, you now have the interpersonal dynamics in the back of your mind and wish that you hadn't dropped psychology back in college.

You do not need to worry. Astrology is the foundation and the backbone of what you are doing. If you rely on your skills as an astrologer, you will be able to deal with all the aspects of the relationship that are within your purvey. For the rest, you indeed may recommend that some clients visit a relationship counselor of some kind.

The chart of the consultation gives you a good overall strategy for how to prioritize things once you have done all the strategizing from your delineation. Now you need to use the synastry as the source of the advice you give to the clients. This also will help you focus on the objectivity of the charts rather than getting caught in the blaming pattern and accepting the subjective view of who is doing what to whom.

The last step after the selection, collation, and strategizing is to describe the interaction and give advice based on the chart:

- *Squares, oppositions, and conjunctions (in that order of priority) describe most of the problems.* Although you are identifying them as problems and describing them in that way, you don't want to give the clients the impression that these are fixed issues that cannot be addressed. They are best understood as *the problems that need to be worked on.* It is sometimes especially relevant when you depict difficult conjunctions as issues on which the clients fail to get a perspective (can't see the forest for the trees) and assume that their own way is right. Here is where they need a third party to help or where they need to use strategies in which external things can help them to understand the problem. The squares are issues where their individual differences in their approaches and goals prevent them from proceeding. They have locked horns and need to develop a new goal or destination that requires them both to make compromises and adopt different methods. The opposition shows where they appear to have opposite approaches or viewpoints that are paralyzing them or creating a vicious circle in which each tries to make things go his or her way. They need to identify and eliminate the most extreme "opposites" in the issue and then try to combine what's best in their differing views and approaches to reach a new common destination.

- *Trines and sextiles (and some conjunctions) should be emphasized as the meeting points between the couple that should be developed and exploited.* This is where they have things in common or where they dovetail easily to function as a couple and to meet some of each other's needs. Conjunctions between beneficial planets show where they instinctively combine forces, where the whole is greater than the combined parts. Sextiles show where their somewhat different approaches naturally dovetail and where each can bring unique talents or viewpoints to the situation to help them achieve the common goal. Trines show where their views are very similar and are easily combined to achieve the goal (or to get along well or whatever the particular situation may be).

- *Connect the difficult aspects to the easy ones*. Try to find easy aspects between a planet involved in a difficult configuration and some other planet. The other planet offers a way in which the difficulty can be worked on. Consider it by house position and house rulership to suggest an aspect of their lives that they can concentrate on that will have the benefit of helping them deal with the problems represented by the difficult aspect. Astrology has the unique ability to connect things together in a meaningful way or to describe existing connections that are not obviously apparent. This simple strategy can be one of the most powerful tools an astrologer has.

- *Don't forget receptions*. This is one of the most important ways to find the true potential of a relationship between two planets (and therefore what they represent to the clients). Receptions connect planets even more deeply than aspects do. Don't look only at mutual receptions; look at one-way reception too. If two planets have a difficult aspect but one is in the other's sign, this provides an avenue for advice as to how the planets may cooperate; there is still a good connection between them, and the planet should defer to the planet that rules it. It also may help you see when one client is *always* deferring to the partner on a specific issue (i.e., one person's planet is ruled by the partner's planet, but not mutually). Generally, when planets are in each other's sign, this dramatically improves the relationship between them, although the reverse can be true if they are in each other's detriment or fall sign.

- *Give practical, realistic advice*. Between all the charts and the clients themselves, you have enough information to ensure that the advice you give based on the charts given their shared life. It's one thing to have a wonderful trine that says they could work together at a professional goal; but it means nothing if one of the partners is needed at home as a full-time parent. Be sure to always look for realistic contexts. Translate the astrology into everyday practicalities; don't expect the clients to feel that having a trine is enough reason in itself to go home and quit complaining!

- *Help the clients set goals*. Astrology is all about time and especially the future. Once again you have a unique tool that helps make that future much more tangible and definable. If your session is to have real benefit, it will not only help the partners deal with existing problems, but will give them some sense of a lasting way to make the changes and improve the future conditions in the relationship. You already have examined the future trends of the relationship; now use your delineations in a practical way to give them something to work toward.

- ***Help them measure their progress.*** It is helpful to suggest assessment points to the clients. These are opportunities for them to actually sit down, take stock, and again apply what they have learned from the charts and from their ongoing shared life. The most fundamental of these are the personal life changes such as the midlife crisis.

  As a couple, the square of Saturn to its position at the time they met is the most important time to assess where the relationship stands and where it is going. Any other transits of Saturn can be used the same way.

  You can propose the transits of Jupiter as a time to focus on the positive and to deliberately share good experiences, such as taking a holiday. Note the transit cycles related to the planets creating challenges and identify them as assessment points, while the cycles of the planets related to their easy aspects and receptions can provide opportunities to reinforce what's good about the relationship, what brought them together in the first place, and perhaps how to sustain their relationship through the thick and thin of the challenges and opportunities they experience.

Wrapping It Up

A relationship is a joint venture. Mostly, the partners come to the astrologer because they want help to make the relationship easier to manage, they want to understand themselves and how they relate to their partners, and they want to know what the future holds for them.

The technique of synthesis allows you to provide a realistic, objective description of the relationship as well as the tools by which it can be enhanced. It is your exciting and rewarding job as the astrologer to use these tools to enlighten your clients and to give them a sense of understanding and possibility based not on vague unknowns or ideals but on real potentials that they sense between them, which may have brought them together in the first place.

Without the need to resort to special philosophies or particular beliefs, without having to develop psychic talents or other mysterious techniques, you are in the position to answer in a tangible and useful fashion the age-old questions that all couples eventually ask: Why are we together? What are we supposed to do together? How do we make this work?

FURTHER READING

The books in this list provide good resources to further your studies. They were all consulted during the writing of this book.

Astrology Basics

Burk, Kevin. *Astrology: Understanding the Birth Chart.* St. Paul, MN: Llewellyn Publications, 2001.

Frawley, John. *The Real Astrology.* London: Apprentice Books, 2001.

————. *The Real Astrology Applied.* London: Apprentice Books, 2002.

Greenbaum, Dorian Gieseler. *Temperament: Astrology's Forgotten Key.* Bournemouth, England: The Wessex Astrologer Ltd., 2004.

Hickey, Isabel. *Astrology: A Cosmic Science.* Sebastopol, CA: CRCS Publications, 1992.

Lehman, Dr. J. Lee. *Classical Astrology for Modern Living.* Atglen, PA: Whitford Press, 2000.

Lilly, William. *Christian Astrology.* Edited by David Roell. Bel Air, MD: Astrology Classics, 2004.

Parker, Julia and Derek. *Parkers' Astrology.* New York: Dorling Kindersley, 2004.

Counseling and Consultations

Sellar, Wanda. *The Consultation Chart: A Guide to What It Is and How to Use It.* Bournemouth, England: The Wessex Astrologer Ltd., 2000.

Tyl, Noel. *The Creative Astrologer.* St. Paul, MN: Llewellyn Publications, 2000.

———. *Noel Tyl's Guide to Astrological Consultation.* St. Paul, MN: Llewellyn Publications, 2007.

———. *Synthesis & Counseling in Astrology.* St. Paul, MN: Llewellyn Publications, 1994.

Relationship Astrology

Arroyo, Stephen. *Relationships and Life Cycles.* Sebastopol, CA: CRCS Publications, 1993.

Davison, Ronald. *Synastry: Understanding Human Relations Through Astrology.* New York: Aurora Press, 1983.

Neville, E. W. *Planets in Synastry: Astrologic Patterns of Relationships.* West Chester, PA: Whitford Press, 1997.

Robson, Vivian. *Astrology and Sex.* Bel Air, MD: Astrology Classics, 2001.

Townley, John. *Composite Charts: The Astrology of Relationships.* St. Paul, MN: Llewellyn Publications, 2000.

Electional Astrology

Hampar, Joann. *Electional Astrology: The Art of Timing.* St. Paul, MN: Llewellyn Publications, 2005.

March, Marian D. *The Only Way to Learn About Horary and Electional Astrology.* San Diego, CA: Astro Comunications Services, 1994.

Robson, Vivian. *Electional Astrology.* Bel Air, MD: Astrology Classics, 2001.

RELATIONSHIP ANALYSIS WORKSHEET

This guide provides a step-by-step summary of all the delineation and analysis described in the book. Items in each section of the table are arranged by priority, so they can function as a checklist and ensure that you properly assess the importance of astrological factors. Page references are provided so you can easily refer to the full explanation of any point at any time.

In this table, the use of the word *aspects* to describe the relationship between planets includes receptions and rulership.

Relationship issues	Delineate in chart	Interpret in regard to
I. Analyzing Each Individual Chart		
1. First impressions		
p. 11	i. The ascending sign	How first impressions are perceived and deliberately created.
	ii. Planets in the first house	
	iii. Element of Mercury	
2. Overall chart impression		
p. 18	i. Hemisphere emphasis	Establish orientation to relationships.
	ii. Identify strong and weak planets	
	iii. Emphasized chart features	
3. Basic needs and essential self		
p. 21	i. Identify needs of each luminary by sign and house	Identify essence of personality and how it is established through early influence. Essential needs always seek to be met.
	ii. Ability of luminaries to meet each other's needs and blend	
	iii. Aspect between luminaries	
4. What is projected		
p. 27	i. Ascendant's ability to project what is needed	Identify how projected persona differs from "true" self.
	ii. Compared with the energy of each luminary	

II. Comparing Individual Charts		
1. Comparison of basic personality determinants		
p. 30	i. Elemental emphasis and whether it mixes with partner's	Basic ability of energies to blend
	ii. Compare Ascendants	Perception of the other as similar and similarity of essential personality factors
	iii. Compare Suns	
	iv. Compare Moons	
	v. Check for similar or compatible signs among all three factors	
2. Comparison of relevant individual characteristics		
p. 34	i. Independence: fire, Uranus, Aries, Sagittarius, Aquarius	Key personality characteristics that remain constant no matter with whom the individual is having a relationship. An emphasis on a number of qualities in each category emphasizes that characteristic. Use these categories and astrological indicators as a starting point—you will find other personal characteristics that also may affect compatibility.
	ii. Dependence/needy: water, weak Moon, Taurus, Cancer	
	iii. Commitment: earth, Saturn, Capricorn	
	iv. Emotionally expressive: fire + water, Moon, Mercury, Mars	
	v. Unexpressive: air + earth, Saturn, Capricorn, Aquarius	
	vi. Sex drive: Venus, Mars, Scorpio, 5th house	
	vii. Jealousy: Mars, Saturn, Pluto, Scorpio, 8th house	

(See previous page)	viii. Extravagance: fire, Venus + Jupiter, Sagittarius, Leo	(See previous page)
	ix. Stingy: earth, Saturn, Cancer, Jupiter/Venus in Virgo, Capricorn	
3. Emotional mindset and communicating feelings		
p. 42	i. Moon-Mercury aspects	Understanding and expressing emotions.
4. Self-worth and the value system		
p. 44	i. Element and dignity of Venus	Critical issues affecting who we attract and are attracted to and how we manage relationships.
	ii. Planets in and ruling 2nd	
	iii. Condition of the Sun	
5. Love, sex, pleasure, and children		
p. 46	i. Planets in and ruling 5th	Issues around sex and children are critical to understand. Partners must know each other's attitudes. Sexual issues profoundly affect intimacy and sharing.
	ii. Condition and aspects of Venus	
	iii. Effect of malefic planets on 5th house is critical	
6. Ability to receive love		
p. 48	i. Planets in and ruling 11th	Difficulties receiving love and other succedent house issues create core issues that can prevent relationship success.
	ii. Aspects between planets in 11th and planets in another succedent house	
	iii. Succedent house planets forming T-square or grand cross	

7. Power issues		
p. 52	i. Planets in and ruling 8th	Power is unequal in relationships. Money and sex can be used to control another person.
	ii. Luminaries and benefics in 8th	
	iii. Aspects between Venus and outer planets	

8. Likelihood and success of marriage or long-term partnership		
p. 54	i. Planets in and ruling 7th	Condition of the 7th house describes the tendency for relationships to follow similar patterns. Thorough analysis describes the partner as well as happiness and longevity in the relationship.
	ii. 7th-house planets representing partners	
	iii. Revise Venus and Moon—natural significators for marriage	
	iv. Difficult planets influencing 7th, Moon, or Venus	

III. Synastry: Interaction Between Charts

1. Basic effect on each other (place one chart in a second wheel around the other)		
p. 63	i. Planets in partner's angular houses	Partner's planets cause house emphasis to change and bring out other characteristics.
	ii. Planets in partner's empty houses	
	iii. Planets emphasizing or changing existing house factors	

2. Basic patterns of interaction (aspects from one chart's personal planets to the other)		
p. 72	i. Aspects between the luminaries	Critical points of contact for ability to relate at deepest level and form a relationship.
	ii. Aspects between angles and luminaries	
	iii. Aspects between angle rulers	
	iv. Aspects between angle rulers and angles	
	v. Aspects between Mercury and luminaries	Communication and understanding.
	vi. Aspects between Mercury and Mercury	
	vii. Aspects between Venus and luminaries	Romantic and sexual feelings and compatibility.
	viii. Aspects between Venus and Venus, Venus and Mars	
	ix. Aspects between Mars and luminaries	Shared or compatible goals and drives.
	x. Aspects between Mars and Mars	
	xi. Aspects between Jupiter and luminaries	Spiritual goals, sharing of ideas, ability to grow together.
	xii. Aspects between Jupiter and Venus, Jupiter and Jupiter	
	xiii. Aspects between Saturn and luminaries	Karma, lessons, limitations, difficulties, lasting bonds.
	xiv. Aspects between Saturn and Venus, Saturn and Saturn	

3. Life issues, challenges, and growth		
p. 91	i. Aspects between succedent house rulers	Succedent houses show core issues and beliefs about self that strongly affect relationships.
	ii. Aspect between ruler of one succedent house with same house ruler in other chart	
	iii. Aspects between succedent house rulers and other planets	
	iv. Key significators in 12th house	Things denied and avoided—also often core issues—can be surfaced by a relationship.
	v. Key significators in partner's 12th house	
	vi. Triggers to partner's 12th-house planets—aspects from positive or negative planets	
4. The outer planets		
p. 98	i. Aspects between outer planets and luminaries	Aspects from outer planets challenge change and growth in often uncomfortable ways.
	ii. Aspects between outer planets and personal planets	
	iii. Aspects between outer planets and relationship significators	
	iv. Aspects between outer planets repeated	
	v. Outer planet in different signs	

5. Lessons, karma, deeper meanings, age differences		
p. 104	i. Saturn-Saturn aspects	These show deep meaning in age differences, which can be stimulating or threatening but represent opportunities for learning and growth.
	ii. Saturn-significant age differences: 3 years, 5 years, multiples of 7 years	
	iii. Uranus enhancing karmic lessons: age difference multiple of 7 years	
	iv. Neptune enhancing karmic lessons: age difference multiple of 7 years and 14+ years	

IV. Charts of the Relationship

1. Composite chart		
p. 116	i. House emphasis	Shows the focus of the relationship, where the partners "meet halfway," and the identity the relationship develops.
	ii. House of the Sun	
	iii. Aspects similar to natal charts	
	iv. Aspects not found in natal charts	
	v. Planets conjunct planets in a natal chart	

2. Marriage chart (or significant moment in relationship)		
p. 121	i. Relationship between rulers of 1st and 7th	A relationship has a life of its own that may not reflect the compatibility of the individuals.
	ii. Relationship between luminaries	
	iii. Aspects of Venus	
	iv. Analysis of the 1st house	
	v. Analysis of remaining houses and planets	

V. Future of the Relationship		
1. Progressions at the time the relationship starts		
p. 126	i. Progressions involving the angles	Progressions are strong indicators of lasting relationships developing.
	ii. Progressions involving Venus or 7th-house ruler	
	iii. Progressions of the Sun	
	iv. Progressed Moon highlights the timing	
2. Transits show all major stages in a relationship		
p. 128	i. 7th-house cusp receiving transits	Transits show precise timing and the nature of the relationship and the changes it undergoes.
	ii. Other angles receiving transits	
	iii. Venus receiving transits	
	iv. Transiting planet shows the trigger for change, type of change, and pace of change	
3. Progressions and transits challenging relationship longevity		
p. 131	i. Relationships begun under transits of Jupiter, Uranus, Neptune	Relationships change when the circumstances that began them change.
	ii. Few connections in synastry charts	
	iii. Synastry not involving luminaries	
	iv. Synastry not involving personal planets	
	v. Relationships begun when one partner's progressions aspect the other chart	

4. Important directions in individual charts		
p. 143	i. "Midlife crisis" Uranus opposes natal Uranus around age 40	These directions may not be specifically about relationships but tend to change many aspects of life, including the relationship.
	ii. Saturn return—Saturn conjoins natal Saturn around age 29	
	iii. Outer planet transits to Venus	
	iv. Directions involving angles, especially 7th	
	v. Directions involving angle rulers or other important significators	
5. Transits to the composite chart		
p. 145	i. Conjunctions to composite planets	Transits to composite indicate simultaneous change or change that affects both parties.
	ii. Other transiting aspects	
	iii. Transits occurring simultaneously in the composite and one of the natal charts	
VI. The Consultation		
1. Deciding what information to use		
p. 165	i. What is accurate and relevant?	Prioritize information and eliminate matters not directly relevant to the relationship at this time.
	ii. What is useful and meaningful?	
	iii. What is urgent and pressing?	
	iv. What is subtle and irrelevant?	

2. Preparing charts		
p. 165	i. Prepare natal, relationship, and directed charts	Use this worksheet as your guide.
3. Collating information		
p. 167	i. Read through and identify themes	Follow what you have established in point 1 of this section to organize your information, and plan how much time to spend on each area.
	ii. Identify repeating chart factors	
	iii. Note other issues that have become apparent during delineation	
	iv. Identify positive and constructive factors to use for advice	
	v. Create an outline or "mind map" and estimate timing of each area of discussion	
4. The astrologer's chart		
p. 169	i. Your planets in clients' houses	Use astrology to alert you to excessive identification with one partner or how the clients trigger your issues.
	ii. Clients' planets in your houses	
	iii. Conjunctions between planets in your chart and the clients'	
5. Role of the astrologer as counselor		
p. 170	i. Be present	Being clear on your own role helps you establish a safe environment for your clients to explore sensitive issues.
	ii. Be neutral	
	iii. Be sensitive	
	iv. Be discreet	
	v. Be professional	

6. The clients' interaction during consultation		
p. 172	i. Covering up (note emphasis on 1st or 12th house)	These "games" occur in many sessions. Use the principles in the previous point to remain aware and neutral.
	ii. Role-play	
	iii. Finger-pointing	
	iv. Drawing you in	
7. Giving constructive advice		
p. 175	i. Identify the hard aspects describing key problems	Unless you have qualifications in counseling, it is wisest to use the charts to give advice rather than your opinions. This also ensures that your advice is specifically meaningful to these individuals rather than just being generally useful.
	ii. Use the easy aspects to suggest good points to exploit	
	iii. Connect the difficult aspects to easy ones involving the same planets	
	iv. Use receptions between planets to understand their interaction and give advice	
	v. Be practical and realistic	
	vi. Help clients set goals (use transits to time them)	

APPENDIX C

CHARTS

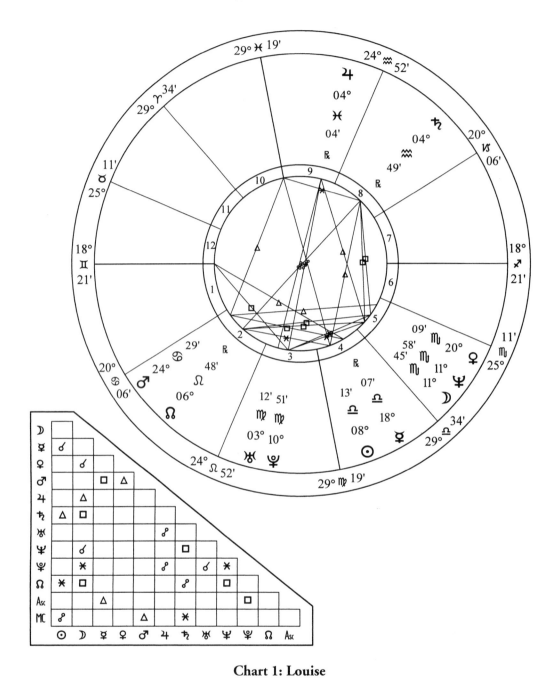

Chart 1: Louise
October 1, 1962 / 11:25 p.m. EET / Johannesburg, South Africa
Placidus houses

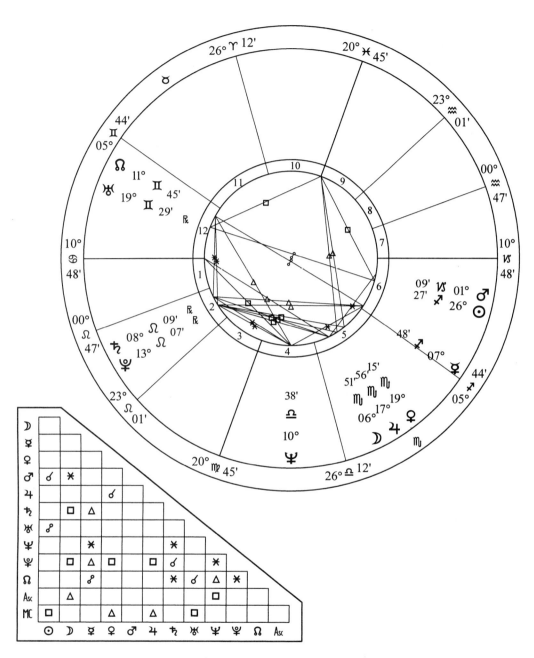

Chart 2: Steven Spielberg
December 18, 1946 / 6:16 p.m. EST / Cincinnati, Ohio
Placidus houses

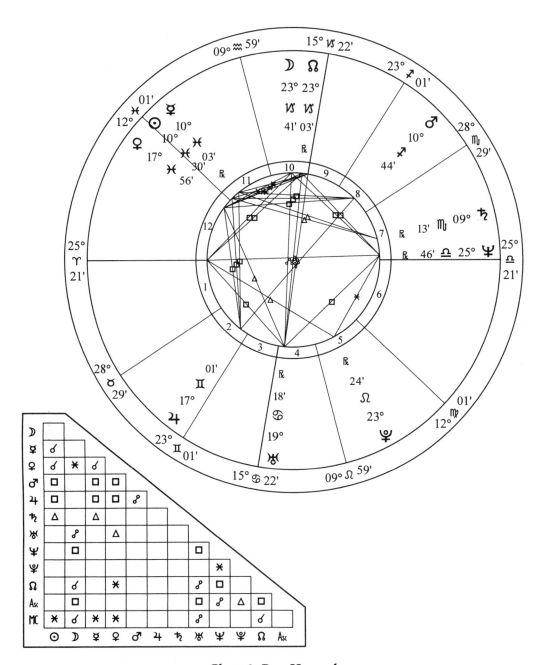

Chart 3: Ron Howard

March 1, 1954 / 9:03 a.m. CST / Duncan, Oklahoma

Placidus houses

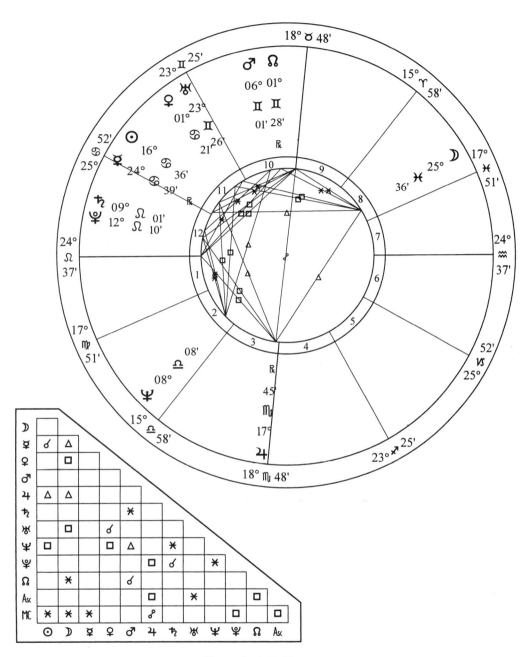

Chart 4: O.J. Simpson

July 9, 1947 / 8:08 a.m. PST / San Francisco, California

Placidus houses

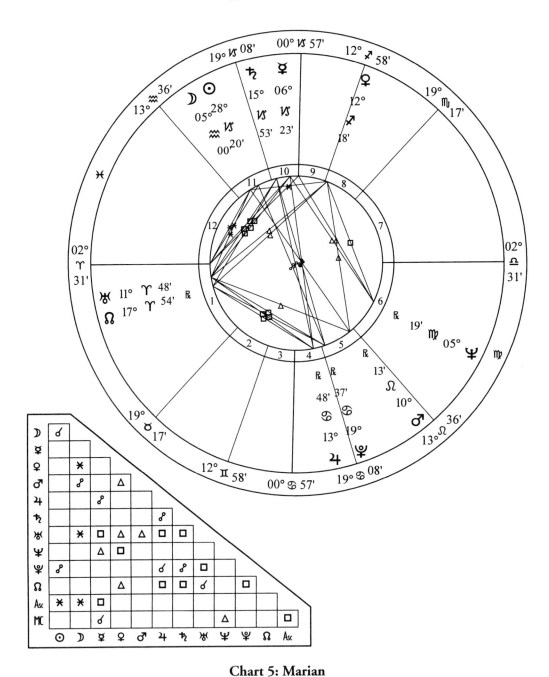

Chart 5: Marian
January 19, 1931 / 9:55 a.m. CET / Lodz, Poland
Placidus houses

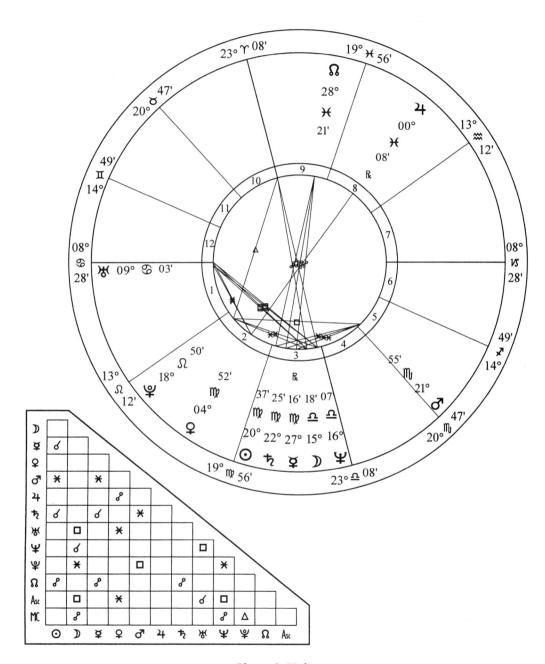

Chart 6: Helen

September 14, 1950 / 2:04 a.m. EET / Johannesburg, South Africa

Placidus houses

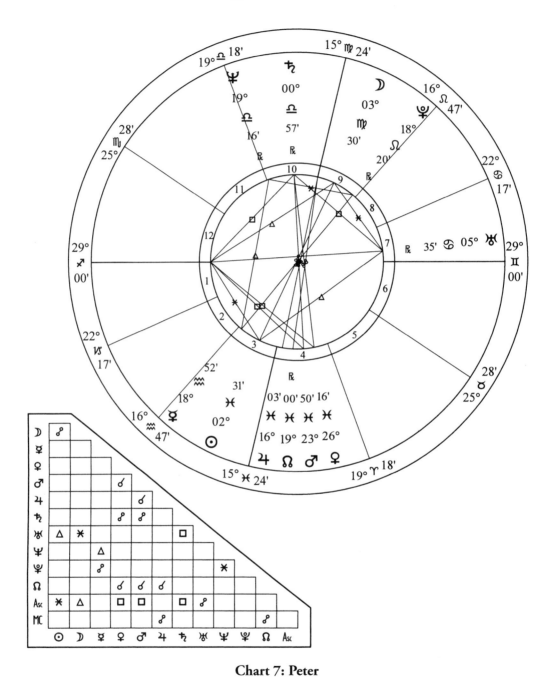

Chart 7: Peter
February 22, 1951 / 1:10 a.m. EET / Johannesburg, South Africa
Placidus houses

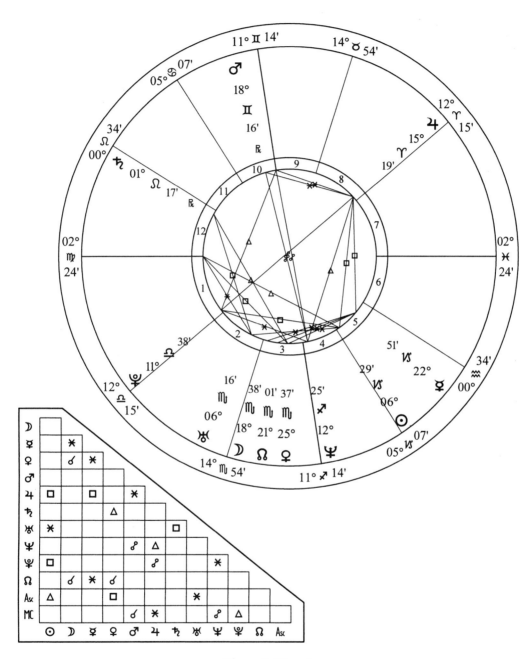

Chart 8: Maggie
December 28, 1975 / 10:20 p.m. EET / Johannesburg, South Africa
Placidus houses

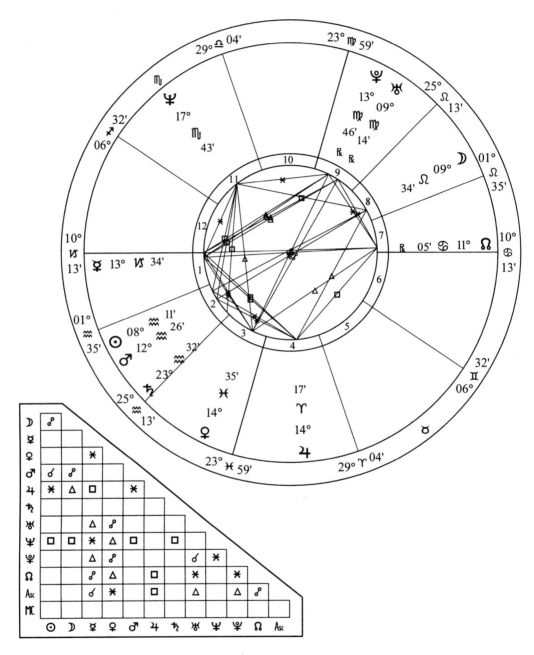

Chart 9: Ken
January 29, 1964 / 3:55 a.m. EET / Cape Town, South Africa
Placidus houses

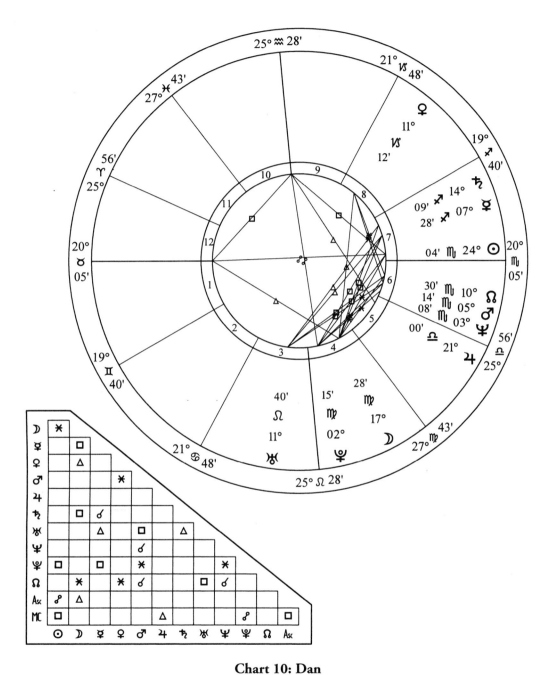

Chart 10: Dan

November 16, 1957 / 6:30 p.m. EET / Kimberley, South Africa

Placidus houses

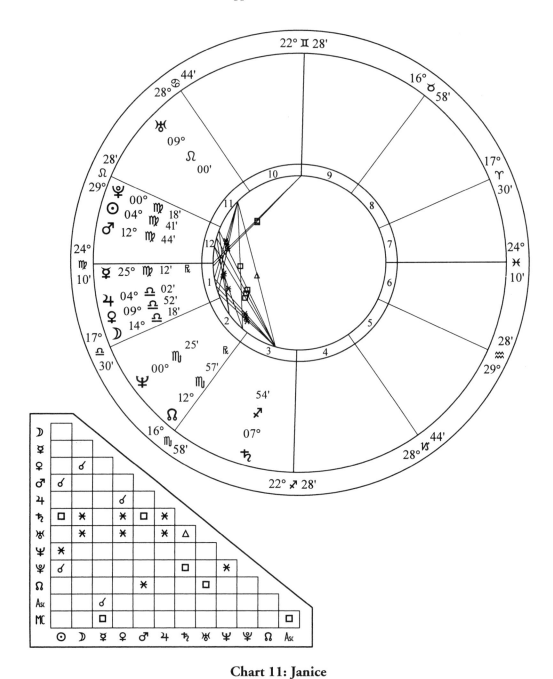

Chart 11: Janice
August 28, 1957 / 7:45 a.m. CET / Brussels, Belgium
Placidus houses

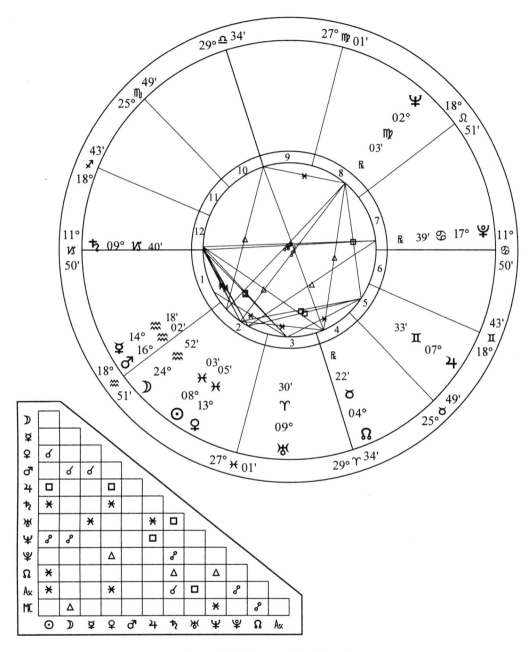

Chart 12: Joanne Woodward
February 27, 1930 / 4:00 a.m. EST / Thomasville, Georgia
Placidus houses

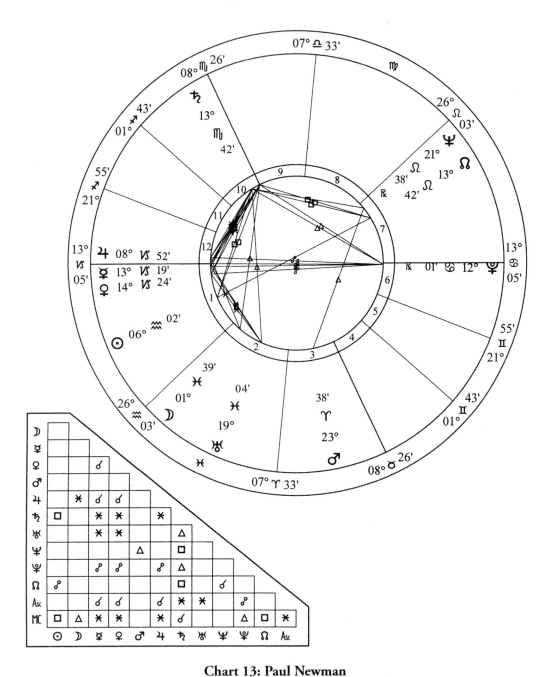

Chart 13: Paul Newman
January 26, 1925 / 6:30 a.m. EST / Cleveland, Ohio
Placidus houses

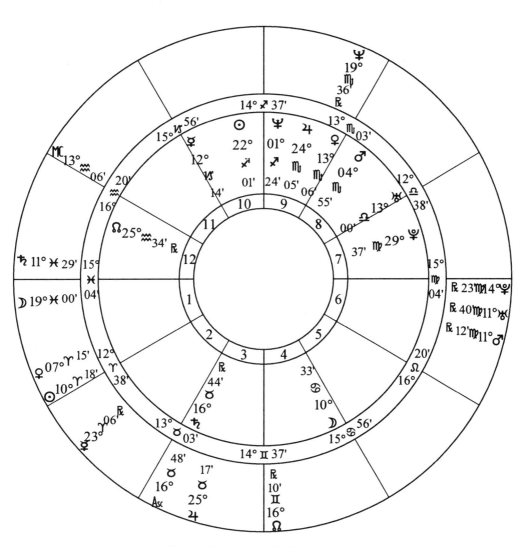

Chart 14: Brett and Alan, synastry

Brett (inner ring)
December 14, 1970 / 12:10 p.m. EET
Keetmanshoop, Namibia
Placidus houses

Alan (outer ring)
March 31, 1965 / 8:50 a.m. BAT
Mombasa, Kenya
Placidus houses

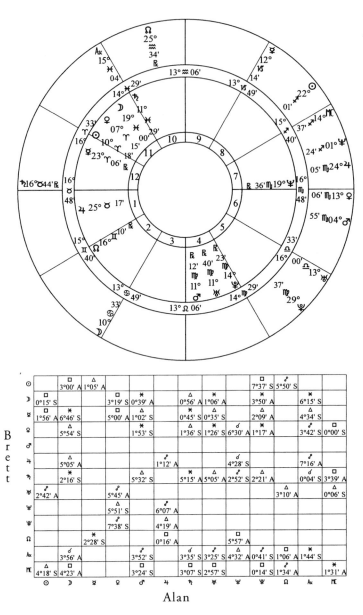

Chart 15: Alan and Brett, synastry

Alan (inner ring)
March 31, 1965 / 8:50 a.m. BAT
Mombasa, Kenya
Placidus houses

Brett (outer ring)
December 14, 1970 / 12:10 p.m. EET
Keetmanshoop, Namibia
Placidus houses

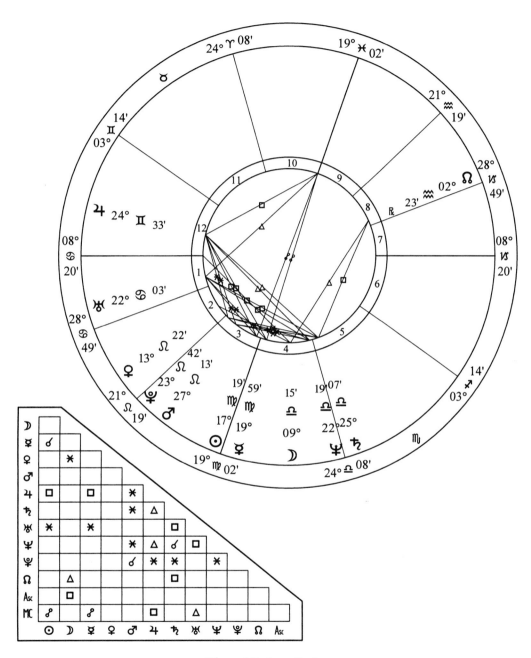

Chart 16: Amy Irving
September 10, 1953 / 1:12 a.m. PDT / Palo Alto, California
Placidus houses

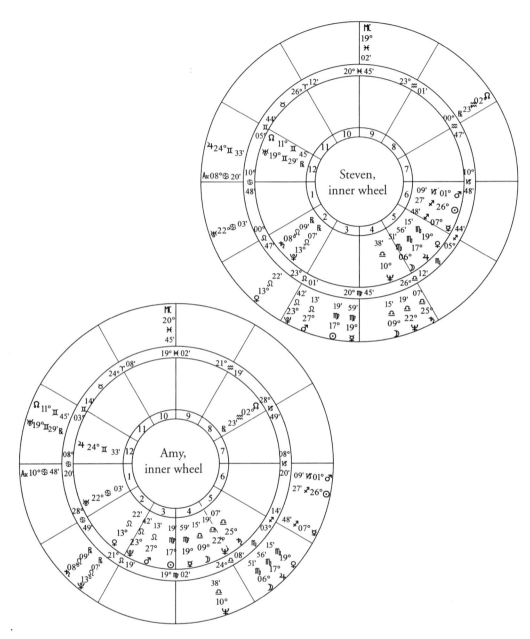

Chart 17: Steven Spielberg and Amy Irving, synastry

Steven Spielberg
December 18, 1946 / 6:16 p.m. EST
Cincinnati, Ohio
Placidus houses

Amy Irving
September 10, 1953 / 1:12 a.m. PDT
Palo Alto, California
Placidus houses

Amy

	☉	☽	☿	♀	♂	♃	♄	♅	♆	♇	☊	Asc	MC
☉	□ 9°08' S		□ 9°31' A	✶ 1°56' A		✶ 0°37' A		□ 2°10' A			□ 5°35' S	✶ 6°32' A	☍ 3°26' S
☽		✶ 1°27' S		□ 8°06' S		✶ 1°06' S	☌ 1°23' A	✶ 3°52' A	△ 2°30' A	□ 1°33' S			
☿	□ 6°28' A			✶ 0°44' S		✶ 2°03' S		□ 0°30' S					☍ 0°46' S
♀		□ 6°32' A	△ 5°34' A	□ 5°52' A		□ 4°34' A	☌ 5°13' S		✶ 2°44' S	☌ 0°16' S	✶ 1°38' S		
♂	△ 0°46' A			□ 7°58' S	△ 3°56' S								
♃	☍ 1°54' S			☍ 6°35' S			☌ 5°04' S						□ 3°48' A
♄	✶ 1°20' S						△ 5°38' S						
♅				△ 2°49' A		△ 4°07' A							△ 1°18' A
♆	✶ 4°08' S						△ 2°50' S						
♇	△ 2°45' S			□ 4°27' A		□ 5°46' A	✶ 4°13' S						
☊		□ 4°27' S	✶ 5°25' S			☍ 5°46' S							
Asc		△ 1°29' S			☍ 7°11' S			□ 2°18' A				☌ 2°28' A	
MC	□ 7°25' A			△ 0°13' A		△ 1°06' S		□ 0°27' A				□ 7°18' S	☌ 1°43' S

Steven

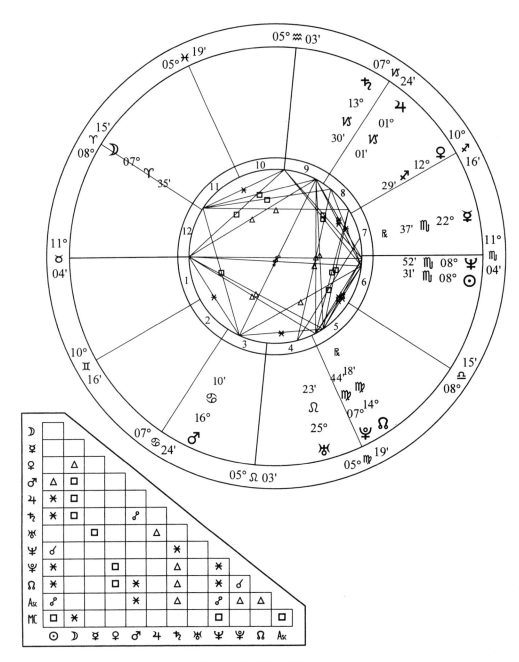

Chart 18: Kate Capshaw
November 3, 1953 / 10:00 p.m. CST / Fort Worth, Texas
Placidus houses

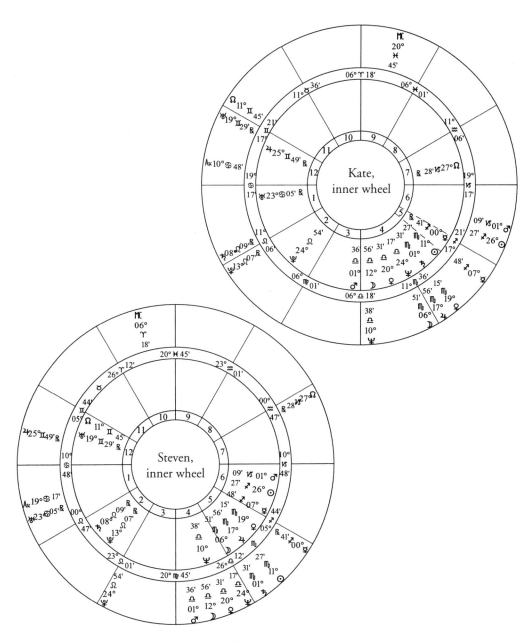

Chart 19: Steven Spielberg and Kate Capshaw, synastry

Steven Spielberg
December 18, 1946 / 6:16 p.m. EST
Cincinnati, Ohio
Placidus houses

Kate Capshaw
November 3, 1953 / 10:00 p.m. CST
Fort Worth, Texas
Placidus houses

Steven (rows) / Kate (columns)

Steven \ Kate	☉	☽	☿	♀	♂	♃	♄	♅	♆	♇	☊	Asc	MC
☉				✶ 5°56' A	□ 5°09' A	☍ 0°38' S	✶ 5°04' A		✶ 2°10' S	△ 1°33' S			□ 9°51' S
☽	☌ 4°36' A						☌ 5°20' S			□ 9°23' S			
☿		✶ 5°08' S	☌ 7°07' S										△ 1°30' A
♀	☌ 7°48' A							△ 3°51' A		□ 5°39' A		△ 0°02' S	
♂						□ 0°27' A	☍ 5°20' S	✶ 0°22' A					□ 5°09' S
♃	☌ 6°30' A							△ 5°09' A		□ 6°57' A		△ 1°21' S	
♄	□ 3°17' S	✶ 4°46' S					□ 6°39' S						△ 1°52' A
♅		△ 6°33' A		△ 1°02' S		☌ 6°19' A		△ 4°48' S	✶ 5°24' S				
♆		☌ 2°18' S											☍ 4°20' A
♇	□ 1°40' A	✶ 0°11' A											
☊		△ 1°11' S											✶ 5°27' A
Asc	△ 0°39' A	□ 2°08' A											□ 4°30' A
MC						□ 5°03' A		△ 2°20' A				△ 1°28' S	

Chart 19: Steven Spielberg and Kate Capshaw, synastry (continued)

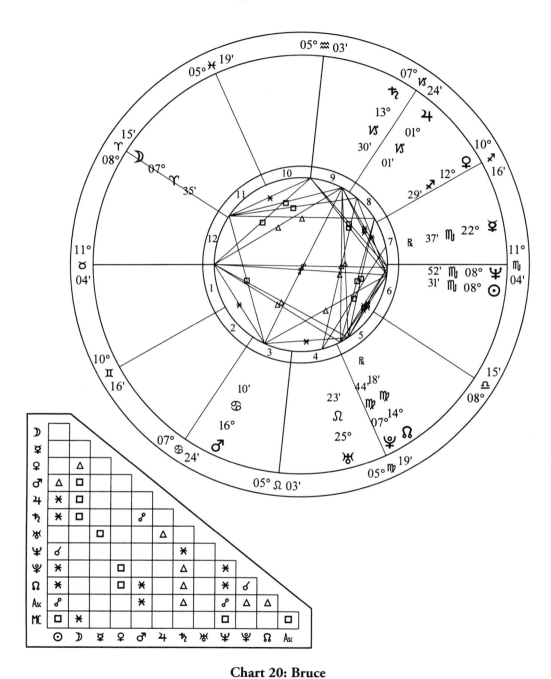

Chart 20: Bruce
October 31, 1960 / 5:45 p.m. EST / Bogota, Colombia
Placidus houses

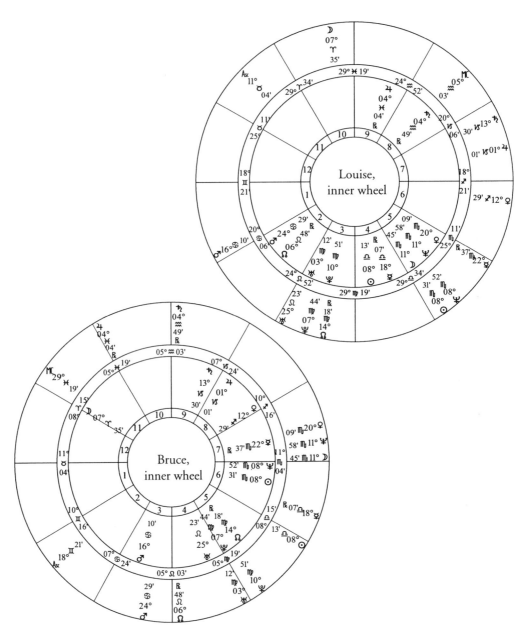

Chart 21: Bruce and Louise, synastry

Bruce
October 31, 1960 / 5:45 p.m. EST
Bogota, Colombia
Placidus houses

Louise
October 1, 1962 / 11:25 p.m. EET
Johannesburg, South Africa
Placidus houses

Bruce (rows) / Louise (columns)

	☉	☽	☿	♀	♂	♃	♄	♅	♆	♇	☊	Asc	MC
☉		☌ 3°14' S				△ 4°27' S	□ 3°42' S	⚹ 5°19' S	☌ 3°27' A	⚹ 2°20' A	□ 1°43' S		
☽	☍ 0°38' A						⚹ 2°46' S			△ 0°47' S			☌ 8°16' A
☿				☌ 2°28' A	△ 1°52' S								
♀	⚹ 4°16' S		⚹ 5°39' A						□ 1°38' S	△ 5°41' S	☍ 5°52' A		
♂	□ 7°57' A	△ 4°24' A	□ 1°58' A	△ 3°59' S					△ 4°12' S	⚹ 5°19' S			
♃	□ 7°11' S					⚹ 3°02' A		△ 2°10' A					□ 1°42' S
♄	□ 5°17' A	⚹ 1°45' A	□ 4°37' A						⚹ 1°32' S	△ 2°40' S			
♅				□ 5°14' A				☌ 7°49' S					
♆		☌ 2°54' S				△ 4°48' S	□ 4°03' S	⚹ 5°40' A	☌ 3°06' A	⚹ 1°59' A	□ 2°04' S		
♇		⚹ 4°01' S				☍ 3°40' S		☌ 4°33' A	⚹ 4°14' A	☌ 3°06' S			
☊		⚹ 2°33' A		⚹ 5°51' S				⚹ 2°20' A	☌ 3°27' A		□ 4°03' S		
Asc		☍ 0°41' A					□ 6°16' S		☍ 0°53' A	△ 0°14' S	□ 4°17' S		
MC	△ 3°10' A	□ 6°43' A					☌ 0°14' S		□ 6°55' A		☍ 1°45' A		⚹ 5°43' A

Louise

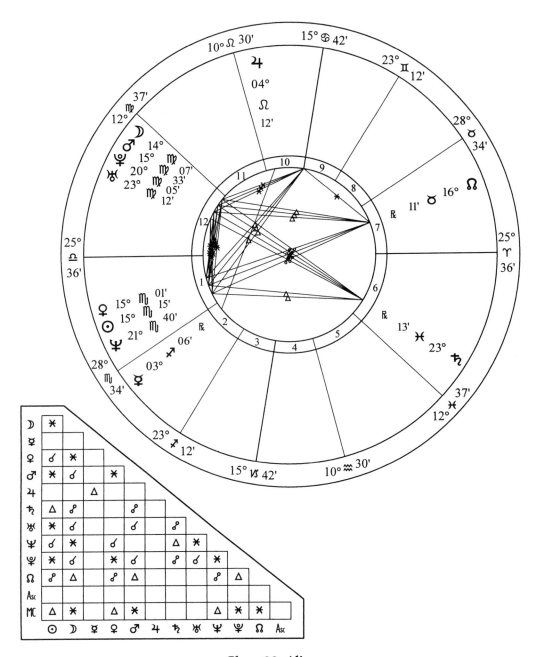

Chart 22: Alice
November 8, 1966 / 4:45 a.m. EET / Paarl, South Africa
Placidus houses

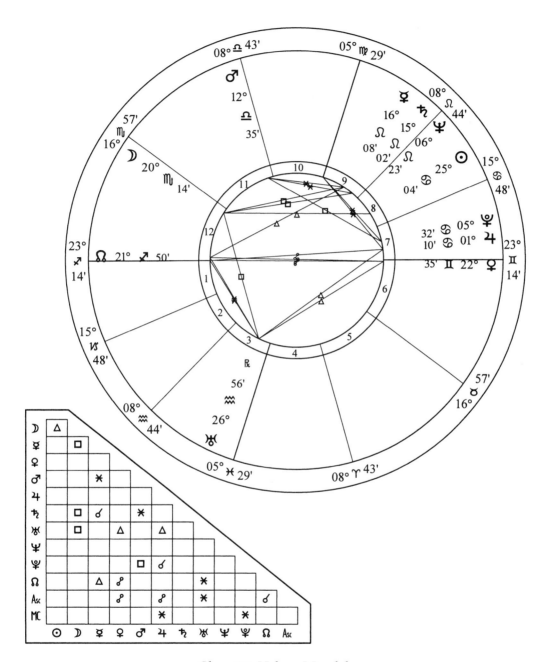

Chart 23: Nelson Mandela
July 18, 1918 / 2:52 p.m. EET / Umtata, South Africa
Placidus houses

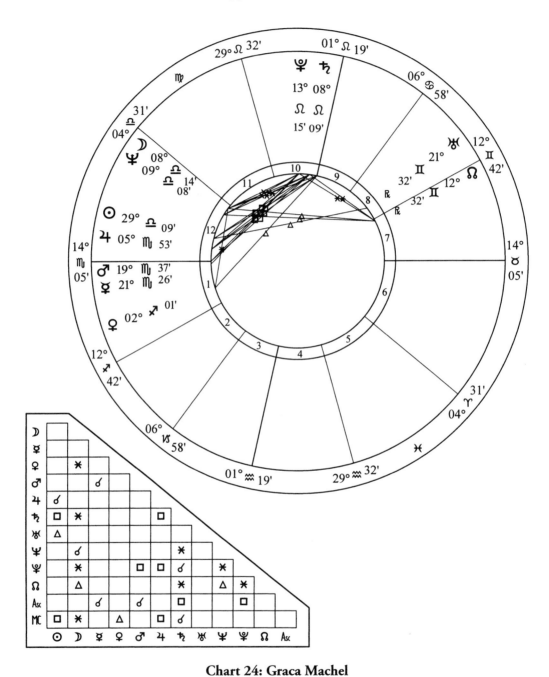

Chart 24: Graca Machel

October 23, 1946 / 6:00 a.m. EET / Maputo, Mozambique

Placidus houses

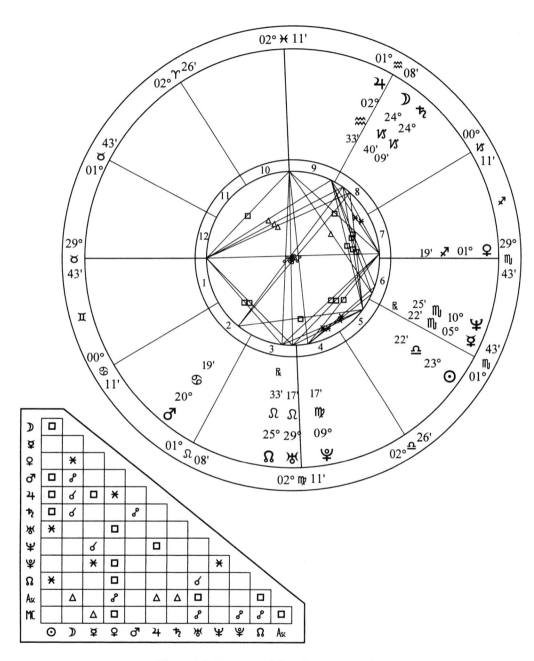

Chart 25: Bruce and Louise, composite

Bruce
October 31, 1960 / 5:45 p.m. EST
Bogota, Colombia
Placidus houses

Louise
October 1, 1962 / 11:25 p.m. EET
Johannesburg, South Africa
Placidus houses

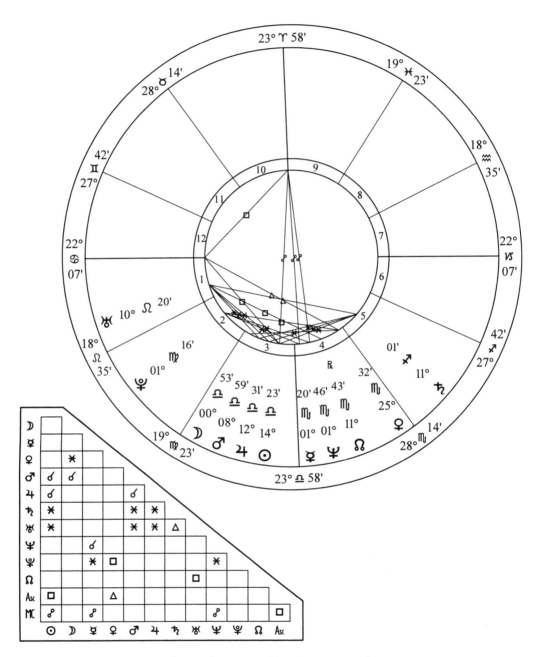

Chart 26: Dan and Janice, composite

Dan
November 16, 1957 / 6:30 p.m. EET
Kimberley, South Africa
Placidus houses

Janice
August 28, 1957 / 7:45 a.m. CET
Brussels, Belgium
Placidus houses

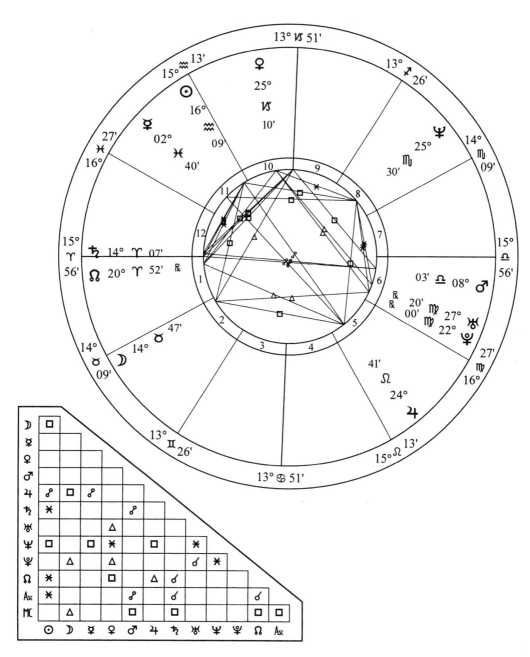

Chart 27: Alan and Brett, composite

Alan
March 31, 1965 / 8:50 a.m. BAT
Mombasa, Kenya
Placidus houses

Brett
December 14, 1970 / 12:10 p.m. EET
Keetmanshoop, Namibia
Placidus houses

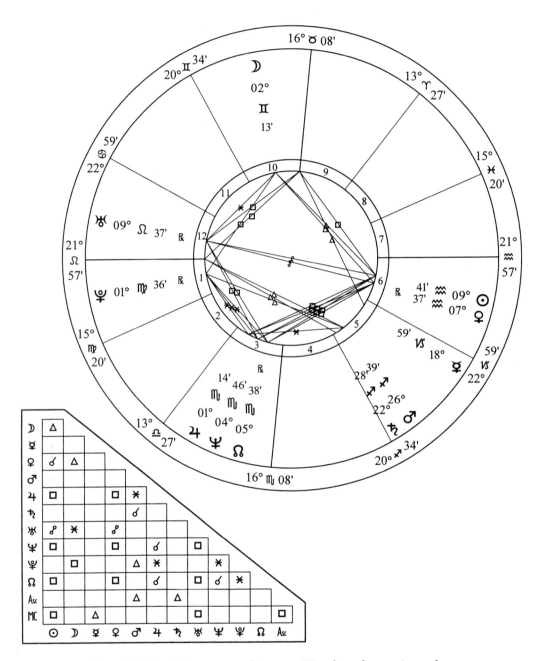

Chart 28: Paul Newman and Joanne Woodward, marriage chart

Paul Newman
January 26, 1925 / 6:30 a.m. EST
Cleveland, Ohio
Placidus houses

Joanne Woodward
February 27, 1930 / 4:00 a.m. EST
Thomasville, Georgia
Placidus houses

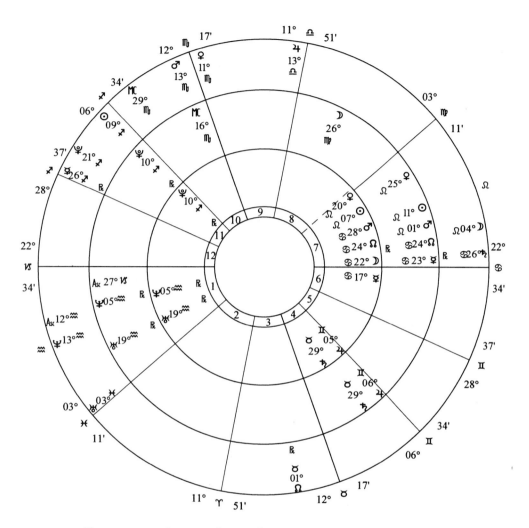

Chart 29: Brad Pitt and Jennifer Aniston, marriage chart plus progressions and transits in late 2004

Marriage chart (inner ring)	*Progressions late 2004* (middle ring)	*Transits late 2004* (outer ring)
July 29, 2000	December 1, 2004	December 1, 2004
7:02 p.m. PDT	12:00 p.m. PDT	12:00 p.m. PDT
Malibu, California	Malibu, California	Malibu, California
Placidus houses	Placidus houses	Placidus houses

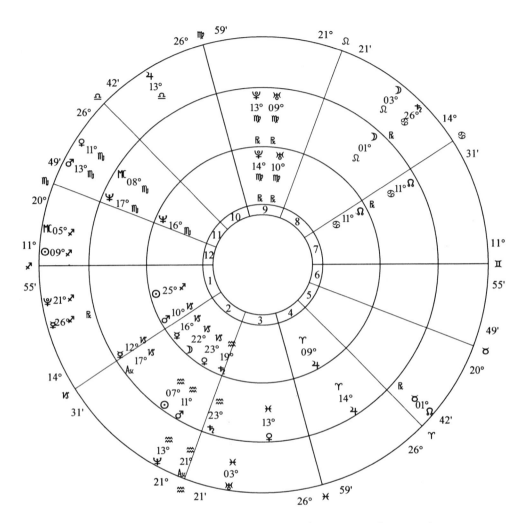

Chart 30: Brad Pitt, progressions and transits in late 2004

Brad Pitt	*Progressions late 2004*	*Transits late 2004*
(inner ring)	*(middle ring)*	*(outer ring)*
December 18, 1963	December 1, 2004	December 1, 2004
6:31 a.m. CST	12:00 p.m. CST	12:00 p.m. CST
Shawnee, Oklahoma	Shawnee, Oklahoma	Shawnee, Oklahoma
Placidus houses	Placidus houses	Placidus houses

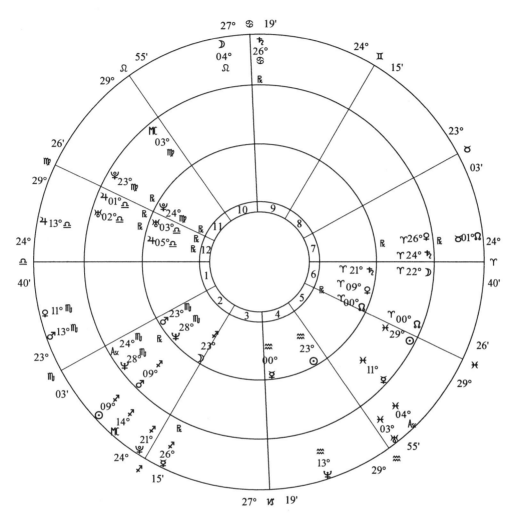

Chart 30: Jennifer Aniston, progressions and transits in late 2004

| *Jennifer Aniston*
(inner ring)
February 11, 1969
10:22 p.m. PST
Los Angeles, California
Placidus houses | *Progressions late 2004*
(middle ring)
December 1, 2004
12:00 p.m. PST
Los Angeles, California
Placidus houses | *Transits late 2004*
(outer ring)
December 1, 2004
12:00 p.m. PST
Los Angeles, California
Placidus houses |

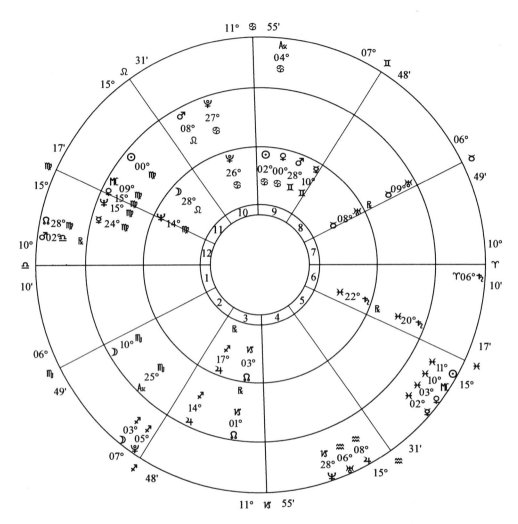

Chart 32: Richard Bach, progressions and transits in year of divorce

Richard Bach	*Progressions in year of divorce*	*Transits in year of divorce*
(inner ring)	*(middle ring)*	*(outer ring)*
June 23, 1936	March 1, 1997	March 1, 1997
12:36 p.m. CST	12:00 p.m. CST	12:00 p.m. CST
Oak Park, Illinois	Oak Park, Illinois	Oak Park, Illinois
Placidus houses	Placidus houses	Placidus houses

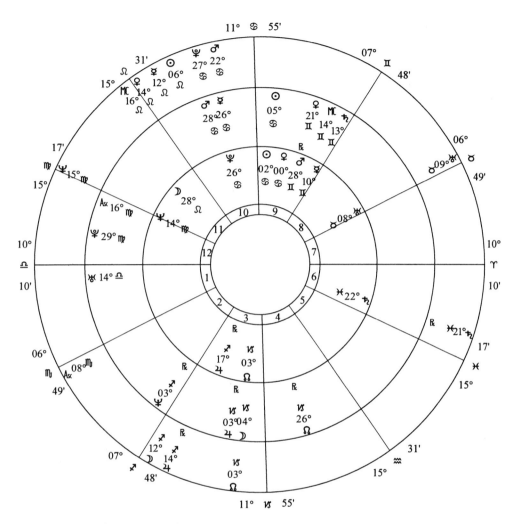

**Chart 33: Richard Bach, transits and progressions when
he first met wife Leslie Parrish**

Richard Bach	*Transits at first meeting*	*Progressions at first meeting*
(inner ring)	*(middle ring)*	*(outer ring)*
June 23, 1936	June 26, 1972	June 23, 1972
12:36 p.m. CST	11:22:40 a.m. CDT	11:22:40 a.m. CDT
Oak Park, Illinois	Oak Park, Illinois	Oak Park, Illinois
Placidus houses	Placidus houses	Placidus houses

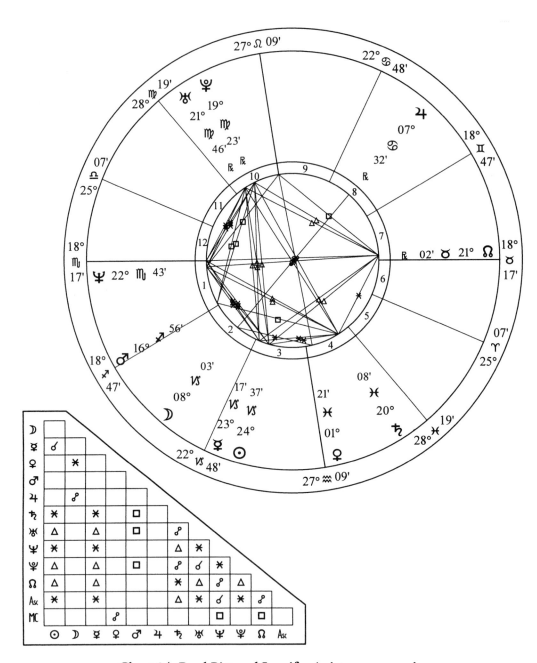

Chart 34: Brad Pitt and Jennifer Aniston, composite

Brad Pitt	*Jennifer Aniston*
December 18, 1963 / 6:31 a.m. CST	February 11, 1969 / 10:22 p.m. PST
Shawnee, Oklahoma	Los Angeles, California
Placidus houses	Placidus houses

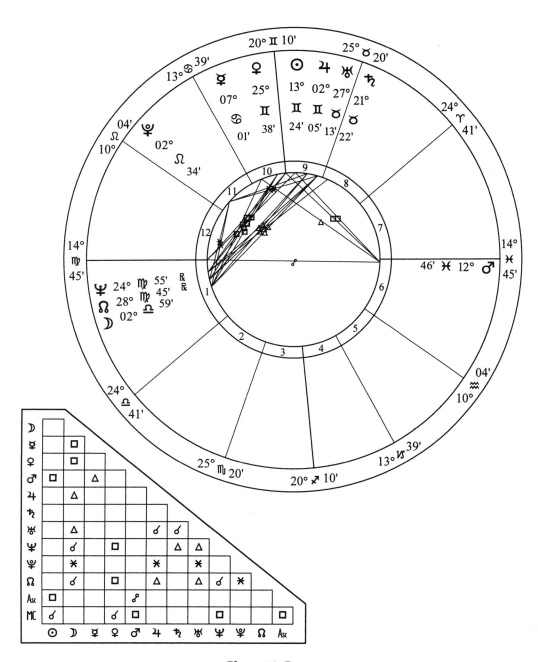

Chart 35: Penny
June 4, 1941 / 12:21:24 p.m. EET / Eshowe, South Africa
Placidus houses

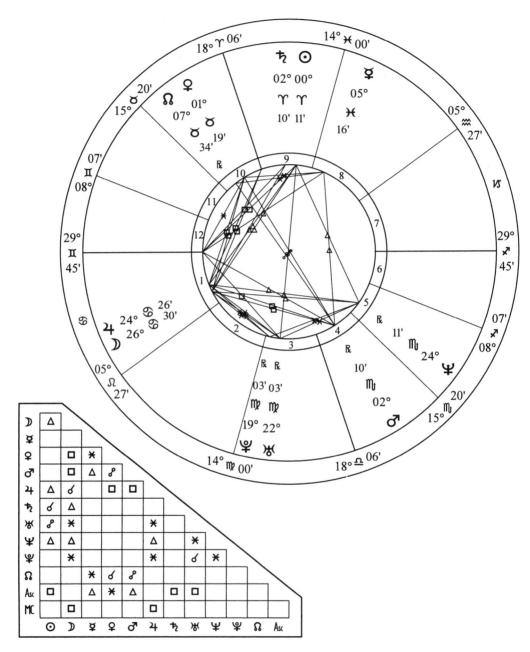

Chart 36: Hayley
March 21, 1967 / 2:00 p.m. EET / Cape Town, South Africa
Placidus houses

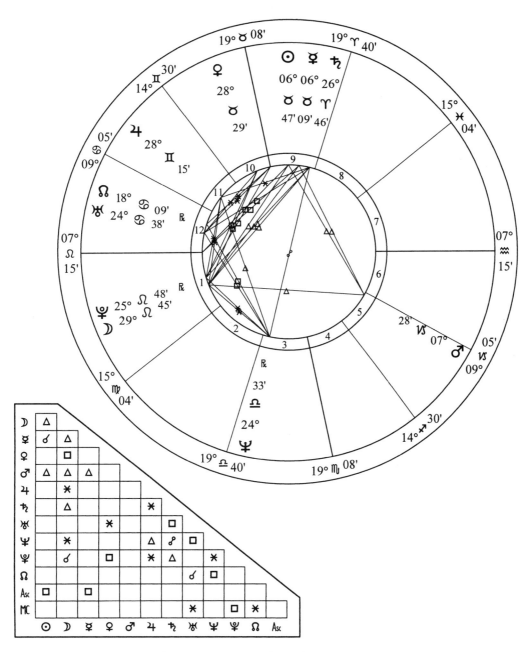

Chart 37: Penny and Hayley, composite

Penny
June 4, 1941 / 12:21:24 p.m. EET
Eshowe, South Africa
Placidus houses

Hayley
March 21, 1967 / 2:00 p.m. EET
Cape Town, South Africa
Placidus houses

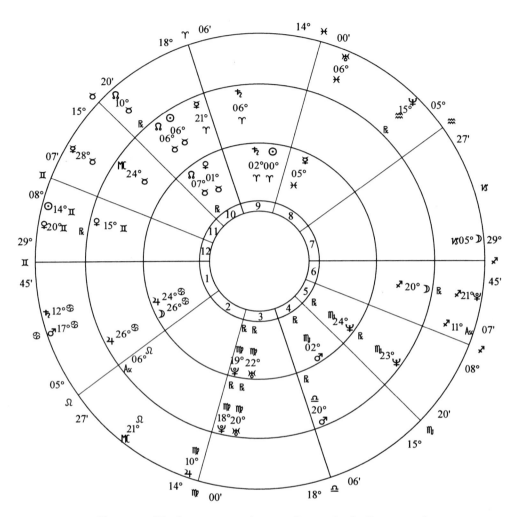

Chart 38: Hayley, progressions and transits in June 2004

Hayley	*Progressions June 2004*	*Transits June 2004*
(inner ring)	*(middle ring)*	*(outer ring)*
March 21, 1967	June 4, 2004	June 4, 2004
2:00 p.m. EET	5:30 p.m. EET	5:30 p.m. EET
Cape Town, South Africa	Cape Town, South Africa	Cape Town, South Africa
Placidus houses	Placidus houses	Placidus houses

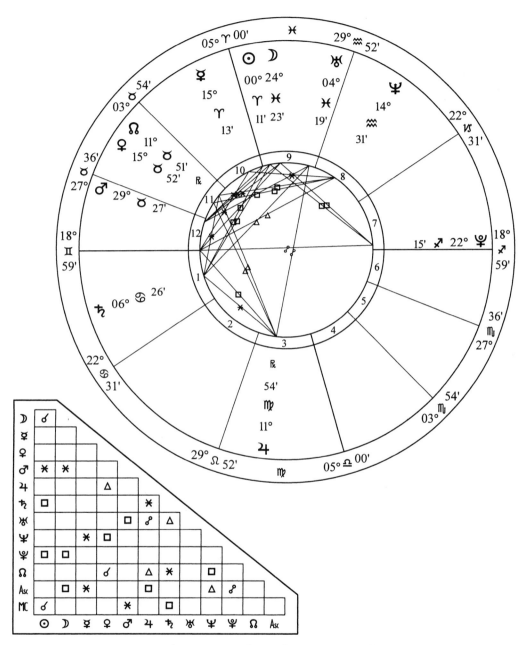

Chart 39: Hayley, solar return 2004

March 20, 2004 / 1:11:34 p.m. EET / Cape Town, South Africa

Placidus houses

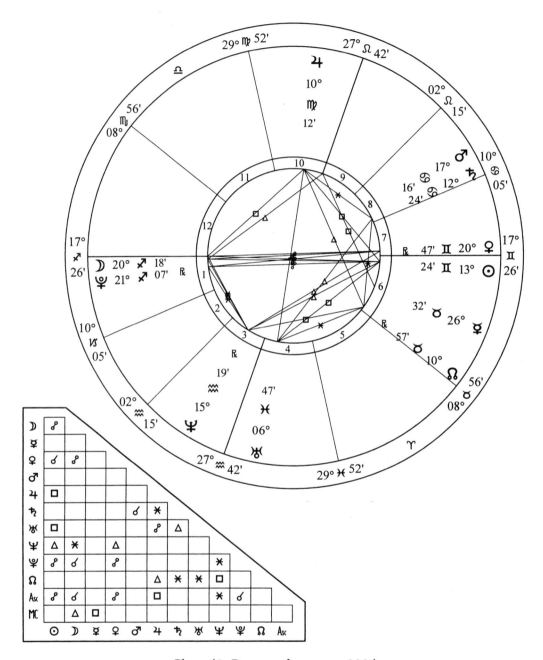

Chart 40: Penny, solar return 2004

June 3, 2004 / 5:56:18 p.m. EET / Cape Town, South Africa

Placidus houses

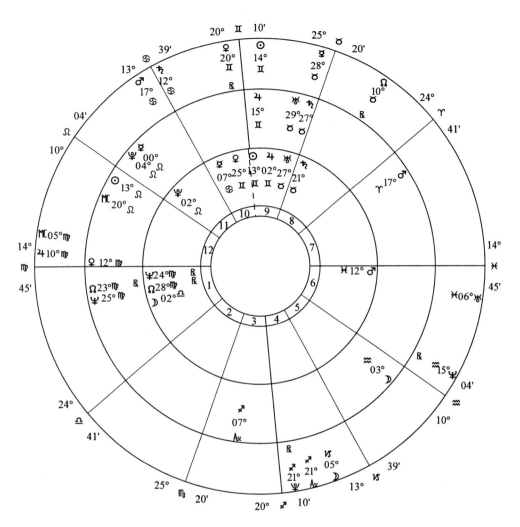

Chart 41: Penny, progressions and transits in June 2004

Penny	*Progressions June 2004*	*Transits June 2004*
(inner ring)	*(middle ring)*	*(outer ring)*
June 4, 1941	June 4, 2004	June 4, 2004
12:21:24 p.m. EET	5:30 p.m. EET	5:30 p.m. EET
Eshowe, South Africa	Cape Town, South Africa	Cape Town, South Africa
Placidus houses	Placidus houses	Placidus houses

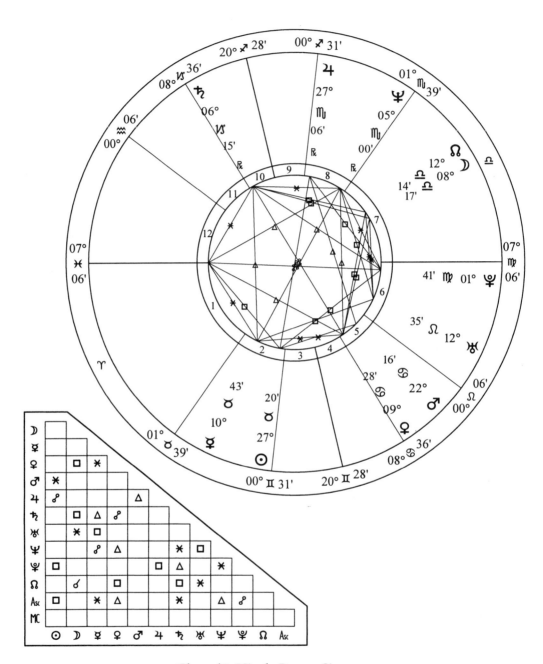

Chart 42: Nicole Brown Simpson
May 19, 1959 / 2:00 a.m. CET / Frankfurt am Main, Germany
Placidus houses

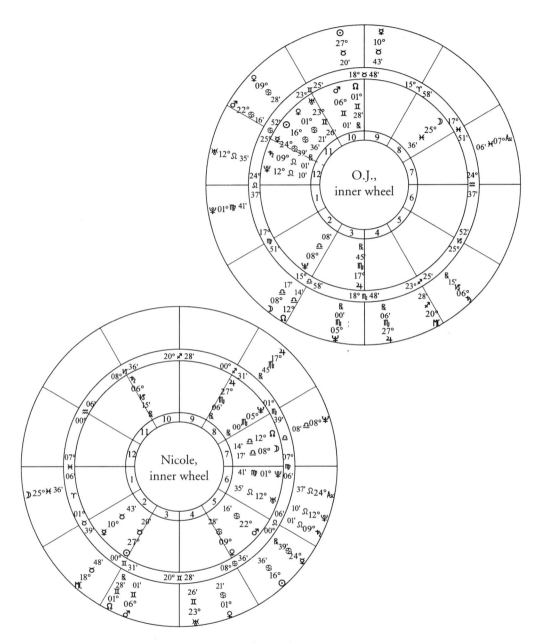

Chart 43: O.J. Simpson and Nicole Brown Simpson, synastry

O.J. Simpson
July 9, 1947 / 8:08 a.m. PST
San Francisco, California
Placidus houses

Nicole Brown Simpson
May 19, 1959 / 2:00 a.m. CET
Frankfurt am Main, Germany
Placidus houses

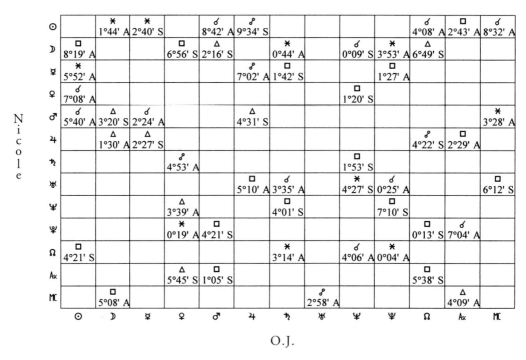

Nicole (rows) × O.J. (columns)

Nicole \ O.J.	☉	☽	☿	♀	♂	♃	♄	⛢	♆	♇	☊	Asc	MC
☉		✶ 1°44' A	✶ 2°40' S		☌ 8°42' A	☍ 9°34' S					☌ 4°08' A	□ 2°43' A	☌ 8°32' A
☽	□ 8°19' A			□ 6°56' S	△ 2°16' S		✶ 0°44' A		☌ 0°09' S	✶ 3°53' A	△ 6°49' S		
☿	✶ 5°52' A				☍ 7°02' A	□ 1°42' S			□ 1°27' A				
♀	☌ 7°08' A								□ 1°20' S				
♂	☌ 5°40' A	△ 3°20' S	☌ 2°24' A			△ 4°31' S							✶ 3°28' A
♃		△ 1°30' A	△ 2°27' S								☍ 4°22' S	□ 2°29' A	
♄				☍ 4°53' A					□ 1°53' S				
⛢					□ 5°10' A	☌ 3°35' A			✶ 4°27' S	☌ 0°25' A			□ 6°12' S
♆				△ 3°39' A		□ 4°01' S			□ 7°10' S				
♇				✶ 0°19' A	□ 4°21' S						□ 0°13' S	☌ 7°04' A	
☊	□ 4°21' S					✶ 3°14' A			☌ 4°06' A	✶ 0°04' A			
Asc				△ 5°45' S	□ 1°05' S						□ 5°38' S		
MC		□ 5°08' A						☍ 2°58' A				△ 4°09' A	

O.J.

Chart 43: O.J. Simpson and Nicole Brown Simpson, synastry (continued)

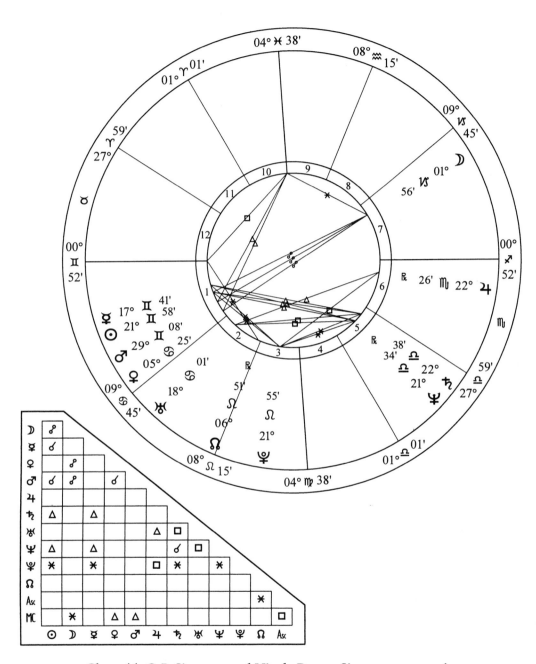

Chart 44: O.J. Simpson and Nicole Brown Simpson, composite

O.J. Simpson
July 9, 1947 / 8:08 a.m. PST
San Francisco, California
Placidus houses

Nicole Brown Simpson
May 19, 1959 / 2:00 a.m. CET
Frankfurt am Main, Germany
Placidus houses

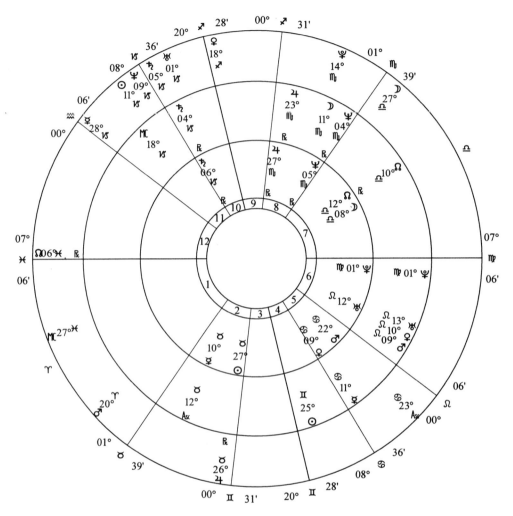

**Chart 45: Nicole Brown Simpson, progressions and transits
for beating in January 1989**

Nicole Brown Simpson	*Progressions January 1989*	*Transits January 1989*
(inner ring)	*(middle ring)*	*(outer ring)*
May 19, 1959	January 1, 1989	January 1, 1989
2:00 a.m. CET	5:30 p.m. CET	5:30 p.m. CET
Frankfurt am Main,	Frankfurt am Main,	Frankfurt am Main,
Germany	Germany	Germany
Placidus houses	Placidus houses	Placidus houses

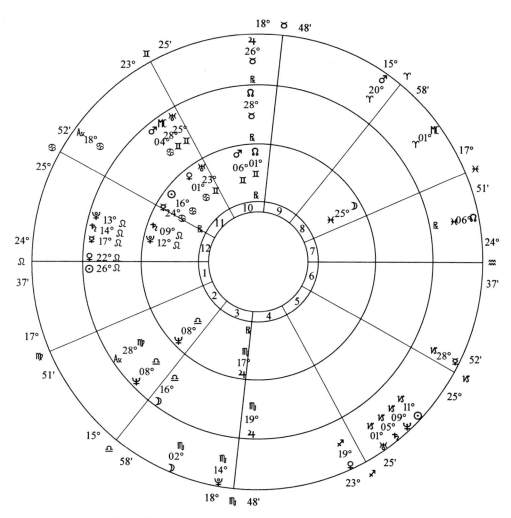

**Chart 46: O.J. Simpson, progressions and transits
for beating in January 1989**

O.J. Simpson	*Progressions January 1989*	*Transits January 1989*
(inner ring)	*(middle ring)*	*(outer ring)*
July 9, 1947	January 1, 1989	January 1, 1989
8:08 a.m. PST	5:30 p.m. PST	5:30 p.m. PST
San Francisco, California	San Francisco, California	San Francisco, California
Placidus houses	Placidus houses	Placidus houses

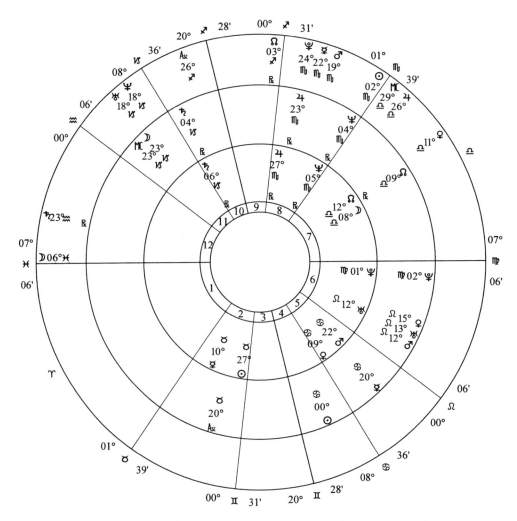

**Chart 47: Nicole Brown Simpson, progressions and transits
when she was threatened in October 1993**

Nicole Brown Simpson (inner ring)	Progressions October 1993 (middle ring)	Transits October 1993 (outer ring)
May 19, 1959	October 25, 1993	October 25, 1993
2:00 a.m. CET	12:00 p.m. CET	12:00 p.m. CET
Frankfurt am Main, Germany	Frankfurt am Main, Germany	Frankfurt am Main, Germany
Placidus houses	Placidus houses	Placidus houses

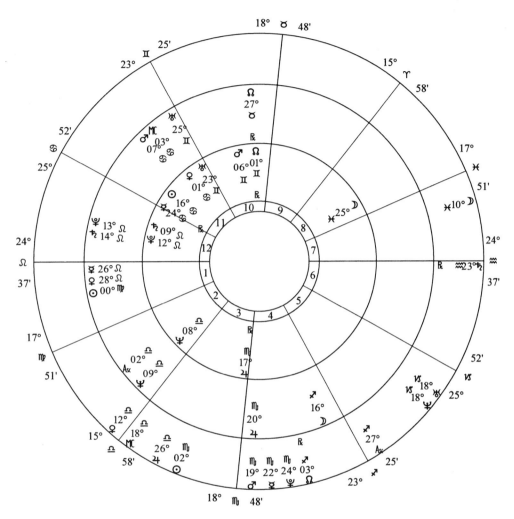

**Chart 48: O.J. Simpson, progressions and transits
when he threatened Nicole in October 1993**

O.J. Simpson (inner ring)	*Progressions October 1993* (middle ring)	*Transits October 1993* (outer ring)
July 9, 1947	October 25, 1993	October 25, 1993
8:08 a.m. PST	12:00 p.m. PST	12:00 p.m. PST
San Francisco, California	San Francisco, California	San Francisco, California
Placidus houses	Placidus houses	Placidus houses

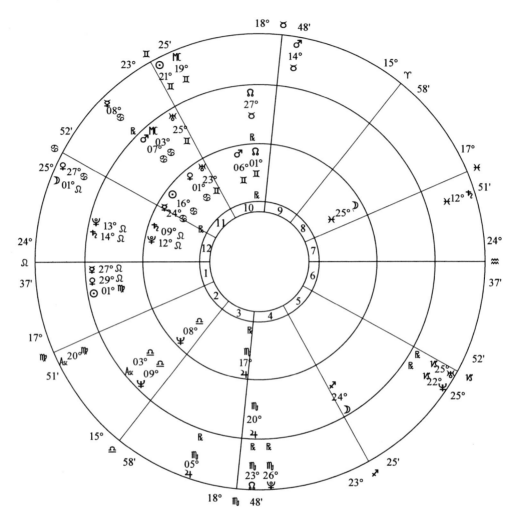

**Chart 49: O.J. Simpson, progressions and transits
when Nicole was killed in June 1994**

O.J. Simpson (inner ring)	Progressions June 1994 (middle ring)	Transits June 1994 (outer ring)
July 9, 1947	June 12, 1994	June 12, 1994
8:08 a.m. PST	12:00 p.m. PST	12:00 p.m. PST
San Francisco, California	San Francisco, California	San Francisco, California
Placidus houses	Placidus houses	Placidus houses

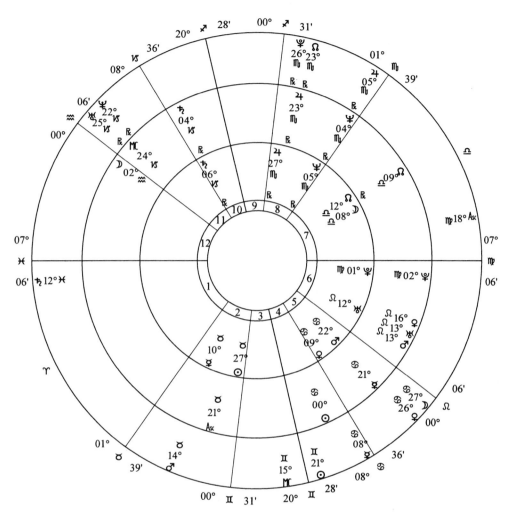

**Chart 40: Nicole Brown Simpson, progressions and transits
when she was killed in June 1994**

Nicole Brown Simpson (inner ring)	*Progressions June 1994* (middle ring)	*Transits June 1994* (outer ring)
May 19, 1959	June 12, 1994	June 12, 1994
2:00 a.m. CET	12:00 p.m. CET	12:00 p.m. CET
Frankfurt am Main, Germany	Frankfurt am Main, Germany	Frankfurt am Main, Germany
Placidus houses	Placidus houses	Placidus houses

To Write to the Author

If you wish to contact the author or would like more information about this book, please write to the author in care of Llewellyn Worldwide and we will forward your request. Both the author and publisher appreciate hearing from you and learning of your enjoyment of this book and how it has helped you. Llewellyn Worldwide cannot guarantee that every letter written to the author can be answered, but all will be forwarded. Please write to:

Rod Suskin
℅ Llewellyn Worldwide
2143 Wooddale Drive, Dept. 978-0-7387-1255-0
Woodbury, Minnesota 55125-2989, U.S.A.
Please enclose a self-addressed stamped envelope for reply,
or $1.00 to cover costs. If outside U.S.A., enclose
international postal reply coupon.

Many of Llewellyn's authors have websites with additional information and resources. For more information, please visit our website at http://www.llewellyn.com.